# THE
# COMMITTED
# MARRIAGE

# THE COMMITTED MARRIAGE

*A Guide to Finding a Soul Mate and Building a Relationship Through Timeless Biblical Wisdom*

REBBETZIN ESTHER JUNGREIS

HarperOne
*An Imprint of HarperCollinsPublishers*

HarperOne

HarperCollins books may be purchased for educational, business, or sales promotional use. For information, please e-mail the Special Markets Department at SPsales@harpercollins.com.

HarperCollins Web site: http://www.harpercollins.com
HarperCollins®, ♦®, and HarperOne™ are
trademarks of HarperCollins Publishers.

*Designed by Joseph Rutt*

Library of Congress Cataloging-in-Publication Data
Jungreis, Esther.
The committed marriage / Esther Jungreis.
p. cm.
ISBN 978-0-06-621374-3
1. Marriage—Religious aspects—Judaism.   2. Interpersonal communication.
3. Marriage counseling—United States—Case studies.   4. Jungreis, Esther.
I. Title.
BM713 .J86 2003
296.7'4—dc21           2002032809

HB 09.22.2023

To my children and grandchildren
the blessings of my life
Rabbi Shlomo and Chaya Sora Gertzulin
Rabbi Yisroel and Rivkie Jungreis
Mendy and Slovi Wolff
Rabbi Osher Anshil and Yaffa Jungreis
How can I ever thank you?
You have given me so much joy, so many blessings.
After Abba of blessed memory was called from on High
It is you and your beautiful children
who sustained me and lent sweetness to my life
I pray that *HaShem* bless you,
your children, and your children's children forevermore
with Torah, *chesed,* and boundless love.
May your homes forever be *Mikdashei M'at*—sanctuaries in miniature,
in which the spirit of G-d resides
and peace and harmony prevails.
Your Mother
whose soul is forever bound with yours
*"V'nafsho keshura B'nafsho"*

In Profound Gratitude

I thank the Almighty
for His many kindnesses.

I thank Him for having granted me
the privilege of writing this book

and teaching His Holy Torah.

I pray that the words of this
book enter people's hearts

so that they may invite G-d into
their homes

and bring peace and harmony
into their lives.

# CONTENTS

# INTRODUCTION

On September 11, 2001, the world changed. As the Twin Towers turned into a hellish inferno, those trapped on the upper floors and those aboard the pirated aircraft desperately reached for their cell phones to get one last message out. Perhaps this was the very first time in recorded history that a group of people, knowing that they were breathing their last, were able to communicate with those who were most precious to them. What do you imagine their final words would be? What would be their last will and testament? Incredibly, they all uttered the same words, "I love you," again and again: "I love you." There was no talk of vengeance or hatred, no recriminations. There were no instructions for running the business or disbursement of assets, nor was there even a trace of anger or bitterness, only the simple awesome words, "I love you."

Those words of the victims touched the hearts and souls of our nation and inspired people to reevaluate their lives. Couples who were on the verge of divorce reexamined their options and decided to give it another try. Career professionals who would stay late at night at their offices now resolved to return home early and have dinner with their families. Young people who had deferred marriage decided to commit, and couples who had postponed starting a family decided to wait no longer. "Life is so uncertain—at least I should have someone to whom I can say with a full heart, 'I love you,'" a young woman confided. These feelings of love spilled over into every area of life. New Yorkers, who are normally brusque, always in a rush, actually became friendly and even stopped to inquire, "How are you?" The country was draped in red, white, and blue in a new surge of patriotism and pride.

A short time after September 11, I was scheduled to speak at an out-of-state university. The quiet at JFK airport was eerie, and I thought nostalgically of the hustle and bustle, the long lines, which only yesterday were so irksome. The plane was half-empty and there was room to stretch out. For the first time, I would have much preferred a full flight. I reached into my purse for my constant companion, my book of psalms. The flight attendant, walking down the aisle, stopped and said, "Put in a prayer for me as well." We started to chat. She related that her husband was a pilot, and after September 11 they had decided to make major changes in their lives.

"I hope I'm not intruding, but may I ask what those changes are?" I was curious to learn how that horrific evil had affected people's lives.

"Well, for one thing," she said, "we became aware of the uncertainty of our lives—how in one split second everything that we cherished and held dear could be just blown away. We decided that we would try to appreciate each other more and to look upon each and every day as a gift."

"Have you been able to maintain those feelings?" I asked.

"Obviously not with the same intensity," she conceded, "but we didn't just talk. We actually did take some concrete steps. We made some changes in our work schedules, even though it meant less income. We also decided not to delay having children any longer. And not just that," she added with a smile, "we go to church now, regularly, not just once in a while. And we visit with our parents at least once a week."

I was impressed, and I asked her if her friends had made similar changes in their lives.

"Oh yes, but then again most of our friends are fellow pilots or flight attendants; we are always in the air, so I guess that makes us feel that we are more at risk."

Although she was probably right in saying that those who work in travel-related professions now feel more vulnerable, I believe that September 11 rendered our entire nation, the entire world, more vulnerable.

In my travels during the days after September 11, I discovered the stirrings of a spiritual renaissance in the hearts of people—a quest for G-d, a yearning for love, marriage, and family. President George Bush reflected the sentiments of America when he took to the airwaves on the night of that fateful day and led the nation in prayer. The President recited Psalm 23: "Even though I walk through the valley of the shadow of death, I fear no evil, for You are with me . . ." That psalm mirrored the feelings of millions of men and women, who, in the midst of their pain, stood strong, united by their faith in G-d and their overwhelming love. But, alas, that awakening was short-lived. When reports from Afghanistan conveyed the success of our armed forces—the surrender and retreat of the Taliban—people heaved a sigh of relief. The nightmare appeared to be over, and by December everything was back to normal. The media reported that church and synagogue attendance had dropped. People reverted to their old ways and once again found their satisfaction in work, shopping, and seeking fun. The much hoped for change in relationships never took off. There was no indication of an increase in marriages, nor was there a decrease in divorces.

I cannot challenge the statistics. They speak for themselves. But I do believe that if people returned to old habits, they did so because no one had inspired them, no one captured that moment of love, that spiritual yearning that could have become a life-transforming experience had it been harnessed to something permanent. I believe that, basically, people do desire more meaningful lives, that deep down they do seek something more than material success. I believe that people are tired of running from one place of entertainment to another. I believe that, more than fun, people yearn for faith, serenity, a higher purpose, and above all, for that love that the doomed victims all spoke of and left as their final legacy.

Despite those yearnings, however, people have difficulty making that spiritual connection. We live in a turbulent world. There are so many voices demanding our attention, so many pulls tugging at us, so many enticements that generate within us feelings of greed and lust. Our minds play tricks and we find a rationale to justify even the basest conduct, the most hateful words. When disaster strikes, for a brief moment we see a glimmer of light, but then we return to our mindless routines and darkness descends once again. Instead of searching our souls and making changes, we feel victimized and sorry for ourselves. "Why has fate treated us so cruelly?" we ask. Once again, we get on our merry-go-rounds and go in circles leading nowhere. Yes, here and there, we may experience brief highs, but they are only momentary and without depth, rooted in taking rather than giving, in entitlement rather than indebtedness, in ingratitude rather than gratitude, in love that is superficial rather than committed. The voices of those doomed souls reverberate and echo in the air. "I love you, I love you!" they cry out. But how to capture that love and integrate it into our lives remains a challenge.

It is with that goal in mind that I have written this book. Although the title suggests that its message is for married couples, the book is geared to the needs of every person, for no matter what our age, background, or status, we are all in need of that faith, that love that can enable us to *walk through the valley of the shadow of death without fear.*

The stories that I relate are based upon real-life situations, but to protect the anonymity of the individuals, I have altered names, locations, and identifiable information. I have written each chapter to stand independently and to impart lessons that can be incorporated into one's life. The teachings that I advocate are based upon the eternal truths of our Torah and the wisdom that I gleaned from my revered parents. My father, Rabbi Abraham Jungreis, was an eminent sage, a descendant of a great rabbinic dynasty. As a child, I had the privilege of always being at his side, and I benefited from the wisdom that he so lovingly dispensed to the many who came seeking his advice. I was nurtured in the cradle of my parents' committed love. I experienced the power of this love in times of peace as well as in days of war and catastrophe. Alas, I am no stranger to tragedy. As a young child, I saw our home destroyed by the Nazis and I lived through the brutality of the concentration camps. The crises in my life never quite abated. Even in the freedom of this blessed country, the challenges continued, albeit in different forms. Poverty, illness, and the death of my beloved husband—I tasted it all, but throughout I was sustained by faith in G-d and the committed love of my parents, my husband, and my children. My husband, Rabbi Meshulem HaLevi Jungreis of blessed memory, was also a survivor of the Holocaust. He was affectionately called "the gentle giant," because that's what he was—a gentle giant, the embodiment of strength, wisdom, and kindness. We were married for forty-four years, and throughout I never heard him raise his voice or express an unkind word. His was a committed love in its purest form.

It is not only I who can testify to this, but our children, grandchildren, and the myriad people who had the privilege of knowing him. I have taken pen in hand so that I might share this love with you, so that those who read this book may build their lives on the bedrock of faith and committed love.

*Rebbetzin Esther Jungreis*

A Roman matron once asked a sage,
"How many days did it take your G-d
to create the world?"

"Six," he answered.


"And since then, what has He been doing?"

The sage replied, "Making matches."

*Midrash Genesis*

# ONE

# FINDING YOUR SOUL MATE

I was sixteen when I made my first *shidduch* (match), for the elder sister of a classmate. It never occurred to me that there was anything remarkable about that until Nadine Blackman, a reporter who was writing a story on matchmaking, expressed her amazement.

"Why would a sixteen-year-old be concerned about making matches?" she asked. For a moment, the question took me aback. I grew up in a home where *chesed* (acts of loving-kindness) were a constant goal. In accordance with our tradition, there can be no greater kindness than to enable two people to meet their life partners. Our faith teaches that G-d Himself is occupied with this *mitzvah* (commandment), for, ultimately, it is He who makes every match. Nevertheless, in His infinite kindness, He invites us to join Him in partnership and act as facilitators. Now who would not welcome such an awesome privilege? Of course I would jump at the opportunity to make a match! To demonstrate further the extent to which matchmaking is part of our tradition, I shared with her a very personal and painful experience that I have often related.

My husband, who had always been in the best of health, overnight succumbed to the deadly disease of cancer. Although he was meticulous about having regular medical checkups, the tumor was not detected until it had metastasized to the entire wall of his stomach. In six agonizing weeks, he underwent three procedures, each bringing him closer to death's door.

I was sitting in the waiting room while he was undergoing his last operation, reciting psalms, looking at the clock, watching the door, waiting for the doctor to appear with some news. There was something surreal about it all. Surely, it was a nightmare from which I would soon awaken, and awaken I did, but not to news that I wanted to hear.

"I'm sorry," the surgeon said bluntly, "but I'm afraid he won't make it. He may have a few more days, perhaps even a week. If you wish, you can see him in recovery now, but don't stay long. He's heavily sedated." And with that, he left.

This surgeon was not someone I knew. He had been highly recommended by our own physician. I had no doubts about his competence as a surgeon, but his matter-of-fact way of delivering a death sentence made the news even more painful. But then again, I tried to be fair and asked myself, Is there a nice way to deliver such news? I just stood there, unable to breathe. Yes, I had suspected all along that I would hear such words, but it's one thing to suspect and something else again to be informed with such finality. I braced myself and buzzed the door to the recovery room. A nurse came and showed me to my husband's bedside. It was devastating to see him that way, lying there attached to myriad tubes. I took his hand, he opened his eyes, and I tried to smile as I fought to hold back the tears. "I just spoke to the doctor," I whispered. "He assured me that you'll be all right."

My husband's eyes filled with tears. "Let's talk *emes*—honestly. Let's talk about things that are possible," he said. "Do you see that doctor over there? He's a very fine young man. He needs a *shidduch*. Find him a nice girl."

I didn't know whether to laugh or cry. It's been more than six years since that day, and that incident has played and replayed in my mind. On each occasion, I have come to a greater appreciation of my husband's words. A man who knows he is dying has choices—to be despondent, to give in to fear, or to look around and search for one more *mitzvah*, one more act of kindness, one more act of love to perform before he departs from this world. My husband chose the latter. Matchmaking is not something out of *Fiddler on the Roof*. It is a *mitzvah* that takes on gigantic proportions, because it's more than just helping two people: it affects generations to come.

Although I made my first match at sixteen, my first experience with matchmaking came immediately after the Holocaust when I was nine. We were in a displaced-persons camp in Switzerland and my parents were desperately searching for news of family members who might have survived the flames. We learned that on my father's side, with the exception of one sister who had been with us in the Bergen Belsen concentration camp, the entire family—grandparents, aunts, uncles, cousins—had perished in the gas chambers of Auschwitz. It was a terrible time. Our grief was beyond words. Before the Holocaust there had been more than eighty-five rabbis by the name of Jungreis in Hungary (my maiden name was also Jungreis—I married a third cousin), and now, overnight, this great rabbinic dynasty that traced its roots all the way back to David, king of Israel, was consumed in the flames. How did my father go on in the face of such a catastrophe? How did he deal with this unbearable pain? He gathered orphans, showered them with love, and, for those of marriageable age, he made matches. And that is how, at the age of nine, I learned that matchmaking is more than introducing two people. It is *tikun olam*—bringing healing to the world, establishing homes, building families.

When we arrived in the United States in 1947, my parents continued their mission. Countless young survivors found their way to my mother and father, who readily assumed responsibility for them. My father accumulated dozens of notebooks, which he filled with names, addresses, telephone numbers, family history, and little tidbits of information that only he could decode. Wherever he went, those notebooks went with him. "You never know who you will meet and for whom you can make a *shidduch*," he would say.

The extent to which my father's notebooks affected people's lives was recently brought home to me by David Moscowitz. My father had introduced him to his wife about thirty years ago, and now he came to see me with his daughter.

"We need a *shidduch* for Alice," he announced, and as I jotted down her information in my notebook, he expressed amazement. "Rebbetzin, I can't believe that you don't have a Palm Pilot. I guess you inherited the notebook method from Zeide." (Everyone called my father Zeide, for although he was a rabbi first and foremost, he was a loving, kind *zeide*—grandpa.)

I had never given it any thought, but I realized that he was right. At Hineni, we have developed all sorts of sophisticated matchmaking programs, which our committee uses, but I am phobic about all of them and use my father's traditional method—the notebook.

A few years ago, a bright, talented young software designer named Sean Saunders walked into one of my classes. His background was totally secular. His father had cut all ties with Judaism, but nevertheless, something impelled Sean to come to my Torah seminar. He connected instantaneously and became an active participant in all our activities. He observed me with my notebook, struggling to find the names that I had entered.

"Rebbetzin," he finally said, "this is a new age. This is no way to do a search. Let me design a program for you." And he did just that. It was truly a marvel. Candidates are photographed with a digital camera connected to a laptop into which the questionnaires that they fill out are scanned. The program does the rest. Simply at the press of a key, likely candidates pop up on the screen! This has become a vital component of our matchmaking program at Hineni. But to be candid, I myself remain as computer-phobic as ever and have yet to use it.

With every passing day, Sean's life altered as he made his way back to his roots. He rediscovered the Jewish family name that his father had discarded and chose Akiva as his given name as a symbol of his journey (Rabbi Akiva commenced his Torah studies late in life). One day he informed me that he was ready to marry and establish a home. Could I help him? He described the young woman of his dreams: she had to come from a good family, because he wanted his children to have grandparents who would be role models of the timeless values of our heritage; he wanted someone who shared his dream of having a large family. It goes without saying that he also aspired to find all the other attributes that young men normally seek—looks, personality, intelligence, sensitivity, and kindness.

I very frankly told him that that was a tall order, that a young woman coming from a solid family would also wish her potential spouse to come from a similar background, but Akiva would not compromise. Then one day Leah, a lovely young woman, came to my class and, after the session, asked to speak to me privately. As we conversed, it occurred to me that she might just be the perfect *shidduch* for Akiva. When I broached the subject, however, she dismissed my suggestion out of hand. "Rebbetzin, I have no interest in meeting anyone. I came here because I want to study Torah as well as to consult you on some issues that I have in my life."

But I wouldn't take no for an answer, and I suggested that she come to our Hineni Heritage Center the following night so that we could talk at greater length. At the same time, I alerted Akiva to be present as well. When Leah arrived at Hineni, I told her that I would be with her momentarily and asked Akiva to show her around our center and museum exhibits. After that short exchange, Akiva definitely felt that this was "it." Leah, however, was still resisting, but with a little warm encouragement from me, her qualms were resolved and a short while later, they became engaged. Today, they have a great marriage; they are the happy parents of a beautiful baby girl and are teaching others the wisdom of our Torah.

Why do I tell this story? Because as accurate as computers are, and as wonderful as the program designed by Akiva is, computers are still only computers. They do not have hearts; they do not prod; they do not encourage; they do not say, "Go for it! It's a wonderful *shidduch!*" In the final analysis, more than technical information is needed to make a match. While a computer can indicate that two people may be compatible, someone has to be there to walk them through the process, to help smooth over difficulties, iron out misunderstandings, and speak to family members. That's what my father's matchmaking notebooks were all about, and that's why I continue to use his method to this day.

Nowadays, there are myriad matchmaking programs all over the world, yet finding one's mate remains the most critical problem in an ever-growing singles population. Perhaps never before in history have there been so many singles with no marriage prospects. Why can't they get married? What went wrong?

As in all such cases, there are no pat answers. Many contributing factors come into play. Years ago, singles lived at home until they married. Parents were actively involved in helping their children find their mates. At the very least, they pressed them to get on with it and establish their own homes. Today, however, things are different. No sooner are young people graduated from high school than they are on their way—from college to their own apartments—and even if they should move back home, parents often adopt a laissez-faire attitude when it comes to their children marrying. Our culture encourages young people to focus on their careers while marriage is placed on the back burner. This has taken a devastating toll. Immersed in their professions, young women have seen their biological clocks tick by. They have been misled into believing that they have all the time in the world, only to discover that the years that have passed can never be retrieved. Although this is a tragedy that afflicts both genders, women are hit hardest, not only because of their biological clocks but because, basically, they are nest builders. Their very bodies cry out the supplication of the matriarch Rachel (who for many years was barren), "Give me a child lest I die" (Genesis 30:1).

The promise of modern science, assuring them that it is possible to have children after the age of forty, is more often hype than reality. Yes, from time to time there are some wonderful stories that make great copy, but reality is quite different. Even if by some stroke of luck a woman in her forties finds her mate, the road to childbearing can be filled with much heartache and painful and expensive medical treatment, resulting more often in frustration than in babies.

A successful young woman in the corporate world came to consult me about finding a mate. "Rebbetzin," she said, her voice full of emotion, "I have an elderly widowed mother. I call her every day and visit her at least once a week, but of late, I'm haunted by a terrible thought. Who will visit *me* when I am her age? I always thought you could have it all—a successful career, marriage, children, the works—but I've discovered that there's a double standard out there. Men can combine marriage and parenthood with a successful career, but it's not so simple for a woman. We've lost the best years of our lives. We've been misled."

Whose fault is it? It doesn't matter. An entire generation has been led down the garden path. Although it may be true that there is a double standard and that men fare better in the singles world, experience has taught me that men are also suffering. Many sincerely desire to marry but can't. Again, there are many factors that render them phobic (and this can apply to women as well). With our new morality, men no longer *have* to get married. They can just as easily have relationships, but these relationships come with a high price and leave indelible marks on their souls. You cannot be intimate with someone and then cancel that person out without consequences. Even if one is in denial, the heart, the mind, and the soul have long memories. It is little wonder, then, that today's singles carry heavy baggage and with each passing year pick up more schtick, all of which mitigates against committing to marriage.

Additionally, the active social lives that many singles lead serve to mask their feelings of loneliness. There is always a plethora of activities to keep them anesthetized and deluded into believing that they are doing their all to pursue a match, whereas in reality they are just going from date to date, gathering to gathering, party to party.

I met Andrew at a United Jewish Appeal (U.J.A.) Young Leadership convention at which I was lecturing. I hadn't seen him in years. "Andrew," I asked, "what's doing with you?"

"I'm still single," he said, laughing. "Any recommendations?"

I thought for a moment and suggested a lovely young woman who had been coming to my classes.

"*Her?*" he said. "Forgive me, Rebbetzin, but I turned down girls who were better than her years ago. I didn't wait all this time to settle now."

I felt sorry for Andrew. The poor guy was unaware of the crassness of his words. He didn't realize that by making comparisons, by living in the past, he was consigning himself to a life of loneliness. With his attitude, even if by some stroke of luck he finally did marry, he would always carry the albatross of past relationships around his neck. "Maybe I should have married her, or her, or her." Second-guessing is always easy to indulge in in times of stress or conflict. Marriage, like life, is not a smooth ride. There are many bumps along the way, and if you come upon a particularly rough stretch, it becomes tempting to blame the vehicle and fantasize that had you gotten a different model or make, you would have been okay. Such rationalization is anathema to marriage—it deludes you into believing that the problem is not with you but with your mate, and if you could only exchange him or her, all would be well.

More than ever, I realized the wisdom of the blessing that we pronounce under the marriage canopy—that bride and groom find the joy and happiness that Adam and Eve experienced in the Garden of Eden. Adam and Eve knew with certainty that they were meant for each other. There was no one else to choose from! Similarly, we wish for every bride and groom to enjoy the same clarity and be free of the burdens that the Andrews of our generation carry—always comparing, always second-guessing themselves, and never being able to make a commitment.

Searching for your soul mate becomes easier when you have faith. It is written that already, forty days before our creation, G-d selects a match for us. That knowledge is very fortifying, for if a potential match doesn't work out, there is no sense of personal rejection. We find consolation in the thought that this person was probably not the one G-d chose for us. So although we must do our part in pursuing a match, if in the process we encounter disappointments, we don't despair. We put it down to its not having been *basherte* (the Yiddish word for predestined).

At a singles gathering in Florida, Peggy Harris, an attractive woman in her thirties, bemoaned her fate: "I've been on more dates than I care to count. I'm suffering from date burnout, and frankly, I'm tired. If indeed everyone has a *basherte,* why is it taking me so long to find him?"

I answered her with two stories—one from our ancient past and one from today. "It is written in the Midrash that King Solomon had an exquisite daughter, and like all fathers, he wanted a very special husband for her—someone who would be truly worthy of a princess. But the king foresaw that his beautiful daughter was destined to marry an impoverished young man from a totally unsuitable family. To ensure that this would never happen, he built a palace on an island and sent his daughter there. He stationed armed guards all around the perimeter and felt quite secure that these precautions would protect the princess from an inappropriate marriage.

"Everyone in the palace loved the princess, for not only was she lovely in appearance, she was also gracious, kind, and wise. Now, one day it happened that despite all the guards and protective walls, a young pauper, barefoot and dressed in rags, miraculously found his way inside the palace. The next morning, when the princess took her daily walk, she came upon the pauper. 'I am a traveler from the city of Acco in the Holy Land,' he explained.

"The princess had compassion for him and secretly arranged for his care. As she came to know him, she discovered that he was a man of great depth and sensitivity, an outstanding Torah scholar, and a gifted scribe. Soon the young man proposed marriage, which the princess readily accepted. In no time at all the secret was out, and in great trepidation the guards informed King Solomon. But to everyone's relief, when King Solomon heard the news, he proclaimed in great awe, 'Blessed be the Almighty G-d who forever brings together the husband and wife who are destined for each other.'

"You see, Peggy," I said, "G-d has many wondrous ways of uniting those who are meant for each other. So, in response to your question, yes, everyone has a *basherte,* and G-d helps you to find him or her, even under the strangest and most inexplicable circumstances. For example, my daughter Slovi went to Israel on a mission for our Hineni organization, and while she was there, her future husband, who was visiting from Brazil, caught a glimpse of her—

and the rest is history. So yes, G-d does bring together souls that are *basherte*, even if they are separated by oceans and live in different parts of the world.

"On the other hand, G-d endows each and every person with free will, and since we live in a world in which values have become blurred, in which Hollywood rather than truth shapes our expectations, it is easy to make wrong decisions and reject our soul mates for superficial reasons when we meet them. We tend to look for fluff rather than substance, for good looks rather than a kind heart, for deep pockets rather than a profound mind, so it's little wonder that our soul mates sometimes slip by. There is a well-known story about a bachelor in his forties who, some years ago, traveled to the Holy Land to consult a great sage about this very problem. Even as you, Peggy, he asked, 'If everyone has a *basherte*, why haven't I found mine?'

"The rabbi gazed at him with piercing eyes. 'You *did* find her, but when you met her, you thought her nose was too long.'"

"What's the answer, then?" Peggy asked. "What measures can we take to ensure that we choose the person who is destined for us?"

"That's a tough one, but since it all comes from G-d, first and foremost we have to pray that when we meet him or her, He will open our eyes so that we may know that this is the *right one*, and moreover, that our 'other half' should recognize us. When my own children were ready to consider marriage, my father would caution us not to beseech G-d for any one specific person. 'The one you might consider to be absolutely perfect could turn out to be a disaster, so place your trust in Him and ask that He guide the children to the one who is destined for them' was his sagacious advice.

"Actually, we can glean this wisdom from the Torah. The first matchmaker, who became the role model for all future matchmakers, was Eliezer, the loyal servant of Abraham. It is written that, when the patriarch was on in years, he called Eliezer and entrusted him with the greatest of all responsibilities: finding a wife for Isaac. Eliezer received very specific instructions from his master about where to go and among which families to search. Additionally, Isaac was what one might call an easy sell. Handsome and wealthy, the scion of a great family, a brilliant Torah scholar, he was the most eligible bachelor of his time. Who would not want him? Yet Eliezer understood that to find your soul mate you need G-d's guiding hand, so he entreated the Almighty to *show kindness* to Abraham by sending the right young woman for Isaac (Genesis 24:12). Eliezer's efforts, however, did not end with prayer. He knew that human beings must exert themselves and do their share as well. When he arrived at Rebecca's hometown, he stationed himself at the well, the hub of activity, where all the people gathered to draw water, and designed the following litmus test of character: 'Let it be that the maiden to whom I shall say, please tip over your jug so that I may drink, and she replies, "Drink, and I will even water your camels," her, will You have designated for Your servant Isaac' (Genesis 24:14).

"We have to appreciate the deeper implication of this test. In those days, drawing and carrying water was hard, backbreaking work, but to do this for a total stranger and his ten thirsty camels was a near Herculean feat. No one would have faulted Rebecca had she politely declined and said to this perfectly healthy stranger, 'Sir, you can get your *own* water.' But not only did she willingly offer to help, she did so without fuss or fanfare, revealing genuine joy at this opportunity to extend kindness. And there were ancillary messages as well. Rebecca proved herself to be sensitive, even to the feelings of animals. Instead of watering each camel individually, which could have caused distress to those waiting their turn, she poured the water into a trough so that they might all drink at the same time. Rebecca also demonstrated that she wasn't pampered or spoiled. As the daughter of a wealthy, prominent family, she could have insisted that one of the servant girls be sent to the well. Finally, she generously extended hospitality to Eliezer and insisted that he come to her home, assuring him that the family would welcome him and make provisions for his camels as well."

"That was quite a litmus test, but if your marriage partner is pre-destined from above," Peggy challenged, "why do you have to go through all this testing in the first place? Shouldn't there be a mysti-cal component, a love that is blind that connects you?"

"That's true. There should be," I answered, "but we are not really in touch with our souls, and therefore not very good at dis-cerning who our soul mates may be. So we have to work with the tools that are available to us and search for values in our marriage partners that the Torah considers vital and indispensable. As for blind love, it definitely has its place in a relationship, but only after marriage. Then, even if mistakes are made, you forgive, but while you are dating, you have to have both eyes wide open and be on the alert for character flaws. This, too, we learn from the story of Isaac and Rebecca. It is written that 'only *after* he married Rebecca did Isaac love her' (Genesis 24:64)."

"But we can't very well go to a well today, and there aren't many camels around either," Peggy said half-jokingly.

"True," I conceded, "we may not have wells or camels, but never-theless, the litmus test remains the same. Eliezer was seeking some-one who embodied loving-kindness, and that is as valid today as it was then. Everything else is negotiable. You don't like someone's appearance, it need not be a problem. There are many ways in which you can enhance looks. You feel a person is lacking in educa-tion and polish—that, too, can be improved upon. In fact, there are makeovers for almost everything, but changing just one character trait, our sages tell us, is more difficult than mastering the intrica-cies of the Talmud."

"Don't you believe that, with love and patience, people can change?" Peggy asked.

"I wouldn't cancel anything out," I said, "but we are cautioned never to rely on miracles. If someone really wants to change, let him or her demonstrate sincerity in the *here* and *now*." And I shared with her a joke I once heard about a poor Jew who was brought before a communist tribunal.

"*Zsid*," they said, "if you had a farm, what would you do with it?"

"I would donate it to the Communist Party."

"If you had a yacht, what would you do with it?"

"I would donate it to the Communist Party."

"If you had a skyscraper, what would you do with it?"

"I would donate it to the Communist Party."

The interrogation proceeded in this manner for quite some time until they finally asked, "*Zsid*, if you had a coat, what would you do with it?"

"That, sir, I would keep for myself."

"*Zsid*," the interrogator said, "I don't understand you—the skyscraper, the yacht, the farm, you give away, but the coat you hold on to?"

"Sir," the poor Jew replied, "the skyscraper, the yacht, the farm, I don't have, but the coat, I *do* have!"

"You get the point, Peggy. It's easy to make a promise when you don't have to deliver.

"Marriage is a lifetime commitment, and you simply can't afford to rely upon empty promises like 'I'll change after we are married.' Such promises usually don't materialize. If anything, after marriage it's downhill all the way. *Chesed* (loving-kindness) is the most important character trait that you can bring to a marriage. The person who possesses this attribute is a selfless, giving individual and will make a great partner and parent. People who are endowed with *chesed* have something more magnetic than beauty or a handsome face. In Hebrew, we call this *chein*, an inner charm that radiates. Kindness illuminates their faces, and even if, with the passage of time, she becomes flabby and wrinkled and he becomes bald and potbellied, the *chein*, the charm, remains, and because of it, they will always find their partners enchanting. And that is the most important ingredient for a good marriage."

# PRELUDE

The eminent sage Rabbi Yochanan Ben Zakkai gathered his most outstanding disciples and requested that they go forth into the world and discover the most important qualities that a man should strive for—qualities that would allow him to live a purposeful and meaningful life. Their conclusions—developing a good eye, finding and becoming a good friend, being a good neighbor, projecting the future by anticipating the consequences of one's actions, and developing a good heart—are the five subdivisions of this book. They speak to us today with new relevance and urgency.

In each category are contemporary stories on marriage and relationships that reflect the timelessness of their teachings and how that wisdom may be applied to our daily lives today.

PART ONE

# A GOOD EYE

Seek the good in everyone,
revere it and bring it forth . . .

*Rabbi Nachman of Breslov*

# DEVELOPING A GOOD EYE, BECOMING THAT DESIRABLE MATE

Nowadays, it is not only introductions to their soul mates that singles require, but also the tools that will enable them to make their marriages work. While I've had the privilege of making countless matches, I've also come to realize that getting married is the easy part. It's the living "happily ever after" that becomes problematic. To help people along the way, I established our Hineni Relationship Seminars.

Hineni is the outreach organization that I founded some thirty years ago to connect Jews with our heritage. Since then, our organization has mushroomed into an international movement with headquarters in New York City, where more than a thousand people attend our weekly Torah seminars and our many other programs.

When I announced that we would be conducting relationship seminars to help singles improve their marriage potential, the response was enthusiastic. Never did I anticipate, however, that the turnout would be so overwhelming. We had to keep bringing in more and more chairs, until the crowd of young people spilled into the hallway, demonstrating that singles are keenly aware of the problems in their relationships and, more than anything, yearn for harmonious marriages. But lacking role models to show them the way, they don't quite know how to go about it.

I opened the discussion with a hypothetical scenario. "Imagine your own funeral," I said. "What will the rabbi say in his eulogy? What stories will he relate about you? How many people will shed genuine tears? How many will miss your presence on planet Earth? What makes some people loved while others have no impact at all? Are people remembered because they achieved the American dream—success, money, fame, power? Is that what endears them to others? Or is there something else?"

Everyone was in accord that that was not the stuff of which memorable eulogies are woven or loving relationships built. There had to be something else, but what exactly that something else was had yet to be defined.

Centuries ago, the great sage Rabbi Yochanan wrestled with this very question. He gathered his five most outstanding disciples and commissioned them to explore the problem. They each came up with a different solution—all of them correct, all of them valid, each of them complementing the others. Taking on all five simultaneously, however, may be overwhelming; but our sages teach us that once you embark on the right path, you go from one mitzvah to another. Thus, if you can master just *one* of the teachings, eventually you will succeed with all of them. Once you decide to improve yourself with one trait, that experience will inspire you to take on the other four.

Rabbi Eleazar, the first disciple, was blessed with an encyclopedic mind and a flawless memory. He posited that the most desirable attribute to develop is a *good eye*. Obviously, he was not referring to 20/20 vision, but to a benevolent and caring attitude—always seeing the good rather than the bad in others. My dear husband of blessed memory had such a *good eye*. He was an erudite rabbi whose wisdom and scholarship were matched only by his compassion and loving-kindness. He taught Torah with a generous spirit, giving of himself freely, without reservation. He personally greeted every worshiper and literally embraced and hugged every man. If someone was missing at services, he knew it. He would immediately call, and if they were ill, he visited them, and he never went empty-handed.

It happened that one Sabbath morning, a man new to the neighborhood came to the synagogue. He wasn't wearing a jacket (the usual Sabbath attire) and to make things worse, two pens protruded from his pocket. All upset, one of the members ran over to my husband. "Rabbi," he exclaimed, "the chutzpah, the audacity of that man, to come to shul (synagogue) this way!"

My husband looked at the congregant and said quietly, "Isn't it a wonderful testimony to the faith and spirit of our people that even those who don't know that we are not permitted to carry a pen on the Sabbath, nevertheless have a desire to come to pray. We must welcome him warmly, make him feel wanted, and share our Torah teachings with him."

A small incident, but a telling one that reveals the power of the *good eye*. There are two ways of looking at every situation. You can see light or darkness, blessing or curse. You can see the world with a good eye or a bad eye. Depending on which eye you choose, you can become either considerate or bitter, patient or angry, giving or niggardly, content or miserable, warm or cantankerous, loving or critical—it's all contingent upon how you train your eye. And that is the legacy that you leave behind. That is your eulogy.

My husband genuinely loved every one. In addition to being the beloved rabbi of his congregation, he was the chaplain of the Nassau County Police Department, in which Jews were a minuscule minority, but he was deeply loved by everyone. When he fell ill, the police commissioner and the members of the force came to visit him regularly at the hospital. Although my husband was suffering from excruciating pain, he never let on. His *good eye* impelled him to impart blessings to all who came to his bedside. On one occasion, I was walking the commissioner to the elevator when, in a voice choked with tears, he said, "The rabbi is a bridge of goodness that connects man to G-d."

The commissioner touched upon a profound truth. Even as goodness is a bridge that connects human beings to G-d, so meanspiritedness banishes us from His presence. People who look upon others with a jaundiced eye are like the serpent in the Garden of Eden. The Garden of Eden was a magical place in which every need was met, yet instead of appreciating all the beauty, joy, and pleasure, the serpent saw only the *one tree* that was off-limits, and with that *mean eye,* he brought a curse upon himself and the entire world.

We all know people like that serpent. They can be at a wonderful celebration, but the only comment they make is that dessert wasn't served fast enough, or something equally petty. A woman can prepare an amazing dinner, but if her husband has a serpentlike personality, he will find something to criticize. People who look at the world with *bad eyes* go through life complaining. They always manage to see problems. Their negativity invades every aspect of their existence. Their relationships, their marriages, their work are all affected. They are never happy, and they can't bear to see someone else happy either. Even if on rare occasions they give someone a compliment, they are unable to give it with a full heart: "You *finally* got it. I don't know what took you so long!" they say. Or, "Your suit looks good, not like the one you wore last week."

Our rabbis identified these serpent personality types as "foolish people" who consign themselves to lives of bitterness and misery.

"Can you imagine," I told the young people, "how different life would be if *mean eyes* could be exchanged for *good ones?* If we could acquire this trait, we could spare ourselves so much distress, so much grief. We could be surrounded by friends rather than enemies, and most important, a good eye could cement our family life and enhance our love for our mates. In the end," I added, "it is within the confines of the family that the good eye is most severely tested. It is easier to show consideration and patience to strangers than to the members of your own household. Strangers come and go, but family members are ever-present—you have to deal with them day in and day out, which is not always an easy feat. If, however, you have a good eye, you won't find their words and actions so irritating. My husband possessed this special gift. His good eye not only enabled him to be a bridge of goodness to all, but he was the personification of goodness to us, the members of his immediate family, always seeing our virtues and never our faults."

"I fully appreciate what you are saying," Eddie, one of the seminar participants, commented. "Having grown up in a home in which there was always much discord, shouting, and fighting, I am in awe of your husband. Please don't take this amiss, but he was a rabbi who lived on a different level. I don't know if I can just look away, be blind to all the stupidity and nastiness that people, including, or should I say, *especially,* members of my family, have inflicted on me, and say, 'It's okay, I'm looking at you with a *good eye!*'"

"Let me answer you on all counts," I said. "Believe it or not, rabbis are also human, just like everyone else. As a matter of fact, our tradition teaches that one's evil inclination is commensurate with one's other attainments, meaning that the higher the level you achieve, the greater your struggle will become. Thus, Jacob had to wrestle with the angel of Esau (the spirit of evil) before he was given the title *Yisrael,* meaning 'righteous with G-d.' Life is one big struggle, and developing a *good eye* is a struggle as well. Start with little things, like learning to say 'Thank you' and not taking things for granted; by noticing the good and acknowledging it; by acting in loving ways and expressing loving words. If you do just that, you will train your eye to see the good rather than the bad.

"Try to develop a sense of humor. When you feel that anger, that meanness, surging in your heart, try to imagine yourself on a highway. Ahead of you is gridlock. No way would you want to be caught in it—better to get off and take another route. So why should you allow yourself to be caught in a gridlock of bitterness from which there is no escape? Put a smile on your face and tell yourself, No way am I going to get caught in this mess."

"Frankly, Rebbetzin, I don't know if I can be so big."

"Of course you can," I told him. "I'll prove it to you. Have you ever done anything stupid, nasty, or mean?"

"I'm sure I have," he responded.

"Well, did you regard yourself as nasty, mean, or stupid because of that? Or did you feel that, basically, you were a *good person* who just happened to have done something stupid? When it comes to judging ourselves, we conveniently manage to see ourselves with a good eye, so why can't we extend this same courtesy to others?—to our wives and husbands, to our parents and siblings, to whomever we come in contact with?

"A Hasidic master, the Ba'al Shem Tov, used to say, 'Man was given two eyes, so that with one, he should see his own faults, and with the other, he should see the virtues of others.' Unfortunately, our generation has reversed the order. We see *our own* virtues and the faults of *others*. So of course we feel dissatisfied, of course we feel victimized. One woman who attended my classes actually said to me, 'Rebbetzin, I have only one fault—I'm too good.' And the pathetic part of it was that she really believed it!

"Most of us would be too embarrassed to articulate such sentiments, but deep down we do harbor similar feelings, so it's little wonder that our relationships are laced with anger, that all kinds of 'issues' plague us. A *good eye* could liberate us from all these constricting emotions and transform us into better people who feel kindly toward others—and no one benefits more from a good eye than the one who acquires it.

"This ability to look for the good, to have a positive attitude and live with hope, has deep roots in our history. It is written in the Talmud that, after the destruction of the Holy Temple, Rabbi Akiva and four of the sages of Israel were walking in Jerusalem. When they passed the Temple Mount, they saw a fox emerge from where the Holy of Holies had once stood. As a sign of mourning, they rent their garments and broke down and wept, but Rabbi Akiva smiled. His colleagues turned to him in shock. 'How can you smile in the face of such a catastrophe?'

"'I smile,' Rabbi Akiva said, 'because now that I have seen the fulfillment of the prophecy which foretold that Jerusalem would be laid waste and wild animals would roam the holy site, we are that much closer to the fulfillment of the second prophecy—that Jerusalem will be rebuilt and the Temple will once again stand in all her majesty and glory.'

"To be sure, Rabbi Akiva also tore his clothing and mourned, but once he did so, he found the inner strength to move on.

"It was not by coincidence that Rabbi Akiva was able to see light in the midst of darkness. Rabbi Akiva had a *good eye*. At the age of forty, he was an impoverished, illiterate shepherd in the employ of Kalba Savua, one of the wealthiest and most prominent men in Jerusalem. It was there that he met his *basherte*—Rachel, Kalba Savua's beautiful eighteen-year-old daughter, a most unlikely match, one that could only have been made in heaven. The odds were against it. Kalba Savua categorically threatened to disown his daughter if she married Akiva, but Rachel was undeterred. She saw greatness in Akiva, but before marrying him she made one stipulation: that he become a Torah scholar. 'I'm forty years old,' Akiva told her. 'I can't even read. Am I to go to school with little children?' Akiva took a walk in the forest hoping to find some insight into what to do. He came upon a large rock in a stream and noticed that the rock had deep indentations. Suddenly, it hit him—he found the wisdom he was seeking. 'If drops of water can make an imprint on a rock, then surely the Torah can make an impact on my mind and heart.' Then and there, he decided to accept Rachel's challenge to study.

"Now surely, myriad people had passed by that very same rock, yet not one of them had stopped to contemplate the significance of its grooves. But Rabbi Akiva had a *good eye* and was able to see hope even in a rock, and at the age of forty he began his education.

"To reach the Torah academy where he was to study, he had to undergo a long and arduous journey. He traveled by donkey and took all his possessions with him: his books, a candle by which to read, and a rooster to awaken him in the early hours of the morning. As night fell, he became tired and hungry and decided to seek lodging in a small town. He knocked on the door of a little house, hoping to be allowed to stay the night. A man opened the door but just as quickly slammed it in his face. 'Strangers are not welcome here!' he exclaimed.

"Akiva was taken aback by this lack of hospitality. Nevertheless, he tried to view his predicament with a good eye and thought to himself that there must be some *reason* that this was happening, even if the reason eluded him. Wearily, he mounted his donkey and made for the forest, where he spread a mat on the ground, lit a candle, opened one of his books, and began to study. Suddenly, he heard his donkey bray. There was a great uproar. Akiva ran toward his beast, but he was too late. A lion had come and devoured it. His luck seemed to be running out. Things were going from bad to worse. Now he would have to travel on foot. 'But no matter,' Akiva murmured to himself, 'there must be some reason for all this.'

"He was about to return to his studies when there was another disturbance. This time it was the cock who fell dead. Was this the reward for a man who undertakes an arduous journey and sacrifices everything in order to be a Torah scholar?

"Akiva could surely have become cynical and renounced his faith. Instead he kindled his candle and continued his studies. But the wind blew so fiercely that it was impossible to keep the candle lit and, finally, in sheer exhaustion he fell asleep.

"The next morning he resumed his journey, stopping at the village where he had been refused lodging the night before. A horrible sight greeted him. Robbers had come during the night and plundered and destroyed everything in sight. With a heavy heart, Akiva whispered to himself, 'G-d's guiding hand is always there. It was meant to be that I was not extended hospitality in this house. It was meant to be that I lost my donkey and rooster, and it was meant to be that the wind blew out my candle, for had the robbers found me, I would not be here now.'

"Despite his many tribulations, Rabbi Akiva became the greatest Torah luminary in Israel, with a following of twenty-four thousand disciples. But the tests in Akiva's life were by no means over. His twenty-four thousand disciples all perished in a terrible plague. Any other man would have given up, but Akiva had a *good eye*—he looked for life amid the ruins and built a second Torah academy, which was even greater than the first.

"At one time or another, we all experience events that are beyond our comprehension, events that may leave us feeling hopeless, cynical, and bitter. On such occasions, our *good eye* can infuse us with faith and fortify us with the knowledge that there must be a reason for what is happening, even if, for the moment, that reason eludes us. Most often, however, we allow these traumas to strip us of our faith and fill our hearts with anger and bitterness. But if we look at our predicament with a good eye, see our difficulties as challenges, as opportunities for growth, we will find something positive on which to focus. This holds true not only in times of crisis, but also in the normal ups and downs of life."

Jessica was in her mid-twenties, the mother of a fifteen-month-old baby, and was having some personal problems. She was visibly nervous and kept apologizing, "Please don't think I came here to complain about my husband. It's just that there are certain things . . ." And before she could finish the sentence, she burst into tears.

"It's okay," I tried to reassure her. "Take a deep breath and tell me what's bothering you." I was prepared to hear the worst. Who knew what this poor young woman had been experiencing.

After a while she regained her composure and related that her husband had two sisters, both married. The family was close-knit and there were many get-togethers, but these occasions were torture to her. Her brothers-in-law were all sharp, successful businessmen, whereas her husband was—and here she paused, and then in a whisper said, "different."

"What do you mean by *different?*" I asked.

She had difficulty defining it. "He's just different—like, when we get together he's always the first to want to leave."

"So, what's so terrible about that?" I asked.

Instead of answering me, she went on with her list of complaints. "He hardly contributes to conversations."

"*That's* not a problem. Our sages teach that 'In much talk, there is also much foolishness,' so perhaps you should be grateful for his discretion."

Once again she bypassed my comment and said, "He just about ekes out a living. It bothers me. I have difficulty respecting him."

I told her to follow the teachings of Rabbi Eleazar and try to look at her husband with a *good eye.*

"How would I do that?" she asked, puzzled.

"Well, you might start by asking yourself if he is a good husband."

"You mean, is he nice to me?"

"Yes, that's exactly what I'm asking."

"Well, I guess he *is* very considerate, and I know he loves me."

"Is he a good father?"

"Yes, he adores the baby."

"Then how can you not respect him? Are there any attributes that are worthy of greater respect?"

She was silent for a while and then reluctantly conceded, "I guess not."

"That's not good enough!" I said. "'I guess not' is too ambivalent a statement. You told me that your brothers-in-law are 'sharper' and 'more successful' than your husband. Let's get away from those euphemisms. What does 'sharper, more successful' really mean to you—that they make more money than he or that they are kinder and wiser? Do you refer to your husband as being *different* because he has difficulty making a living? Come on, you know better than that. You envy your sisters-in-law, but how do you really know what's going on in their homes? How do you know what sort of husbands and fathers your brothers-in-law are? If you learn to look at your husband with a *good eye*, you will come to appreciate the priceless blessing of having an attentive, caring, loving father and husband at your side."

And with that, I told her the story of a man whose store was failing, while his competitor, who was located just a few blocks away, was thriving. Upset, he went to consult his rabbi.

"Why is he succeeding while I am failing?" he asked.

"You are overworked. You have undertaken too much, running two businesses at the same time," the rabbi told him.

"What do you mean?" the man protested. "I have only this one little store."

"So why are you watching the other one? Focus on your own store, and if you do so, you will discover how to bring it to its full potential."

"Similarly," I told Jessica, "stop comparing your husband to others. Look at him with a *good eye* and bring forth that which is best in him. A woman can make or break a man—that's your challenge."

Time and again, I have resolved marital conflicts by encouraging people to exercise their *good eye*.

Paula and Malcolm came to see me because they were constantly fighting. "But we love each other," they insisted. Malcolm added: "We don't want to separate or anything like that. We are just two opposites. I am neat. I like an orderly house, but Paula, she couldn't care less."

"Of course I care," she interjected. "It's just that I don't go crazy like you do when there's a mess."

"It's not a matter of going crazy," he shot back, "but I think I'm entitled to come home at night without having to walk through an obstacle course of toys, bottles, shoes, and sweaters. The other night, I almost broke a leg."

"If you look at your problem with a *good eye*," I told him, "you will realize that what you are complaining about is a wonderful blessing. Do you know how many men would literally give their right arms to return home to find children's toys strewn about? Instead of becoming annoyed and feeling sorry for yourself, you could say, 'Thank G-d I have lively children and a wife who is relaxed with them.' And if the mess really bothers you, you could say, 'Honey, you must have had a stressful day. Let me give you a hand with the kids.' It all depends on whether you look at things with a good or a bad eye.

"A *good eye* can resolve many different little things in a marriage. A man can be late coming home from work—his wife can be outraged. 'Why are you so late? Dinner is ruined!' Or she can say, 'You must have had a tough day, sweetheart. Do you want to tell me about it?'"

When I shared these thoughts with the seminar participants, one of them, David, interjected: "I hate to sound cynical, but if you ask me, it's more likely that he was late because he was just plain inconsiderate, and the house was a mess because she had spent the day on the phone or coffee-klatching at Starbucks with one of her friends."

Not surprisingly, most of the people in the room agreed with David, so I invited the group to look at another scenario. "Let's play it David's way. A man comes home late from work and his wife accuses him of being inconsiderate, or a man comes home from work, finds the house a mess, and berates his wife for neglecting their home. True, this couple may be looking at their domestic problems realistically, but where will that get them? One hostile accusation will lead to another. Tension will beget more tension, and before you know it, the peace and harmony of their home will be destroyed. You know, it's always more difficult to rebuild something that has been destroyed than to fix something that is still functioning. The idea is to evoke the positive in your mate rather than the negative. When a husband or a wife expresses concern rather than criticism, more will be accomplished than if inflammatory accusations are made. In one instance, anger and resentment will dominate the home, whereas in the other, feelings of tenderness will be awakened. In the final analysis, the most basic need of human beings is to be loved, cared for, and appreciated, but whether that love will be forthcoming will largely depend on the development of that *good eye*."

"Still, I'm a realist," David argued. "I don't know if I could be so understanding and forgiving."

"Rabbi Eleazar was certainly a realist, but that did not prevent him from looking for the good in people and behaving toward them with compassion, and that's what committed love is all about. One can face the facts head-on in their stark reality and still see the good rather than the bad. Try practicing it, David," I said. "At first, like all new exercises, it will take much effort, but eventually, your *eye* will be conditioned to see good, and your way of thinking will change as well."

Marriage can be a minefield. Every step, every word, every deed can be misunderstood, so what better way can there be to prepare for it than to develop that *good eye*.

# THREE

# MARRIAGE IS HERE TO STAY

Jason Miller was a forty-two-year-old investment banker who founded his own start-up company and made it big. From time to time, he would drop in on one of our Hineni Torah classes, but he never came with any serious intent to study. He would scan the room, stay for a few minutes, and then leave. As brief as his visits were, they always made an impression on the single women. Many of them would approach me and ask for an introduction. "What do you know about him?" I would ask. "Why him and not someone else? Just because he's good-looking and has money doesn't mean that he'll be a good husband or father, and when it comes to marriage, that's what counts."

But my words would fall on deaf ears. "I just want to meet him. Could you please set me up?" I tried to make the introductions that they so eagerly sought, but it seemed that no one was good enough, and I began to wonder if Jason would ever make it to the *chuppah* (marriage canopy). When I heard one day that he had become engaged to a woman in his office, someone he had dated on and off for a number of years, I was pleasantly surprised. Sometime after his marriage, I ran into him at JFK. I was on my way to Los Angeles to speak and he was bound for the same destination on business. Our flight had been delayed, so we had an opportunity to chat.

"How is your beautiful bride?" I asked.

"Bride?" he questioned. "We've been married for over five months."

"We have a tradition," I explained, "called *shana rishona*—which means that throughout the entire first year, you are considered bride and groom. It's a year of celebration, and every day is your wedding day. This is so that the joy of the first year may set the pattern for your entire married life. As a matter of fact," I went on, "had you asked, I would have advised you to avoid trips that preclude your wife being at your side during this first year."

"Well, then, I'm glad I didn't ask," was Jason's surprising answer. "I could have sent someone from my office, but I just had to get away."

"I'm sorry that you're having problems. Would you like to talk about it?"

"Why not?" Jason shrugged. "Actually, a few times I've thought about coming to see you."

"Maybe that's why our flight was delayed," I said.

"Maybe," he agreed. "So where should I begin?"

"When people ask me that question, I always suggest that they begin at the end, because that sort of sums it all up."

"Well, I guess I could sum it up in two sentences: The marriage is no good. I want out."

"I can also give you some one-liners," I told him. "'Marriage *is* good—it's *people* who mess up.' 'It's never too late to have a new beginning.' Want to hear some more?" I asked.

"Not really. I'm familiar with all those clichés. They sound great in a marriage manual, but in real life they just don't work."

"Well, of course they don't if you don't give them a try."

"Rebbetzin, I've tried. There's no talking to her. It's no use."

"Before you throw in the towel, tell me what the problem is."

"I can't even say. We just fight continually about everything."

"Still, try to give me an example."

"Well, for one thing, we have an ongoing battle about my working late at the office."

"That's no fight at all. Remember what I told you about the first year of marriage. Our tradition requires that during this time husbands make an extra effort to be home early for their wives. So you see, you have argued a moot point—she is right. Besides, I would regard Dana's request as a compliment. If she weren't in love with you, if she didn't want to spend time with you, she wouldn't make a fuss about your coming home on time."

"Trust me, Rebbetzin, this is not about wanting to be with me. This is about control and criticism."

"I don't think you're reading it right. In our psychology-oriented society, sometimes we just get too analytical, and we attribute meanings to words and behavior that aren't there."

"It's not only about my coming home late that she argues; she's always on my case. I'm not a kid out of college, and I don't need to be told what to do. Wherever I go, people respect what I say. The only place I have a problem is at home."

"I don't think that you have a problem. You may be miscommunicating, but it seems to me that you and Dana are a perfect match."

Jason looked at me uncomprehendingly. "Rebbetzin, are you being facetious?"

"Not at all," I said. "I'm just quoting the Torah." And with that, I took a Bible from my carry-on and turned to Genesis 2, sentence 18. "Read this passage, Jason."

"But I don't understand Hebrew," he protested.

"That's okay. Read it in English and I will help you with the Hebrew."

"'It's not good for man to be alone,' Jason read. 'I will make him a helpmate.'

"Okay," he said, "how does that make Dana my perfect match?"

"Like you said, you don't read Hebrew, so you missed the word after helpmate, *k'negdo,* which, literally translated, means a help-mate *against* him."

"Thanks a lot!" Jason said. "That's exactly what I needed to hear—Dana being on my case is a biblical injunction! I could have lived without this good news."

"It *is* good news, Jason, but you will have to listen with your heart if you are to absorb the true meaning behind it."

"I'm all ears," Jason said somewhat sarcastically.

"Please don't think I'm nitpicking, but listening with both ears won't quite do it. I want you to listen with your heart."

"Rebbetzin, heart . . . ears, really! What's the difference? I'm here, aren't I? And I'm listening."

"There's a great difference, Jason. There is listening and then there is *listening.* King Solomon," I went on, "was known through-out the world as the wisest man. He was twelve years old when he ascended the throne of his father, King David—an awesome, fright-ening challenge for a child. G-d appeared to him in a dream and told him that he could ask for whatever he wished and it would be granted. What do you think Solomon requested? I mean, here's a boy of twelve becoming king of Israel. If you were in his place, what would you have asked for?"

"I don't know—an empire, a triumphant army, success, riches, smarts . . . you know, the works."

"You're right. Solomon could have asked for all of that, but he didn't. Instead, he beseeched G-d for the gift of a *listening heart,* which at first may sound rather odd, because it is with our ears that we listen. Very often, though, the message that we listen to with our ears goes in one ear and out the other. The mind is also tricky. It hears only what it wants to hear. The heart, however, is different. The heart recognizes the truth, and therefore listening with your heart can be a life-transforming experience. As a matter of fact, I would venture to say that most of the problems in our relationships could be resolved if we learned to listen with our hearts. But most often, when our spouses or children speak to us, we don't hear them, and the gap widens. G-d sends us many wake-up calls, not only through formal teachings, but through everyday occurrences—little incidents, even casual remarks from strangers. Usually we don't give even a moment's thought to them, but if we learn to listen with our hearts and absorb the words, the sounds, the experiences that come our way, then every day can be a new opportunity for growth and development. For example, this chance meeting can serve as a wake-up call if you wish. Of course," I added, "many people who get wake-up calls turn off the alarm and go back to sleep."

Jason laughed good-naturedly. "I'm not turning off the alarm. I'm ready to listen."

"Good! Let's start with your telling me what you think marriage is all about."

"Wait a minute. I thought I was supposed to be listening, and now you're telling me to talk."

"That's true," I agreed, "but I want you to listen to your own words and contrast your notion of marriage to that which our Torah teaches."

"Well, I guess to me marriage means having someone in your life who will make you feel real good about yourself."

"For that, you don't have to get married," I interjected.

"What do you mean?" Jason asked, surprised.

"Well, a girlfriend or, for that matter, a good shot of scotch can achieve the same thing."

"Come on, Rebbetzin, that's not fair."

"Why not?" I asked

"It just isn't."

"Look, Jason," I explained, "if G-d made the institution of marriage a commandment and declared that *it is not good for man to be alone,* He must have had something more in mind than for us to feel good about ourselves. From the passage that you just read, 'It is not good for man to be alone,' our rabbis deduced that if a man lives without a wife, he lives without joy, without goodness, without blessing—in fact, he's *half a man.*"

"Isn't this just semantics? I mean, what's the difference between wanting to feel good about oneself and what you just said?"

"There's a world of difference, Jason. Your goal of wanting to feel good about yourself is self-focused. On the other hand, the teaching of the Bible reminds us that without marriage we are only a half, and we need our other half to feel fulfilled and grow into a better person. That is why the Torah teaches us that G-d created the first man as an androgynous being (Genesis 1:27), and only later divided him into two. G-d could certainly have created Adam and Eve separately at the very outset, even as He did the animals, but G-d wished to program within man not only a need for physical intimacy but, more significantly, a yearning for completion that can be achieved only when you are connected to your other half. You need your helpmate to fulfill your higher purpose in life. True, at times it may appear as if your helpmate is against you, but in essence, she is challenging you. Blessing in marriage is not just having a wife who will 'yes' you, bolster your ego, or, as you said, make you feel good about yourself but, more significantly, having one who will motivate you to be a better person. Her task is not only to make you feel loved and cared for, but to inspire you to be more loving and more caring. For that to happen, however, it is very often necessary for her to become a *helpmate against you.*

"A wise man once taught that there is no greater joy than the joy of developing and improving your character traits. That's what growth is all about. That's the meaning of fulfilling your potential. Marriage is the perfect venue for that. It demands that you think in terms of *we* rather than *me*, and that you dig deep into your soul to bring forth the tenderness, affection, and forgiveness buried there. I know that this may seem rather grandiose," I told him, "but a nation is only as strong as its individual families. That is why it was patriarchs and matriarchs rather than monarchs or politicians who were the architects of our people. So try to listen with your heart to the criticisms that Dana sends your way. Granted, you may find her words irritating, but that's because she lacks Torah skills in communicating, not because she feels hostility toward you."

Jason remained silent, but his expression told me that he was not convinced.

"Do you realize what a blessing it is to have someone in your life who can say, 'Honey, you're wrong. Honey, you have to change.' Only a wife can do that; only a wife can be a helpmate *against* you and motivate you to examine your life."

"Well, in that case, Dana sure has all the makings of a good wife," he said sardonically.

"You're being sarcastic, Jason," I said. "Go back to listening with your heart and consider that Dana was given to you by G-d to bring out the *best* rather than the *worst* in you. But because our minds are filled with the divergent voices of our culture rather than with our biblical wisdom, you are not communicating. Look back on your school years. Who did more for you, the teachers who let you get away with murder or the ones who really got on your case and made you work? Sure, you may have resented the latter, but they helped you develop good, strong character traits and learning skills. Similarly, when Dana criticizes you, she is prodding you to examine your life and grow."

"It sounds good here in the airport, but believe me, when she gets going, she doesn't sound very inspirational."

"That's because, as I told you, she doesn't know how to criticize the Torah way. The Bible doesn't only say *against* him, but to be a *helper* against him, meaning that one's words have to be couched in such a way that they are *helpful*, and if one doesn't know how to do that, it's best to remain silent.

"Let me tell you about a great lady from our past. She was a prophetess and a judge, respected and honored by everyone. Her name was Deborah, but she was also known as *Aishet Lapidot*, which, literally translated, means 'the wife of light.' She was given that name because she used her feminine ingenuity to be a *helpmate against him*. Her husband was a good man, but not well versed in Torah, so she had the formidable task of inspiring him to become a scholar. But how was she to accomplish that without damaging his self-esteem? Should she confront him with his lack of knowledge? Should she cajole or nag? What is the best way to reach a man? Deborah, in her wisdom, chose none of these options. Instead, she fashioned wicks to light the lamps in the Tabernacle and asked her husband to deliver them. At the same time, she alerted the High Priest to keep an eye out for her husband and involve him in learning when he came on his errand. With the passage of time, her husband became a great Torah luminary, but the credit for his achievement was given to Deborah, and it was for this reason that she was known as The Wife of Light.

"You can see from this story, Jason, the enormous power of a wife, so let's establish that the method through which Dana has been communicating may be all wrong, but her motivation is sincere."

"What's the difference what her motivation is? The fact is, she makes me sick!"

"There's an enormous difference, Jason. It's the difference

between looking at your wife with a *good eye* and looking at her with a *bad eye*, seeing her as a partner or as an adversary. If she's your partner, then you will welcome her honesty and her insight because you realize that she has your welfare at heart. But if you look upon her as your adversary, then nothing she does or says will be good. Let me illustrate.

"One day, when my children were small, they watched a *Sesame Street* video. There was something so touching about that tape that it never left me. It was the story of a little boy who lost his mother and cried bitterly, 'I want my mommy.' No one could console him. Not knowing what to do, the neighbors took him to the king, who was renowned for his compassion and wisdom. 'Don't worry, little boy,' he said, 'we'll find your mommy. But tell me, what does your mommy look like?'

"'She is the most beautiful lady in the entire world,' he gasped between sobs.

"'Well, that should be easy enough,' the king said, and he ordered all the beautiful women in the kingdom to come to the palace. 'Is this your mommy? Is this your mommy?' he asked the little boy as the women filed past them. But no one filled the bill. Evening came, and still the little boy's mommy could not be found. The king was about to give up when suddenly the boy cried out, 'That's my mommy. That's my mommy!' and joyously ran to a woman who was bent and disheveled.

"'But, little boy,' the king protested, 'you told us that your mommy is the most beautiful lady in the world.'

"'But she *is*, Your Majesty, she *is!*'

"A mother, no matter what she looks like, is the most beautiful lady in the world to her child, for no other reason than that she is the mother. Similarly, your wife has to be the most beautiful, the most special person in your life for no other reason than that she is your wife, your other half. If you keep this in mind, it will be easier, and the words that you now find so objectionable will no longer be so cutting."

"That's a nice story, Rebbetzin, but there's a difference between a mother and a wife."

"That's true, but they also have much in common. When you were a little boy, it was your mom who was out there watching and protecting you, and now let's hope that in Dana, G-d sent you a partner who will continue to bestow the same loving care, albeit differently."

"Rebbetzin, I was looking for a wife, not a mother."

"I understand that. Nevertheless, it's important for every person to have someone in his or her life who really cares, someone who will say, 'You're working too hard!' 'You're not getting enough rest,' and even silly things like 'That tie doesn't go with that suit.' The trick, of course, is to try to emulate Deborah, the prophetess, who communicated this in an unobtrusive, sensitive manner. Yes, there has to be a difference between wives and mothers. That which a mother can get away with, a wife cannot and should not, but the loving care must remain. No, I don't think your marriage is over, but I do think that you and Dana will have to learn to relate the Torah way, so before giving up, why not give it a try? Start looking at Dana with a *good eye* and listen to her with your heart."

"Are you seriously suggesting that there is a Torah formula for relationships?" Jason asked.

"That's exactly what this conversation has been about. And it is logical. Did you ever purchase a gadget without an instruction manual? Similarly, how can you imagine that G-d would have propelled us into this world without some sort of manual? If G-d made marriage a commandment, then it follows that He must have given us guidelines on how to make our marriages happy, harmonious, and fulfilling. 'Turn the pages, turn the pages, everything is in it' (the Bible) is the wise counsel of our sages."

"So how is it that no one knows about it?" Jason challenged.

"Well, just as there are people who discard instruction manuals because they think they know better and require no guidance, so there are people who have chosen to disregard G-d's instructions. And the tragedy is that, after generations of neglect, people no longer know that an instruction manual ever existed. The 'gadget,' marriage, remains broken; they try every which way to fix it, but nothing works, so either they learn to live with broken gadgets or they throw up their hands in frustration, until in anger and bitterness they discard it. Before giving up on your marriage, however, I think you owe it to yourself to study that instruction manual. It is the single most important document in your life."

"I think it's too late for that. I missed the first year—what did you call it in Hebrew?"

"*Shana rishona*. And if you will it, Jason, every year of your life can be a *shana rishona*. That's what's so amazing about the compassion of G-d. He is forever prepared to give us an opportunity to start anew, and that, too, is part of the instruction manual, so if you will it, it's never too late for anyone."

"I don't know if I can do it," Jason declared.

"Of course you can. Forgiveness is built into your spiritual genes."

"My spiritual genes?" Jason repeated quizzically.

"Let's go back to the Bible. Remember Adam and Eve? How Eve prevailed upon her husband to partake of that forbidden fruit and how, as a result, their entire world collapsed? Adam could hardly have been blamed had he been furious with his wife, but instead of berating her, Adam gave her a new name, Chava, which means 'the mother of all life' (Genesis 3:20). Adam did not allow bitterness or resentment to dominate his emotions. He focused on that which was good in his wife and blessed her for being the source of life. So you see, Jason, it is in your spiritual genes to see good rather than bad. When G-d saw how Adam *acted*, He *reacted* in kind and made them clothing to protect them (Genesis, 3:21), teaching us that when peace and harmony prevail between husband and wife, G-d clothes them in garments of blessing and dwells in their midst. From Adam's example we can all learn how to deal with the conflicts and hurts in our marriages. Concentrate on the positives and allow the negatives to pass. And mind you, I will relate the same to Dana should you decide to come and see me with her. I can assure you that she will have her own story to tell. But what is significant, what is important, is that you become wiser from your experience, that you forgive each other, get on with your lives, and establish a home in which sons and daughters will be nurtured in an atmosphere of respect and love."

Jason and Dana did come to see me, and they did discover that timeless instruction manual that changed their lives.

# START YOUR FAMILY
# WITH A LEGACY
# OF SONG

J anie and Kenny called for an appointment. They were a sweet young couple who had recently begun to attend my classes. As they walked into my office, I hoped it wasn't marital difficulties that had prompted them to come.

"So how can I help you?" I asked after we had exchanged some small talk.

"You start, honey," Janie said. But Kenny passed the ball right back to her.

"As far as I'm concerned, I don't think we have a problem. This was your idea, so I think it would be better if you speak," Kenny said.

Janie appeared somewhat hurt, but she plunged into her story. "Rebbetzin, I've just passed my thirtieth birthday. We've been married for two years and I would like to start a family, but Kenny wants to wait. He feels we need more financial security."

"I'm not saying that we have to be millionaires," Kenny interrupted, "but parents *do* have a responsibility to provide a good life for their children, and I don't feel that we are in that position as yet." And with that, he turned to me and asked, "Have you ever considered how much it costs to raise a child these days?"

I found his question jarring. How do you measure life in dollars and cents? Has it come to that? Have children become just another expenditure? What has happened to the love, to the pure joy that enters a home with the birth of every child? But I felt that, for now, it would be wiser not to become confrontational, so I simply told him that that question had never occurred to me.

"Well, it has occurred to me. The costs are astronomical, but even apart from financial considerations, having a baby places a terrible strain on a marriage. Right now, we can come and go as we please, but a baby complicates everything."

"The greatest blessing that you can have," I said, "is children. Our tradition teaches that every child brings its own *mazel* (luck) into the world. If you have faith in G-d, He will help you provide for them. Besides, it's not as if you're not earning a living. So you make some budgetary changes—you don't have to go out to dinner so often; you don't have to buy that new set of golf clubs or whatever else you are spending on. Focus on those things in life that are *really* important, and you will discover that there are no obstacles to having a baby.

"As for coming and going as you please, where are you running, and to what end? Another trip? Another place of entertainment? And then what? What does that do for you? But if you have a baby, your life will take on meaning. You will realize what a blessing it is to come home and find that little bundle of joy waiting for you—guaranteed that it will give you dividends of happiness that you never anticipated. People who have babies always tell me, 'I'd heard that having a baby is amazing, but I never imagined that it could be this wonderful.'"

"Rebbetzin, you make it sound as if I don't want to have children. Of course I do, just not yet."

"Kenny," I said, "I have heard many couples voice the same concerns as you did and delay having a family, and when finally they felt ready, nature wasn't ready for them. People assume that the moment they decide to have a baby, presto, it will happen. Well, there may be a lucky few for whom it works that way, but that's not reality, and there has been much sad documentation on that. In any event, you want to have your children while you are young. You want to see them grow up and marry, and then enjoy your grandchildren. You are worried about your security? Having children is the *best* security. That's the way to go if you want to plan your future. Nevertheless, I will agree that you are justified in being concerned. Not, however, about whether you will have the wherewithal to support your children—that comes from G-d—but rather, whether you will have *something of value* to transmit to them. If children are to make it, they will need much more than a bank account to draw upon."

"I'm a realist, and before I would consider having children, I would have to feel financially secure," Kenny insisted.

It was obvious that either my words had flown by him or he had deliberately chosen to ignore them, but I was not about to let go, so I told him that the only real security that parents can offer their children is to inculcate in them spiritual values, faith in G-d, and a positive outlook on life.

"Oh, Rebbetzin, that's what I've been saying all along," said Janie. "Of course, I didn't quite put it as you did, but I've been trying to tell him that money is no guarantee of anything. Many of our friends who thought they had it made have lost it all and are really struggling now."

"That's all the more reason to wait," Kenny interjected, using Janie's argument to buttress his own position.

"I think that what Janie is trying to tell you is that money is round—today you have it, tomorrow you don't—and even more significantly, money is a two-edged sword. It can enrich, but it can also corrupt."

"I would be very happy to be corrupted by it," Kenny muttered under his breath.

"Money, Kenny, has destroyed too many lives, broken up too many families, built too many walls of jealousy and greed for you to be so flippant about it. Some time ago, I read an interesting essay tracing the many ills of our society to a virus identified as 'affluenza.' This virus, the article related, is so potent that even those who are not infected by it have somehow become bitten by the bug. To understand the symptoms, we just have to think of the lyrics of 'If I Were a Rich Man': 'I'd build a big tall house with rooms by the dozen. . . . There would be one long staircase just going up and one even longer coming down, and one more leading nowhere just for show.'

"That's our world today: people driving themselves frantic, building staircases that go nowhere *just for show*—trying to outdo their neighbors, expending their energies on fruitless and meaningless pursuits. And it doesn't end there. When money is an obsession, it becomes more important than life itself."

"What are you going to do?—that's the world today."

"It may be the world today," I agreed, "but why should you get enmeshed in all that craziness? You are fortunate to have a wife who wants the *real* things out of life. Be grateful for it." And to help put things into perspective, I shared a parable with them.

"Once, there was a poor man with a large family who just couldn't make a living. One day his wife told him that she'd heard of a far-off island where diamonds were lying on the streets, available to all for the picking. Desperate, the man set out and, after an arduous journey, arrived at his destination. Sure enough, everything that he had heard was true. He couldn't believe his eyes. The streets were strewn with diamonds! He couldn't gather them fast enough.

"When night fell, he sought lodging at an inn, prepared to pay for his room and board with his newly acquired gems. The proprietor laughed in his face. 'Diamonds have no value on this island,' he explained. 'Here you pay with chicken fat.'

"'Chicken fat!' the man exclaimed incredulously.

"'Yes, chicken fat,' was the reply.

"'But where do I buy chicken fat?' the man asked, not quite comprehending what he had been told.

"'Sir, I told you—it's the currency. You can't buy it, you have to earn it.'

"Having no choice, the man slaved to gather chicken fat, and as time passed, he forgot the reason he had come to the island in the first place. After many years of toil, he became wealthy and prepared to set sail for home, taking huge vats of his newfound fortune with him. After a long journey, the boat reached port. His wife and children were waiting at the dock.

"'I'm sorry that I was away so long, but it's all been worthwhile. Wait until you see the treasures I've accumulated. We will never have to worry again.'

"As the porters unloaded the heavy vats, a terrible stench filled the air. The chicken fat had rotted in the heat. His wife and children looked at him in disbelief. 'Is this what you sacrificed for all these years?' she cried. 'Was it for *this* that you slaved and labored? Was it for *this* that you stayed away from home?'

"The man, realizing the absurdity and the futility of his life, broke down and wept. How could he have forgotten the true purpose of his mission?

"Exchange the word *money* for *chicken fat,* and the word *diamonds* for *children, mitzvahs, and good deeds,* and you will get the picture. There can be nothing more tragic than to wake up and hear a voice ask, Was it for *this* that you slaved? Was it for *this* that you gave up having a family? Was it for *this* that you gave up Torah and good deeds? Was it for *this?*

"G-d propels us into this world to gather *diamonds*, but too often, like this man, we forget our true mission and end up with foul-smelling chicken fat."

"I must admit that that's a powerful story," Kenny conceded, "but I have no intention of ending up with chicken fat! It's just that, for the time being, I have to put certain things on hold. The type of business I'm in is volatile. Additionally, as you said, we live in a crazy world."

"It's not only your business that is volatile," I said. "Life itself is volatile and uncertain. But children are security. They are forever. Let me share with you a beautiful *midrash*.

"It is related that when G-d was about to bestow the Torah upon the Jewish people, there was much consternation in the heavens above.

"'Almighty G-d,' the angels pleaded, 'You are about to give away Your most sacred treasure, the Torah, and yet what guarantees do You have for its safekeeping?'

"G-d considered the words of the angels and found them to be just. But what can mere mortals offer the Creator of the universe? What guarantees can they possibly give?

"There were those who counseled that the prophets, the sages, the rabbis, be held as surety. But G-d did not accept.

"Then there were those who advised that the matriarchs, the ancestors of the nation, act as guarantors, but still G-d did not accept.

"Finally, someone suggested that the children, the little ones be offered to vouchsafe for the nation. Immediately, G-d assented, and gave the Torah to the Jewish people as an eternal inheritance.

"Thus, our children became more than children. They became the guarantors of our survival, the links to our future, as our sages taught—the builders of our world. And that's your security, Kenny."

"That's a nice story, but it doesn't pay the bills, it doesn't offer a real solution."

"The solution, Kenny, is to do your best, and to know that ultimately it's all in G-d's hands. This is one of the first lessons that we had to absorb when we were formed into a nation. For forty years in the desert we subsisted on manna. The manna had to be gathered daily (except for the Sabbath). It couldn't be stored. If anyone attempted to save it, it became putrid and wormy, teaching that having 'the good life' means placing your trust in G-d, for it is He who provides for our daily needs. Unfortunately, we have forgotten this basic principle. We have allowed the pressures of contemporary society to play upon our insecurities. We live in fear of that 'rainy day' and can never save quite enough to feel solvent."

"But these pressures are *real*—they reflect real needs."

"Real? We make up our own realities and then become victimized by them. Yesterday's luxuries become today's necessities. Let me tell you about my own childhood. My parents didn't have much money. As you know, my father was a rabbi who came to this country right after the Holocaust. His income was limited, but do you for a moment think that I would have been better prepared for life had I inherited a million dollars rather than a legacy of Torah?

"I don't know what your financial situation is, Kenny, but for argument's sake, would you feel any more secure if you were earning three hundred thousand annually instead of one hundred thousand?"

"You'd better believe it!" Kenny responded without hesitation.

"Don't be so quick to answer, because you know very well that the more people have, the more they require. As their income escalates, so does their lifestyle, and whereas they once made it on one hundred thousand, today they can't manage on three. There is as much insecurity on the Upper East Side as on the Lower East Side, and children who come from affluent homes are as much at risk as those who do not. It's inner strength and faith that people need, and that is something that money cannot buy. On the other hand, people to whom money is the be-all and end-all will never be satisfied.

Thousands of years ago, King Solomon taught, 'He who loves money will never be satisfied with money' (Ecclesiastes 5:9). Our sages taught us how we might become rich: 'Who is wealthy?' they challenged. 'He who is content with his lot' *(Ethics of the Fathers)*. A man can be a multimillionaire, but if he is not content with what he has, he is indeed poor. On the other hand, a man of moderate means who appreciates life is truly rich. At the risk of sounding trite, I once heard a saying, Wealth is a city in the state of the mind.

"As for the craziness in our world, from time immemorial, every society has had to confront its own craziness. Just consider ancient Egypt. Male Jewish babies were killed; our people were robbed, abused, and enslaved. In desperation, the chief rabbi of the community, Rabbi Amram, made a painful decision. He decided to separate from his wife and urged all the other men to follow suit. Now wouldn't you say *that* was a legitimate reason for not having children?"

"I sure would," Kenny agreed.

"Well, what if I tell you that the Torah was not supportive of Rabbi Amram's position? And the one who challenged him was his little daughter, Miriam. One of the remarkable things about Miriam was that her name derived from the Hebrew word *mar* (bitter), reflecting the sorrow, the pain of the period into which she was born. Yet, despite it all, she always managed to look at the world with a *good eye*. She even went so far as to tell people to call her *mazel tov* (good luck), because that is how convinced she was that, ultimately, everything would turn out to be good. So it was not surprising that one day she said, 'Father, I don't mean to be disrespectful, but where is your trust in G-d? Your decision is even crueler than Pharaoh's. Pharaoh issued a decree against male infants, but your mandate precludes girls from being born as well. Besides,' Miriam said, 'how do you know that G-d will not grant you a son who will redeem us all and become a blessing to the world?'

"Rabbi Amram perceived the wisdom of his daughter's words; he remarried his wife, Yocheved, and thus Moses was born.

"The Torah testifies that from the moment Moses came into this world, a special light permeated the house of his parents. Our people never forgot that lesson, and to this very day, children are regarded as a source of light and blessing in the home. My father always called us *lichtige kinder* (Yiddish for 'special lights'), and we children were buoyed by the knowledge that we were the lights of his existence.

"The teaching that every child is a source of light and blessing has shaped our attitude toward our children. No matter how desperate our situation, our sons and daughters were our hope and strength. So you see, Kenny, you have it all wrong. Children are never a strain. If anything, they are the cement that keeps a marriage together."

"It all sounds very good, but Moseses are not born every day," Kenny objected, "and not every child is a blessing. As a matter of fact, children can turn out to be real disappointments."

"That's true," I agreed, "but even under the most painful circumstances, children remain our answers. And once again, we find illumination in the Bible. Adam and Eve had two sons, and one day their son Abel was murdered by their son Cain. Can you envision anything more devastating than that? How can parents go on after such an experience? What would you have done, Kenny, if, G-d forbid, you were in their place?"

"It's beyond me," Kenny shrugged. "It's a tragedy I can't even fathom."

"Well, I'll tell you what Adam and Eve did. They searched for light in the midst of the darkness. They used their *good eye* and had another son, Seth. As a result, life continued, and we are here today.

"Bringing children into the world is not just an expression of love between two people, an act of nature, or a mere accident. Rather, it is the fulfillment of G-d's commandment: 'And ye shall be fruitful and multiply' (Genesis 1:28). So you should never be afraid, Kenny, to have children. G-d will be there to help you. You need only invite Him."

"Maybe you're right," Kenny conceded grudgingly.

"*Maybe* is the wrong term. You have to *know* that this is right if you're going to succeed as a father and, in years to come, a grandfather."

"Hold on!" Kenny protested. "I'm weighing the possibility of parenthood, and you're already casting me in the role of grandpa."

"It goes hand in hand," I told him. "As I said earlier, the sooner you start parenthood, the greater the likelihood that you will enjoy grandchildren when you are still in your prime. You may not understand this now, but grandchildren are a great blessing that give much joy and brighten up your middle and senior years."

"Rebbetzin, Kenny just doesn't get it," Janie interjected. "He sees problems everywhere. That's him!"

"Well, that's why we are here. Let's see if we can change all that, Kenny. It's important that you cultivate a *good eye*—a positive attitude—and you can start by learning to sing."

"Sing?" Kenny laughed. "I can barely carry a tune."

"That's okay," I assured him. "I'm not suggesting that you sing on stage, but that you sing in your heart and make your home a place of faith and song. Learn to do this for your own sake as well as for the sake of the children who will be born to you one day. You may wonder what this has to do with preparing for parenthood—but children are very sensitive, and even the youngest among them can sense when problems erupt. And problems are one thing that you cannot insulate them against. Like you said, you never know what tomorrow will bring, but if you show them how you sing away your worries and anxieties, you will bestow upon them an inheritance that is priceless, by far more precious than gold.

"Some years ago," I told them, "I spoke in Israel in a small settlement. I met a woman there, the mother of four, expecting her fifth. Her husband had been killed two months previously in a terrorist attack while driving to work.

"'How do you manage?' I asked, overwhelmed by her story.

"'I have no choice—I have to manage. I have a family to support, so I get up every morning and go to work.'

"We chatted for a while, and I walked with her to her car. I was dumbstruck. The car was riddled with bullet holes.

"'Aren't you frightened to drive to work?'

"'I'm terrified,' she replied.

"'So what do you do?'

"'I roll up the windows tight and sing songs from the psalms at the top of my voice, and the more I sing, the less frightened I am.'

"How is it that some people respond to crises with a song, while others become paralyzed? Like anything else, it's a matter of conditioning. If your parents put you to sleep with the song of faith, the *Shema* (bedtime prayer), and if they awakened you with a song of thanksgiving, *Modeh Ani* (the morning prayer), if they hummed as they went about their daily tasks, if they studied Torah with a melody and taught you to sing the psalms of King David, then chances are that you, too, will begin and end your day with a song that will allow you to see the sunshine rather than the shadows in life.

"One of my fondest childhood memories is of awakening in the morning to the delicious aroma of bread baking in the oven and my mother singing. Now, mind you, those were difficult days. World War II had erupted, and although the Nazis had not as yet invaded Hungary, persecution of Jews was rampant and our home became a gathering place for refugees. It was for them that my mother baked bread. My mom's heart may have been breaking, but nevertheless, she always sang, and her songs gave us courage.

"Singing is an integral part of our faith. All of G-d's creations are commanded to sing (Psalm 148). Adam, the first man, sang in the Garden of Eden: 'It is good to give thanks unto the L-rd . . .' (Psalm 92). And Moses led all the men, and Miriam, all the women, in song following the miracle of the Red Sea.

"Miriam not only sang, she played the drums and the tambourines as well. Our sages asked from whence she obtained those musical instruments. Obviously, there were no shops in the desert, but Miriam's faith was so powerful that in the midst of the Egyptian darkness, when all seemed hopeless and lost, she went forth to search for drums and tambourines because she was convinced that one day there would be cause to play music, dance, and sing.

"The sweetest singer of all was King David of Israel. His life was filled with untold pain and suffering. Persecution, betrayal, personal tragedy—he experienced it all, but he never ceased singing and creating psalms."

"I'm just an ordinary guy," Kenny objected. "You can't expect me to sing away my worries. I mean, life is complex. There are real problems out there."

"That's exactly what this is all about. The psalms of David are not mere songs or poetry. They speak to every person and reflect the anguish in his or her soul. David introduces his psalms with the word *Mizmor* (song), which is etymologically related to the Hebrew word that means 'pruning.' If a tree is to live and grow, its decayed branches and dead bark must be pruned lest disease infect the entire tree. David composed psalms for every life situation so that, with a song, we might prune away the poisonous effects of greed, jealousy, fear, anger, depression, and worry. There is no torment or pain that David did not experience, but he triumphed over it all with his psalms, and those psalms have sustained not only our people but all of humankind throughout the centuries.

"It's not only in cataclysmic moments that the psalms of David sustain us. They nourish our souls every day and are there to fortify us in every life situation. You, Kenny, are worried about supporting a family. Try reciting Psalm 55: 'Cast your burden upon G-d and He will support you.' Or Psalm 145: 'You (G-d) open Your hand and satisfy the desire of every living thing.'

"I realize that this may sound simplistic, but a song speaks. Memories of a melody remain and they don't let go. They enable us to retain our faith, and perhaps it is for this reason that the Torah itself is called a song.

"During the years of the Holocaust, some young Jewish children were hidden in monasteries throughout Europe. At the end of the war, Jewish rescue organizations tried to reclaim these orphans.

"Rabbi Eliezer Silver of Cincinnati, Ohio, was among those who took upon himself the responsibility of searching out these children. He came to a hermitage in the Alsace-Lorraine region of France, where he had been told Jewish orphans were hidden. The monk in charge, however, said that he didn't know of any Jewish children on the premises.

"Rabbi Silver asked for a list of the refugees. The Jewish-sounding names, he was told, were all German. Not at all convinced, Rabbi Silver asked if he could come back to say a few words to the children before they went to sleep.

"That evening Rabbi Silver, accompanied by two aides, returned to the large dormitory room. He started to sing *Shema Yisrael*, the prayer that Jewish children have sung at bedtime throughout the centuries. Suddenly, from six beds in the room, little voices were heard. They remembered the song and ran to the rabbi, who embraced them and took them home to their people. I related this story at one of my speaking engagements, following which a young man approached me and told me that his Hebrew school teacher had been one of those children.

"This story reflects one of the most tragic periods in our history, but because there was a song of faith in the hearts of the children, they were able to survive and start anew.

"What I'm trying to tell you, Kenny, is that children should have songs that connect them to their families, to their homes, to their heritage, to a greater vision, and *that*, not money, is security. When I tell you that you have to learn to sing, I'm not suggesting that you sing in the shower or that you have music blasting from a tape deck. Rather, I'm asking that you impart a heritage with a melody. And if you do that, then your children will have the tools with which to lighten their daily burdens and tackle the many ups and downs of life."

"Rebbetzin," Kenny said, "what you have said has touched me deeply, but what do I know about singing songs of faith and hope? It's beautiful, but where do I shine in?"

"Of course you shine in," I answered. "Every man does. Let me tell you a story of my favorite singer, my husband, and you will see how it works.

"Jewish etiquette requires that we announce ourselves before entering a house so as not to frighten the occupants, and this applies even to one's own home. We learn this teaching from the High Priest of the Holy Temple, whose coat was trimmed with bells to signal his approach.

"Whenever my husband of blessed memory returned home, I always knew that he was at the door—not because he knocked, rang the bell, or rattled the doorknob, but because as he approached, I would hear him sing.

"Now G-d knows, he didn't always have cause to sing. A survivor of Bergen Belsen who came to this country orphaned and destitute after the war, he had much to contend with. He was the pioneering rabbi of a Long Island congregation, which was a challenge fraught with many obstacles and heartaches. Nevertheless, he always sang or hummed a tune. Sometimes it was just *Bim, bam, bim,* but sing he did.

"People who were in slave labor and concentration camps with my husband told me that he sang even there, and with his songs, he gave everyone hope. Just as he lived with a song on his lips, so, too, he departed from this world with a song. In his last days, we, his entire family, children and grandchildren, stood vigil at his bedside. He summoned all his strength and sang one final song to us. It was the song with which the patriarch Jacob blessed his children in his final moment. 'May the angels who redeemed me from all evil bless the lads . . .' (Genesis 48).

"And when he could no longer speak, my children and grandchildren gathered at his bedside and sang the song to him. The nurses on the floor at Sloan Kettering stopped by the room and listened in awe.

"Did my husband hear that final song? Ask my grandchildren and they will tell you that Abba Zaide (a loving title, father/ grandfather, by which they called him) raised his hands and tried to clap, and only then did he depart.

"So, yes, Kenny, learn to sing. Life is filled with ups and downs. There is so much pain, so many uncertainties, but it all becomes meaningful if you leave behind a legacy of song for your children to sing. Don't be afraid, Kenny, to bring children into the world. They are your diamonds."

# PART TWO

# A GOOD FRIEND

Two are better than one. . . .

For should they fall, one can raise the other;

but woe to him who is alone.

When he falls, there is no one to raise him.

*King Solomon—Ecclesiastes*

# FIVE

# WHEN THE MARKET
# DROPS AND YOU
# HIT BOTTOM

Rabbi Yehoshua, the second disciple of Rabbi Yochanan, was blessed with impeccable character. He was respected and loved by everyone. It is said that when his mother carried him during her pregnancy, she visited every study hall and asked the rabbis to bless her unborn child so that he might grow up to be a Torah scholar and devote his life to the welfare of others. She did not relax even after he was born but continued to carry her infant in his cradle to houses of study so that he might absorb the holy words. Perhaps it was because his mother exposed him to spiritual nurturing early on that Rabbi Yehoshua had a cheerful, loving way about him. It was his belief that the most important goal for a person to strive for is to become a *good friend*, and at the same time, to be worthy of having a good friend. It was regarding Rabbi Yehoshua that the famous Talmudic adage was coined: "Blessed is the one who gave life to him," giving his mother credit for his sterling character.

In Hebrew, the word for friend is *chaver*, which is derived from the word "connected." A true friend always remains connected to you in good times as well as bad. A true *good friend* is someone to whom you can open your heart and reveal your most sensitive secrets, confident that your relationship won't be compromised and that you will be given good advice.

Our sages teach that a friendship based on any one thing cannot last, for as soon as that *thing* disintegrates, the friendship also disappears. Thus, friendships that are based solely on organizational or recreational interests, attending the same university, or living in the same community will fall apart once that interest flags or one of the parties relocates. Although it is perfectly acceptable for friendship to be initiated by mutual goals and concerns, if it is to endure it will have to transcend those narrow confines and evolve into a relationship of unconditional love. This principle is especially true for marriage.

The woman that Saul was going to marry couldn't just be sweet or charming. She had to be *stunning*, and he spotted her while on a ski trip to Aspen. Amy was everything that Saul had ever dreamed of. He pursued her ardently, and soon enough they were married, and could have had a happy marriage were it not for a freak skiing accident that left Amy scarred and disfigured. As Amy's beauty faded, so did the love for her that had once obsessed Saul. After a while, he started looking elsewhere and had Amy served with divorce papers.

Under the *chuppah* (marriage canopy) we pronounce a special blessing that renders the couple *loving, kind* friends, always at each other's side, always encouraging each other, and when necessary, criticizing and gently showing where the other erred. G-d has endowed each of us with unique gifts. When our mates become our best friends, we pool our spiritual resources and strengthen each other. In such a relationship, life's trials become less threatening, and even the most formidable challenges become manageable. "Two are better than one" is the wise teaching of King Solomon. If one falls, the other is there to pick him/her up. If one is attacked, the other is there to rescue him; if one is depressed, the other is there to buoy her spirits.

When we feel that the rug has been pulled out from under us, when our problems are so overwhelming that we can no longer go on—at such times, we need a *good friend* to help us pull through. Michael Berkman discovered that friend when he plummeted from the top and hit bottom.

I first met Michael in Israel. He and his family were spending the summer in Jerusalem. He came to the seminar I was conducting at our Bill and Jill Roberts Hineni Center and introduced himself.

"You don't know me, Rebbetzin, but my wife, Jackie, attends your Torah classes in New York."

"Of course," I responded. "She is a very special lady—not only beautiful, but wise and sensitive."

"You don't know the half of it," Michael said.

"I'm sure I don't," I agreed. "So tell me, what are you doing here in Jerusalem?"

"We've decided to take the summer off and study."

"That's great!" I said.

"Thank you," Michael said, smiling, "but it's not so simple. There's a long story behind it. Would you like to hear it?"

I told Michael that I was always ready for a good story, and with that he reached into his pocket for his wallet and took out a piece of paper.

"You see this? I carry it with me wherever I go. It saved my life. It was written by my *best friend*—my wife—and I think that it is a story that you could make good use of."

Of all the stories that I've heard about friendship between husband and wife, perhaps Michael's touched me the most.

"A few years ago," he began, "I was making money hand over fist. It was coming in faster than I could spend it. A couple of guys and I invested in high tech stocks and IPOs, and overnight, we became wealthy—and I mean wealthy. Jackie and I bought an apartment on the Upper East Side and a home in the Hamptons. On winter breaks we took the kids skiing in Aspen. But then, the bottom fell out of the market and my money was gone faster than it had come.

"Rebbetzin, I didn't lose a *lot* of money—I lost *all* my money!" Michael said. "I don't think I'll ever forget the day it happened. I was sitting at my desk watching the computer screen. Suddenly, I couldn't breathe. Right there in front of my eyes, everything I had was disappearing. I started to bang on the monitor. I felt sure I was going to have a heart attack. I yelled, I cursed, but it was no use. There was no one to yell at! I could be angry only at myself. As the awful truth sank in, I broke down and wept. Even now, when I think about it, I feel sick. What was I going to do? How could I tell Jackie? How could I face my kids and my elderly father, who had trusted me and given me money to invest. I wanted to commit suicide. Believe it or not, I actually walked over to the window and opened it. I started to fantasize about how it would feel to jump from the twenty-second floor. But, thank G-d, I was a coward."

"You didn't think of calling someone, just for support?" I asked.

"Actually, my wife called me, but I was afraid to speak to her, so I told my secretary to tell her that I'd call her back. I just stood by the window, paralyzed by fear. Over and over, I asked myself how I could have been such an idiot. The month before I had twenty million—I could have gotten out. Why did I reinvest? I tried to convince myself that my intentions had been good, but I couldn't escape from the terrible reality. The money was gone, and it was my fault. I was left with this sick feeling and I just wanted to die. If only I had gotten out. If only I hadn't been so greedy, if only, if only. The words kept playing like a broken record in my mind.

"Meanwhile, Jackie heard the news. She kept calling until I had no choice but to take the phone. As soon as I heard her voice, I burst out crying. I hadn't cried like that since I was a kid. I didn't have to say anything. She understood. She told me to get hold of myself, that we'd manage. I tried to make her understand that there was nothing left to manage, but she couldn't comprehend it. She kept insisting that we had twenty million and there had to be something left. You can't imagine how I felt when I told her that I'd reinvested all of it. It was supposed to be a sure thing, and I was certain that I could double our money. My plan was to get out of the market when I hit forty million."

At this point, Michael paused, reached into his pocket for a handkerchief, and blew his nose. His eyes filled with tears. "I'm sorry, but I still get emotional when I think about it. I thought that Jackie would curse me out; instead, she said, 'Hang in there, honey. I'm coming right over,' and sure enough, in no time at all she was there."

"That's quite a woman you have there," I told him.

"Wait, this is just the beginning of my story. Jackie walked into my office and took charge. She literally took me by the arm, led me to the elevator, and told me that she was taking me home.

"She warned me that I shouldn't allow the children to see me this way. 'We'll figure out something. It's not the end of the world. It's not terminal illness.'

"Somehow Jackie managed to get me home," Michael continued. "I was a total mess. I got down on my knees in front of her and told her that if she wanted to leave me, I'd understand. I deserved it. Her response was to take me in her arms and rock me like a baby. 'There's no getting away from it, you did a really stupid, irresponsible thing, but I learned in Torah class that *life is all about forgiveness and starting anew.* Even as we would like G-d to forgive us, so we must forgive each other, and above all, we must learn to forgive ourselves.'

"She tried to lift my spirits by reassuring me that she loved me for *myself*, and not for the money I had made, that yes, we were in for some hard times, but with G-d's help, we'd make it. We had each other, we had great kids, and at the end of the day, that was most important. We'd be okay."

"Did you believe her?" I asked.

"To tell you the truth, Rebbetzin, I heard her voice, but I didn't hear what she said. I could only focus on my losses. How could we be okay? I kept asking. There was *nothing left!* How could I face people?

"'Who cares about what people will say?' she told me, infusing me with strength. 'So they'll talk for a few days and say, Michael Berkman lost his money. Big deal! Those who are true friends will stick with us, and those who don't—who needs them anyway? If you are confident and strong, then people won't have reason to talk, but if you walk around like a basket case, like your world has come to an end, then for sure you'll evoke gossip.' Those words stood me in good stead. Every time I got a panic attack and was afraid to face people, I would hear Jackie's voice, 'Pull yourself together, honey. Don't allow people to see you this way.'"

Slowly, and with much patience, Jackie taught Michael to accept reality. "Face the fact," she said, "that the money is *really gone,* but that doesn't mean that your life is gone." She helped him come to terms with what had happened and prodded him to move on.

Jackie demanded that Michael quit the market, which was easy enough since there was nothing left with which to play. But what he found more difficult was her insistence that they sell the house in the Hamptons and the apartment in Manhattan.

"The thought of giving up our home and our apartment was dev-astating. I sort of felt that I was losing my manhood, but Jackie kept assuring me that the house and the apartment had nothing to do with what I was—that we'd use that money to invest in a business.

"I went through a year of hell," Michael continued. "The nights were the worst. I would fall asleep from sheer exhaustion and then wake up in a sweat with a panic attack. I was certain that I was going to have a coronary. On a few occasions we even went to the emergency room at NYU Medical Center. I had nightmares. I started to take medication, but I didn't like the feeling of being dependent on pills, so I weaned myself off them, and the nights remained long and torturous. I would wake up Jackie for reassurance. She never complained and was always there to give me hope and encouragement.

"The toughest thing for me, though, was telling my father. He had given me money to invest, and now that, too, was gone. He had always been a strict disciplinarian with high expectations of all of us. I just didn't know how to approach him, but Jackie offered to go with me. As expected, my father launched into a tirade, but once again Jackie saved the day. 'Dad, Michael is sick about this. Please don't make it worse. It's bad enough we lost the money, we don't want to lose Michael as well. Come on, Dad,' she said in her very special way, 'Michael is looking to you for strength. This is your opportunity to bond with him.'

"Jackie calmed down my father, and although he gave me a long lecture, it wasn't half as bad as it could have been. We sold our house and the apartment and invested in a small business. Of course, it wasn't as easy as it sounds. Every day was another struggle. I had panic attacks at work and kept calling Jackie for reassurance. So one day she put it all down on paper, and that's the note that I showed you when we met. I carry it with me wherever I go. Would you like to read it?" Michael asked, handing it to me.

I hesitated, thinking that by reading it I would be intruding in a very private place.

Michael saw my reluctance. "It's okay," he said. "You can read it."

I took the crumpled paper. It was obvious that it had been folded and unfolded many times. "My dearest Michael," it read. "You are my soul mate, my best friend, my partner in life. I married you because I loved you and not for the money that you would one day make. My love is constant and doesn't fluctuate with the market. You are my husband, the father of my children, and with G-d's help, we'll see this thing through. So hang in there. Forever yours, Jackie."

"So now, Rebbetzin, you know why she is my best friend," Michael said.

I told Michael that he was one lucky man, and that it must have been women like Jackie that the sage Rabbi Akiva had in mind when he taught, "Who is rich? He who has a wife who is lovely in her deeds" (Talmud).

"I'll second that! There isn't a day that goes by that I don't thank G-d for Jackie."

Michael went on to tell me about his new life. "I don't have a lot of money anymore, but that's all right. I've discovered that I can manage with less. But more important, my values have changed. I have a whole different way of looking at things, which would probably never have happened if I hadn't crashed. And I owe you a debt of gratitude for that, because it was a teaching from your Torah class that Jackie shared with me that enabled me to do it. The lesson was from the story of Noah and his ark. Do you know what I'm referring to?" Michael asked.

For over forty years I have been teaching Torah, and among my most gratifying moments have been those occasions when people came back to me and shared how a particular teaching enabled them to overcome the crises in their lives. This lesson to which Michael was referring has proved to be a source of inspiration to countless people who felt that they could no longer go on.

If there was anyone whose world had fallen apart, it was Noah's. Everyone and everything vanished. He confronted a total Holocaust. How does a man survive in an ark while the entire world is disappearing in front of him? G-d commanded Noah to place a *tzo-*

*har* in the ark for illumination. What the exact translation of this word is, is open to debate. Some of our sages suggest that it was a special jewel of such brilliance that it illuminated the entire ark; others say it was a window that brought in light. We have a tradition regarding varying biblical interpretations of our sages: they're *all* correct, for they all represent the living word of G-d. Therefore, even if there appears to be a disparity, they are equally valid.

The word *tzohar* contains the same Hebrew letters found in the word *tsores* (terrible problems). When someone says, "I have *tsores*," it's never a matter of simple difficulties. It's more like you've run out of gas and have nothing left—that's *tsores!*

Noah had that type of *tsores*, so G-d told him to make a *tzohar* to convert his pain into a "window of opportunity" through which he would see his mission in the world with clarity, and once he learned to view his life through this window, then his *tsores* would become a brilliant jewel that would illuminate his path and enable him to grow. It was that teaching that Jackie shared with Michael: "Look at your losses as a window of opportunity—a learning experience through which you can reevaluate your life and thus convert the *tsores* into a *tzohar*, a jewel." And that's exactly what Michael did.

"Jackie inspired me to examine my life," Michael now said. "She pointed out that if I went to pieces and became suicidal, it was because I had no beliefs to sustain me.

"I came to understood how important it is to have G-d in my life, so I began to explore my heritage, and as I studied, I began to realize that more than a house in the Hamptons and a luxury apartment in Manhattan, my children and I needed the direction that only faith in G-d can provide. In the past, my moods would go up and down with the market. My kids were actually afraid to talk to me before checking with Jackie to see if the market was okay that day. In retrospect, I realize how sad that was.

"I discovered the magic of *Shabbos*. From the moment that Jackie kindles the Sabbath lights, peace enters our home and my heart is filled with serenity. The telephone, the computer, the TV are all silent, and we, as a family, enter a different time zone and connect with G-d.

"You should see the magnificent table that my wife sets," Michael continued. "Jackie even bakes her own challah (special Sabbath loaves). On Thursday nights, the challahs baking in the oven give our home the flavor of the Garden of Eden. And when the Sabbath arrives, we sit around the table telling stories, sharing wisdom from the Torah, and singing songs, and no one is in a rush to leave. Our family has really grown so much closer. You know something," Michael said, "when I sing *Shalom Aleichem* (Welcome, you angels of Sabbath), I look at my Jackie and the children and I really see angels in my home.

"I bless the children,[1] but more than I bless them, it is they who bless me. My favorite Sabbath song," he continued, "is King Solomon's 'A Woman of Valor, who can find . . . she is far more precious than rubies . . . her husband's heart trusts in her . . . she openeth her mouth in wisdom and lessons of kindness are on her lips'. . . That song speaks to me."

Not only was I overwhelmed by Michael's story, but I was impressed by his willingness to give his wife credit, something that not every man is capable of doing.

"Would you like to hear more?" he now asked, interrupting my thoughts.

"Please," I said. "I find your story fascinating."

---

[1] Every Friday evening at the dinner table, prior to making Kiddush (the blessing over the wine), parents place their hands upon their children's heads and invoke the ancient priestly blessing from the Torah: "May G-d bless thee and keep thee . . . (for girls) May G-d make thee like Sarah, Rebecca, Rachel, and Leah. (For boys) May G-d make thee like Ephraim and Menashe.

"Jackie and I had a dream—to spend a summer studying in Jerusalem, something I could never have envisioned doing in my previous life. In the past, even when I went on vacation, I was glued to the computer, watching the market. Looking back, I can't understand how I could have lived such a crazy life.

"So here we are in Jerusalem, having an incredible summer. The children go to day camp while Jackie and I study. Every day at dawn I have a most special experience. I go to the Wall to pray.

"Have you ever been at the Western Wall as the sun rises over Jerusalem?" he asked. "It's awesome, it takes your breath away. There, at the Wall, I talk to G-d in a way that is impossible anywhere else on earth. I don my phylacteries and I proclaim the ancient words from the Bible: 'I will betroth you to Me forever; I will betroth you to Me in kindness, in righteousness, in love and in mercy. I will betroth you to Me in faithfulness and you shall know the L-rd . . . ' (Hosea).

"I love those words. They have special meaning. I would never have believed that this could happen to me—I have become a new man, and I have Jackie to thank for it. I still have my bad moments. It still hurts when I think about the twenty million, but I also realize that losing the money wasn't that bad after all. It enabled me to put my life into proper perspective. It forced me off the fast track and connected me in a bond of love with my best friend, my wife, and it opened my heart to my ultimate Friend, the Almighty G-d, who, I now know, watches over me day and night. It enabled me to make a *tzohar* out of my life and put my *tsores* into proper perspective."

I related Michael's story to the students at my Relationships Seminar. When I finished, there was total silence until someone finally said, "Wow! Is Jackie for real?"

How sad, I thought, that when we hear the story of a wife who is a *true good friend* to her husband, we have difficulty giving it credibility.

"Not only is Jackie for real," I assured him, "but she is someone whom we would all do well to emulate. So let's try to dissect her story and see how we can relate it to our own lives. When the tragedy hit, Jackie had three options: to follow Michael's example and fall apart, to berate Michael and destroy their marriage, or to be a good friend to her husband. She chose the third option, and solidified her marriage."

I went on to discuss what exactly constitutes a good friend. A true friend does not make painful accusations. Jackie could certainly have castigated Michael for his disastrous investments, but she realized that there was nothing to be gained from rehashing the mistakes of the past. A *good friend* understands that you don't kick the wounded when they are down, that when friends collapse, you have to revive them, not pounce on them in anger.

As a *good friend*, Jackie understood that if Michael was to survive this trying period in his life, it was not only her love and support that he would require, but some positive, constructive guidance to help him get on his feet again.

As a *good friend*, Jackie understood Michael's vulnerability. Having lost his self-esteem, he needed something tangible to remind him that he was still loved, so she wrote that special note that he showed me in Jerusalem.

A *good friend* remains connected even in the most trying times. Jackie was there to hold Michael's hand throughout this, the most difficult period in their lives.

A *good friend* looks at the total picture and tries to give good advice—not just for the moment, but for the future. Jackie perceived that if Michael was on the verge of a breakdown, something was desperately missing in his life, and she inspired him to embark on a spiritual journey.

Our tradition teaches that husband and wife are meant to be loving, kind friends, and if they are, then the Almighty Himself will become their loving friend and dwell in their midst.

# SIX

# HOW TO BUILD A LOVING RELATIONSHIP

The blessing is given under the *chuppah*, but whether husband and wife become *loving, kind friends* will depend upon *them*. If there is a breakdown in communications, if they confide in others rather than in each other, if instead of giving they make demands, then that special friendship will not materialize.

When I voiced these concerns to Beth and Benjamin, who came to consult me about their troubled marriage, they conceded that I was right. Still, Beth seemed to have difficulty accepting responsibility for their problems and said to me half in jest, "If being 'loving, kind friends' is a blessing given under the *chuppah*, how come it eluded us?"

Early on in my work I discovered that, very often, hidden behind laughter are real issues, and I sensed it to be the case here. Beth, like many young marrieds who had been conditioned to believe that happiness is an *entitlement*, was wondering what had happened to all her dreams. Why hadn't all those blessings under the *chuppah* worked?

"Blessings," I told her, "are effective only if you act upon them. We have a teaching, 'I shall bless you in everything you *do*.' The key word is *do*. My revered father would explain, 'If you do yours, my children, then the blessing will come from G-d.' Marriage takes a lot of hard work, and if someone tells you differently, that person is either lying or living in a state of denial. So, Beth, if you want your relationship to be that of *loving, kind friends*, you have to work at it."

To inject a light note, I shared an anecdote with them about a poor fellow who was a *schlemozzel* (the paradigm of Murphy's Law—if something could go wrong, it would happen to him). He was beset by mishap after mishap and his bills kept piling up. "If only I could win the lottery," he would cry to G-d. Finally, the angels interceded on his behalf, "Almighty G-d," they pleaded, "please grant this poor chap his wish."

"I would be happy to do so," G-d answered, "but he never bought a ticket!"

Similarly, many people bemoan their problems but are not ready to take the steps necessary to bring about a change.

"Okay," Beth said, smiling, "I get the point. What do I have to do?"

"Well, maybe you could start by explaining your feelings to Benjamin. Tell him what you meant when you said to me that you feel unloved."

"Oh, Rebbetzin, if I have to do that, it's no use."

"I wouldn't say that at all. Benjamin may just not fully understand what's bothering you." And to prove my point, I turned to Benjamin. "What do you think Beth meant?"

"What do I think she meant?" Benjamin snapped. "I really don't have patience for this. I work very hard and put in long hours at the office. I think I'm a good husband, and I don't have the time for conjecture about what she did or did not mean. She's a big girl now, and if she has something to say, let her say it and stop griping."

"You see, Rebbetzin," Beth said, "it's no use."

"Let's not give up so quickly. Let's see if I can help you clarify some of your issues. The reason you may have difficulty understanding Beth," I told Benjamin, "is because women communicate differently than men. Very often, rather than explicitly articulating their needs, they tend to hint about their feelings, anticipating that those who love them will automatically understand. But if that understanding is not forthcoming, they feel unloved and rejected, and that may be one of the reasons why Beth is so upset.

"When husband and wife are *loving, kind friends*, they perceive each other's feelings so totally that there is no need for explanations. Their relationship is virtually symbiotic. There is total empathy with the needs of the other, so if you would like to benefit from this blessing of being loving, kind friends," I said, "you will have to make an effort to plumb the heart and mind of your spouse and define yourself by focusing on the other person's feelings rather than on your own. Such was the relationship of my parents. When I visited my father in the hospital after his coronary, he hastened to assure me that all was well and bade me return to my family. But when my mother had a kidney stone attack, he called in tears and asked me to come immediately. He loved my mother with such intensity that her pain was more real to him than his own."

"It's a very touching story, but every situation and person is different," Benjamin said. "If Beth has something on her mind, let her tell me."

"That's true," I concurred. "Beth should learn to articulate her feelings. Nevertheless, this sense of oneness is a goal that you should strive for. Until a man is one with his wife, his marriage bond is incomplete. But let's backtrack. Is it possible," I continued, "that Beth has difficulty expressing herself because she feels rebuffed and intimidated by you?"

"With all due respect, Rebbetzin, that's nonsense. I'm always ready to listen, but Beth never has anything to say. She just clams up, gets teary-eyed, and expects me to guess what she is upset about."

"Perhaps," I suggested, "instead of addressing her in such a cold, adversarial tone, if you'd speak to her in a warm, loving manner, and say, 'Honey, I feel something is bothering you. Would you like to tell me about it?' she might just open up."

"I wasn't trying to be adversarial, and if I come off sounding like that, I'm sorry, but this has been going on for a long time, and I don't have patience anymore."

"You'll have to try to find the patience," I said, "and give it all you've got, because this is about *your marriage, your wife, your life.*" And with that, I turned to Beth, "You see, Benjamin is sincere, he's sorry, and he has no clue as to why you are so upset, so why don't you try to explain yourself again?"

For a moment Beth was silent. Then she took a deep breath. "This is going to be really hard, but okay, I'll try. For one thing, I would like us to spend more time together, to feel connected"—and looking at Benjamin, she hastened to add, "I know how hard you work, and if it means doing with less, it's okay with me."

"Sure, I can just see you doing with less. What would you cut out?" Benjamin asked sarcastically.

"You don't have to make such a choice," I said. "This is not about giving up things, but it *is* about elevating your relationship to that of *loving, kind friends.* Let's recapture the blessing that escaped you under the *chuppah.* But before you can recover that which you lost, you have to know what you are looking for. The Hebrew term for 'loving, kind friends' is *r'eim v'ahuvim.* The word *r'eim* is derived from the Hebrew *ro'eh,* which means 'shepherd.' The relationship of husbands and wives should be that of shepherds, always there for each other, always keeping a loving, watchful eye on the other, always expressing interest in the concerns of the other, and always there to protect and help."

"But what if your spouse is not appreciative of your watchful eye and protective care?" Benjamin asked.

"Shepherds," I said, "find their fulfillment in caring, so even if it appears that your spouse is *unaware* or unappreciative, you nevertheless remain a shepherd. The Hebrew word for 'loving,' *ahuvim*, underscores this, for it is derived from the root word *hav*, to give. To love means to give, so it's not what my spouse is doing for me but what I'm doing for my spouse that counts. A love that is not based on giving is bound to deteriorate into an exploitive relationship. It's like when people say they love chicken. What does that mean? Does it mean that they will take the chicken for a walk and speak endearingly to it, or does it mean that they will consume the chicken for their own gratification. If love is to prevail between husband and wife, it cannot be chicken-love. Rather, it must be like the love of a shepherd who finds pleasure in caring and giving."

"I really ask for so little," Beth interrupted. "I like to visit my parents. I'm an only child, and it means so much to them when we come. But whenever I ask Benjamin to join me, he balks, so I've stopped asking. But when it comes to visiting *his* mother and father, he expects me to be there for him."

"You are both wrong," I said. "Love is not tit for tat: I'll visit your mother if you visit mine. You do what you do because it's *the right* thing to do, because it's your pleasure to give, and because it *makes your spouse happy*. Honoring parents is the fifth commandment. Therefore, visiting them is the right thing to do, and if it makes your spouse happy, that's all the more reason to do so.

"We live in a capitalistic society and our culture mitigates against the idea of giving for the sake of giving. We have come to view our relationships from a business perspective: the dividends have to justify the investment. But if that's the way we run our homes, we will need live-in accountants to keep track of who gave what, where, and when; and then, every once in a while, we will call for an audit, because there will always be a feeling of mistrust, a suspicion that we're being taken advantage of. Marriage is not a business partnership—it's not even give-and-take, but it's *give* and *give more*. Giving is a prerequisite to genuine love, although people mistakenly believe that just the opposite is true, that love is a prerequisite to giving.

"When husbands and wives give of themselves fully, they quickly discover that they have gained much more than they invested, but should they fail to do so, then genuine love will elude them, for as giving stops, demands begin, and a downward spiral commences that can lead to divorce. On the other hand, when couples give to each other unconditionally, then intuitively, they sense each other's needs and they rejoice in the knowledge that they were able to bring pleasure to their mates.

"Let me tell you about my own husband. He was unquestionably my shepherd, my loving, kind friend. Our love wasn't anything we ever discussed, but it was manifested through deeds. Sometimes it was through small and seemingly insignificant things, such as the way he said hello or good-bye. When I left the house, my husband not only accompanied me to the door, but he would wave from the porch until the car turned the corner.[1] Consider how different your day would be," I told them, "if you extended this little courtesy and walked each other to the elevator or to the door.

"Our sages teach that we should greet each person with a 'warm and loving countenance' (*Ethics of the Fathers*). This doesn't mean just a smile or a kind word; it also means that when you say hello or good-bye, you *focus completely* on that person. It doesn't have to take more than a few seconds, but those few seconds should be totally devoted to your mate. Instead of mumbling something under your breath and letting your eyes roam, give your full attention and say hello or good-bye like you mean it.

---

[1] Torah dictates that we accompany whoever leaves our home. We learn this from the patriarch Abraham who escorted all those who crossed his threshold.

"Then there will be moments when your spouse will wish to share some thoughts with you—nothing earthshaking, just normal conversation. When your spouse approaches you, you may be at the computer, watching TV, or reading a book or newspaper, and without looking up, you will say, 'Go on, I'm listening.'

"Oh, Benjamin always does that," Beth interjected.

"So do you," he shot back.

"Well, then," I said, "I'm glad I brought it up, because if you want to recover the blessing of *loving, kind friends,* you will have to learn to focus on each other. Stop for a moment, leave whatever you are doing, look at the other person, and show that you care. So you see, it's not so much that you have to give more time, but rather that the time that you *do* give be *full-hearted and undivided.* Even as a half-baked cake is inedible, so, too, is a half-hearted greeting or conversation ineffective. Besides, it's just plain rude. I once visited a high-powered person in her office, and throughout my visit, her eyes remained glued to her computer monitor."

"Well, I agree. That's impolite," Benjamin said. "But I think that husbands and wives should be sufficiently confident in each other's love that things like that should not bother them."

"Listen to what you are saying, Benjamin. Are you suggesting that you should be more considerate of a stranger than of your wife? Who deserves more of your attention?

"Our rabbis teach that if there is a man who devotes himself to service, acts of kindness and philanthropy, he is certainly to be commended, but if at the very same time he neglects his family and relates to his wife in an arrogant, condescending, hostile manner, his good deeds and charity will have lost their worth and meaning.

"Yes, husband and wife should be confident in each other's love, but never should that confidence be confused with disrespect. Besides, simply from a practical point of view, you cannot do two things well at the same time, and this, too, we learn from the Torah.

G-d sent three angels to Abraham, one to heal him, one to announce the birth of Isaac, and one to destroy the twin cities of Sodom and Gemorah (Genesis 18). Surely one angel could have fulfilled all three missions, but G-d wanted to impress upon us that if we wish to succeed, we can do only one task at a time."

"Rebbetzin, when you quote that Torah stuff, you're one up on me," Benjamin laughed.

"That may be true," I said, "but Torah is one up on all of us. That's the beauty of Torah guidance.

"You and I can be wrong; every generation creates its own credos and beliefs. For example, not too long ago, the pundits advocated feminism, careers, and independence. As a result, many young women renounced motherhood and marriage. Today, the pendulum has swung the other way. Today, marriage is in again. This same type of fluctuation is evidenced in every area of life. When my children were born, breast-feeding was discouraged; today, it's the thing to do. When it came to child rearing, camaraderie was advocated over discipline. You may think that these issues are of no real consequence, but for those who lost the opportunity to marry and for those who raised their children without proper guidelines, the damage can't be undone. Life is just too precious to play games with. We owe it to ourselves to consult a higher authority for guidance."

"You must admit, Benjamin, that that makes sense," Beth said.

"Maybe it does, but it's not our lifestyle. We're not religious."

"Every human being is religious. That's what spirituality is all about. There is a yearning within the soul of everyone to connect with G-d. It's just that some of us don't know how to go about it. Hidden within the Torah is a fount of wisdom that is life-transforming, so if you really want to solidify your marriage, to raise it to another level, then get into the habit of studying Torah. It will do more for you than any other experience."

"But we don't have the background," Beth protested.

"That's okay, you can acquire it. Just as you have a personal trainer, you can have a Torah teacher, and in an instant, the Book will open up for you and change your lives, and I must tell you that even the couples who live by Torah principles would enhance their relationships if they set aside time to study together."

"Let's try it," Beth urged.

"What exactly are we talking about?" Benjamin asked.

"Well, there are several options. You can join our Torah classes or you can have a teacher come to your home—just start and the blessings will follow. In the interim, let me give you some good, easy tips that will make an immediate difference in your life.

"Let's begin with small things, because very often it's the small things that make our relationships what they are. Beth, let's start with you. Remember what we said about focusing—if it should happen that you are on the phone when Benjamin walks into the house, don't just wave to him; get off that phone and let him see that *he* comes first. If he has a favorite dish, make it for him. I knew a woman whose husband loved lasagna, but she never found time to prepare it for him. One day, he walked into the house and was hit by the aroma of lasagna baking in the oven. Wow, he thought to himself, my wife finally made it for me! But before he could even say 'Honey, thank you,' she warned, 'Don't touch the lasagna! I made it for the PTA's supperette.' Now, what kind of message does that send to a husband? And this holds true in many areas, like when a woman dresses up for strangers but greets her husband in a sloppy old outfit."

"I'm glad you brought that up," Benjamin said, "because Beth walks around in this old sweat suit that drives me crazy."

"I'm sorry, but when I'm at home I like to relax, and I can't see why I should get all dressed up," Beth protested. "Besides," she added, "I thought we were going to do this the Torah way, so why all this emphasis on appearance?"

"No one ever said that you can't relax, or that you have to be all dressed up, but pleasing your husband *is the Torah way* and should be your priority, so if your sweat suit bothers him, why wear it?"

"Well, you should see how he schleps around in his underwear."

"If that's the case, then this holds true for Benjamin as well. It's important that you accustom yourselves to being properly dressed at home because it is one of the ways in which you convey respect to each other and the home that you establish. Bear in mind that the manner in which you dress sends a message to your children and sets the tone of your home."

I told them a story about a sage in Jerusalem who was accompanied to his home by one of his disciples. At his doorstep, the rabbi took a few moments to arrange his beard and straighten his jacket and hat. Puzzled, the student asked, "Is there someone special waiting for the rabbi?"

"Yes," he replied. "The *Shechina*" (presence of G-d).

The young man looked at his rabbi uncomprehendingly, so the rabbi explained that, in the merit of his wife, the presence of G-d rests upon a man's home.

"If we can keep that in mind," I continued, "then not only will we dress appropriately, but we will conduct ourselves in that spirit as well.

"The Torah way, the spiritual way, doesn't mean neglecting the physical, but rather, sanctifying and elevating it. Nothing is as holy as the love between husband and wife. As a matter of fact, the prophets viewed this relationship as a metaphor for the most sacred of all relationships—that of G-d to His people."

"What does that have to do with my sweat suit?" Beth asked.

"If your love is sacred and holy, you will want to safeguard it and avoid everything that will diminish it. So, like I said, if that sweat suit irritates Benjamin, why don't you just get rid of it? What's the big deal?"

"It's a matter of principle!" Beth said. "He should love me for what I *am*, not for what I *wear!*"

"Of course he does," I assured her. "Otherwise, he would never have married you. But love is like a plant that needs watering and nurturing lest it die. When you were dating, you wouldn't have dreamed of wearing something that Benjamin found unattractive, so why do it now?"

I told Beth of the time a middle-aged couple, who were each in their second marriage, came to see me. The husband was very proper and well groomed, whereas she was terribly overweight and neglectful of her appearance. He wanted her to go on a diet and, in general, to be more put-together. In a way, she had the same attitude as you, Beth. 'He should love me for what I am.' But she went even a step further, and right then and there, she reached into her handbag, took out a huge chocolate bar, turned to him, and started to munch! Needless to say, the marriage didn't last.

"One of the most spiritual things that you can do is to please your mate. When G-d commanded the construction of the Tabernacle, He instructed Moses to build a basin for ritual washing. The women came forth and offered their mirrors for this purpose. Moses was hesitant. Would it be appropriate to use mirrors, a symbol of vanity, to fashion the basin for the Holy Tabernacle? Whereupon G-d proclaimed that those mirrors were holy because, through them, the love of husbands for their wives was enhanced."

"Okay, I learned something," Beth conceded.

"So you see," I told them, "to be a *loving, kind friend* doesn't mean that you have to make radical changes in your life, or sacrifice all that much time. It's the little, ordinary things that we normally take for granted that can make all the difference. Let's go back to those ideas that I mentioned earlier: listening to each other and expressing interest in your mate's activities, and if anyone should plead lack of time or the wherewithal to do that, then chances are that he or she is just copping out.

"No one was busier than my husband. Professionally, he wore many hats, and he was a caring and devoted father and always there to empathize with my feelings and anticipate my needs. I often returned home late at night after a speech or a session at Hineni—and when I say late, it might even have been one or two in the morning, because after my programs, I would speak to people individually, and I never left until I had addressed everyone's concerns. When I finally got home, my husband would be waiting for me with a smile on his face. Mind you, I often woke him up, because he would doze off in his chair with a volume of the Talmud in his hands, but as soon as he saw me, he would smile and sleepily say, 'What's new? How is everything, *shefele?*' (a Yiddish term of endearment meaning 'my little lamb'). On the kitchen table I would find my favorite snack waiting, and he'd sit down with me and we'd talk. Then later, on my night table, I would discover clippings from the daily paper that he thought I might find interesting, with significant sentences highlighted with a colored marker. My husband knew that I lacked the patience to read the daily papers from cover to cover, but he also knew that it was important for me to keep current with world events. So you see, it is the small things that do not require much time or money that are major, because that's the fabric from which the relationship of *loving, kind friends* is woven.

"And now to you, Benjamin. Our sages teach us that more than material possessions, it is friendship that a woman desires from her husband. Just knowing that her spouse is there to listen to her means so much. And it's not necessarily because she is looking for some solution or answers from him but because she needs a sympathetic, listening ear, someone to share with."

"That's exactly what I've been trying to say all along," Beth exclaimed. "Benjamin never has the patience to listen to me."

"It's not that I don't want to listen to her," he protested, "but Beth has this way of kvetching, of going on and on and not coming to the point, and frankly, it grinds on my nerves."

"Benjamin," I said, "if you had an important client who kvetched and ground on your nerves, you would somehow summon the patience to hear him out."

"Say no more," he interrupted with a smile. "I got it the first time. My wife deserves the same consideration."

"Well, Beth, I think that's major. You can't ask for more than that. You have the makings of becoming loving, kind friends after all. It will take work and there will be glitches along the way, so bear in mind that when Benjamin appears inattentive, it's nothing personal; it's one of those gender differences. Men like brevity. They have no patience for drawn-out conversations, and this, too, is in the Torah. At Mount Sinai, when G-d gave us the Commandments, He instructed Moses to speak to the women in soft, inspirational words, but the men were to be addressed in precise, succinct language (Exodus 19)."

"Do you really think that those gender differences are valid today?" Beth asked. "I mean, this is the twenty-first century and girls are doing everything boys do."

"That has nothing to do with gender differences. I'm talking about emotions and reactions. Males and females respond to and see things differently, and that doesn't change with time. I remember reading an interview given by the male coach of a female soccer team. You can't lead women with your intensity, he said. Rather, you have to inspire them with your humanity. Men should be coached with their egos; women, through the quality of their relationships. Female players, he said, are more likely to take criticism personally. With women, if you tell the team that they are not as fit as they need to be, they assume the coach must be talking about *me*, but if you say the same thing to a group of men, most of them will think, The coach is right. I'm the only one that's fit here. The other guys better get off their butts.

"Men and women just see things differently," I continued. "For example, has it ever happened that Benjamin went to a dinner or party that for some reason you couldn't attend, and when he came home you asked, 'How was it?' and he answered, 'Okay'? But that's not what you were looking for. You wanted to know every detail. Who was there? How was the music? What was the color scheme? What was on the menu? But a man sums it all up with one word: 'Okay.' You see, Beth, it's not that Benjamin lacks the patience for you. Men and women just communicate differently. But if you give to each other unconditionally and become loving, kind friends, you will feel each other's needs. You, Beth, will learn to be more concise, and you, Benjamin, will learn to be more patient and sympathetic.

"When Adam beheld Eve for the first time, he said, 'She is bone of my bone, flesh of my flesh. She shall be called woman—*isha*—because she was taken from man—*ish*.' What is significant about this first declaration of Adam is that before he identified himself, he identified his wife, teaching us that it *is only through recognizing our other half that we can define ourselves*. Once you absorb this concept, your quarrels and differences will fade. You will find it easy to forgive each other because, in essence, you will be forgiving yourself. You are one, and even as you would not take revenge on your hand if you dropped a heavy package on your toe, so you would not take revenge on your mate, for your mate is 'bone of my bone, flesh of my flesh'—you are *loving, kind friends*."

Benjamin said, "It sounds almost poetic, and it makes sense, but can you legislate feelings? I don't know if I can get to feel this bone-of-my-bone, flesh-of-my-flesh stuff."

"We have a wonderful teaching, so simple yet so profound: 'A man is shaped by his deeds.' *When you act in a certain way, you become that way.* Your conduct has an impact on your emotions. That's why I spoke about those little things—giving your spouse your wholehearted attention, learning Torah together, extending kindness, giving pleasure to each other; those things will cement your relationship and enable you to become *one.* Act like one, and you will become one; act like loving, kind friends, and you will become loving, kind friends.

"The relationship that G-d designed for us through marriage is not just having someone with whom to share a home, to satisfy our physical and material needs, nor is it a matter of companionship or overcoming loneliness, for if that had been the case, G-d would not have had to create Eve. After all, Adam had an array of angels taking care of him, answering to his every need—he literally lived in the Garden of Eden and had everything he needed to keep him entertained. But that is not the purpose of man's existence. Man can fulfill himself only through the act of giving, and that is what marriage is all about. Only through giving to his other half does he become complete and realize his mission in life. It is through this union, the uniting of two halves in loving, kind friendship, that man fulfills himself and joins G-d in the partnership of creation. And there can be no more sacred calling than that."

PART THREE

# A GOOD NEIGHBOR

Love your neighbor as yourself.

*Leviticus 19:18*

# SEVEN

# BEING YOUR OWN PERSON

R abbi Yossi, the third disciple of Rabbi Yochanan, advocated
that one should strive to be a *good neighbor* and find a *good
neighbor.* The Hebrew word for neighbor, *shochein,* is related to the
word *Shechina* (presence of G-d), teaching us that the presence of
G-d rests on homes in which a spirit of good neighborliness prevails and in which relationships are forged in a bond of love, kindness, and understanding.

A further correlation between these two concepts (*Shechina* and
*shochein*) is that, even as an awareness of G-d's ever-guiding, protective presence imbues us with a sense of security and peace, similarly,
albeit on a different level, the knowledge that there is someone
close by who is reliable and kind imparts a sense of well-being.

Rabbi Yossi was known to be a *chosid*—meticulous in his piety.
His love of his people prompted him to go above and beyond the
letter of the law. He lived by the dictum "What is mine is yours and
what is yours is yours"—meaning that he took delight in seeing
people enjoy his possessions, but at the same time he was careful
not to take advantage of that which belonged to others. He did not
keep a tally of favors rendered; his relationships were not based on
tit for tat. "My neighbor was nice or mean to me today. Therefore I

will react in kind." Rabbi Yossi found delight in sharing, fulfillment in giving, and that was all the reward he required. He was truly the paradigm of a good neighbor.

If there is anything that would render one a perfect marriage partner, it is the development of this character trait of Rabbi Yossi—being a *good neighbor*. When husband and wife can give freely of themselves and measure their own happiness by that of their spouse, then you can be assured that their marriage is built on a solid foundation.

I have said this previously, but it bears repeating that *ahava*, the Hebrew word for love, is connected to the root word *hav*—to give. In our culture, however, this view of love has been interpreted in reverse. Somehow, we have come to believe that love is a prerequisite to giving, whereas, in essence, it is *giving* that is the prerequisite to love. We see this principle reinforced in nature. The ultimate love is that of a mother for her child; it is in that relationship that we witness the greatest giving and sacrifice. From carrying the child under her heart for nine months, to nursing and nurturing, the bond of love keeps growing, and even should the mother be hurt or rejected by her child, her love will nevertheless remain constant. Sadly enough, we have failed to apply this simple lesson to our own lives. We desire to *get* rather than to *give*, and when we are disappointed in love, we are convinced that the fault lies with the other and not with ourselves. Self-righteously we declare: he/she doesn't give me what I need, so it's time to bail out.

Douglas, a young writer who studied at our Hineni Torah classes, told me that he was writing a book about marriage and had interviewed his grandparents.

"Why your grandparents?" I asked.

He thought about it for a minute and then said, "To my mind, they are the perfect couple, totally happy with each other. As a matter of fact, I don't think I've ever seen them fight, and believe me,

Rebbetzin, I've observed the grandparents of many of my friends: they can really be difficult, arguing over all kinds of nonsense. So I figured that my grandparents would be a good story."

"Tell me about it. I would like to know."

"Well, I decided to speak to them individually, and what an experience that was! First, I asked Grandma how it was that I never saw her fight with Grandpa.

"'What's there to fight about?' she said. 'I'm happy if he's happy.' And as a case in point, she told me that when they fly she would much prefer to have the window seat, but she knows that Grandpa likes it, 'So I let him have it. No big deal. Like I said, I'm happy if he's happy.'

"Now what was remarkable about this conversation," Douglas continued, "was that later, when I interviewed Grandpa, he cited the same example. 'I know that your grandmother likes the aisle seat on the plane, so I always let her have it, even though I prefer it.'

"To be honest with you," Douglas confided, "at first I thought that was real dumb. All those years sitting in seats they didn't want thinking they were pleasing the other! That could never happen to someone of my generation. We would just say outright, 'I want the aisle seat' or 'I want the window seat,' and we would expect to be accommodated. But Grandma and Grandpa have only one agenda—making each other happy—and that's kind of touching, don't you think?"

"I sure do. But tell me, did you ever enlighten them about their misunderstanding?"

"I almost did, but then I realized that that would be cruel. For the past forty years they've been going down to Florida, and every time they got on a plane, they thought they were giving each other a gift. I wouldn't want to spoil that. That's what makes their love so special."

If you stop to think about it, you will realize how right Douglas was. His grandparents' love is so special because they live to give to and please each other. Once you grasp that, then as Douglas's grandmother said, there's nothing much to fight about, and "what's mine is yours and what's yours is yours" becomes easy.

Rabbi Yossi's teaching regarding a good neighbor can be understood not only metaphorically but literally as well.

Paul was a participant in our Hineni Young Leadership classes. One day, he was summoned for jury duty. He told his superior at the brokerage firm where he worked that he wouldn't be coming in. That night, as he was preparing for bed, he collapsed. For five days, he lay on the floor of his apartment without food or water. There was no neighbor to knock on his door, no one missed him, no one wondered where he might be. His family lived in Chicago, and at his workplace it was assumed that he was still on jury duty. By the time his doorman, who came to drop off a delivery, found him, he was near death. He spent many days in the ICU, followed by a long stay at a rehab center. Sadly, he was left with some permanent damage. If only someone had knocked at his door, if only he had had a good neighbor, this tragedy could have been averted.

In our impersonal, faceless society, it is possible to live in homes or apartments for years without knowing the next-door neighbors, and in marriage, it is possible for spouses to live under one roof and pass each other like ships in the night, never knowing what the other feels. At one of our seminars for married couples, I asked the participants to list what they thought their mates cherished most in life—their hopes, their aspirations, their visions—and also what they thought their mates struggled with most painfully. Not surprisingly, most of their answers were way off the mark.

Husbands and wives who are *good neighbors* know what is in the heart of the other. They are sensitive to each other's thoughts and emotions. They will call each other in the middle of the day just to say "Hello, how's it going? I love you." My father often told couples that the easiest and most inexpensive way to make your spouse happy is to make a call. Nowadays, with the advent of e-mail, this has become even easier. And yet, there are so many who fail to avail themselves of such opportunities. How often do I hear a man say, "I have a business to take care of," or a woman complain, "I have been running the entire day—who has the time for such things?" Little do these husbands and wives realize that it is they who are losing out.

Hannah was a school friend. We sat next to each other in class, married in the same year, and had our children at more or less the same time. Hannah's husband, Abe, was a brilliant educator with very high standards, demanding excellence of himself as well as those in his employ. One morning, out of the blue, I received a shocking call. Abe had had a massive heart attack while he slept. Things like that were not supposed to happen to people our age. Abe was the first of our circle of friends to die, and it was devastating. I braced myself for the shiva (condolence) call, wondering what I could possibly say to Hannah and her children that would be of comfort, but I didn't have to worry. It was Hannah who offered *us* consolation.

"Esther," she said, when I sat down next to her, "you knew my Abe well—what a perfectionist he was, how he drove himself. Very often he made me crazy with his attention to detail, but one thing I will tell you. No matter how the day went, I never went to sleep without telling him 'I love you.' I'm so grateful for that now. Can you imagine how I would feel, if that night I hadn't said 'I love you'?"

The death of a loved one is always traumatic, and it never comes at an opportune time, but if husband and wife regard each day as a gift and offer each other love, then the pain is easier to bear because there are no regrets. Hannah was always there to express her commitment to Abe, and therefore she was able to pick up the pieces and go on.

There are many ways to deal with difficult challenges. Sometimes it's having a sense of humor that best enables us to cope. My husband had this ability and was able to inject laughter into every situation, even when recollecting his Holocaust experiences. Before the Nazi invasion at the beginning of World War II, he and many other young Jewish men were rounded up by the Hungarian Zsandars (Gestapo) for slave labor. Over the years, I have met fellow survivors who told me that my husband kept everyone going with his optimistic spirit and Torah wisdom. As they marched, carrying heavy boulders on their shoulders, he would share with those laboring alongside him teachings from the Talmud. Even under those horrific conditions, he managed to be a *good neighbor* and buoyed the spirits of those who were fortunate enough to be near him.

Despite subhuman conditions in the labor camp, my husband never compromised the laws of *kashruth*. Now this was not as simple as one might imagine, for the authorities demanded that all prisoners eat their daily ration of soup made with pork fat so that they would have the energy to labor. Nevertheless, my husband managed to defy them, and by the war's end, his six-foot two-inch frame had become skeletal.

On one occasion his work detail was trudging along carrying their heavy loads when they passed some apple trees along the road. My husband spotted a few apples that had fallen to the ground. He quickly snatched them up and hid them in his trousers. Unfortunately, on that day, a *bad neighbor,* the one mean-spirited person in the group, was marching alongside him. He resented my husband's Torah teaching and adherence to the laws of *kashruth,* and informed on him to the guard. When the group arrived back at the camp, they were lined up as usual for roll call; the guard ordered my husband to come forward and do a hundred push-ups in the middle of the parade ground.

"You should have seen those apples roll. Oy, was that a sight!" my husband would laugh, telling us the story. Yes, believe it or not, when my husband related this incident, he laughed wholeheartedly. There wasn't even a trace of bitterness in him. The experience never jaundiced his view of people; it never caused him to shut down. On the contrary, it made him more determined than ever to reach out and be a good neighbor.

I have shared this story with you because, despite all our hopes and aspirations, sometimes our mates are not the *good neighbors* that we hoped for, and often, the best way to respond is to develop a sense of humor. If you know how to laugh at your troubles, then you will laugh your troubles away. Injecting a little humor into tense situations can lighten intense moments and serve as an antidote to anger and bitterness.

If your husband is the type who never hangs up his coat but just drops it on the nearest chair or couch, and if you have asked him year in and year out to put his things away to no avail, you can either continue to berate him and increase the tensions between you, or you can learn to laugh.

If your wife never balances the checkbook, and if she fails to record the checks she writes even after you have repeatedly requested that she do so, you can either have a major fight and throw up your hands in frustration, or you can learn to laugh. My husband chose to laugh. Against all odds, he retained his warm, loving disposition, and throughout his life he remained a good neighbor to everyone.

Our home was always open. No one had to make an appointment; you just rang the bell and walked in. People came for all sorts of reasons—the elderly, who felt lonely and sought companionship; the troubled, to unburden themselves; and still others who sought knowledge and direction.

One morning, one of our neighbors came running in a panic. "Rabbi, Seymour is not well!" she gasped.

My husband rushed the man, his wife, and his elderly mother, who lived with them, to the nearest hospital. Seymour had suffered a coronary, and he was hospitalized for quite a long while. His wife didn't drive, but she and his mother wanted to visit him every day, so who do you suppose drove them? My husband, the good neighbor, of course.

In marriage, too, you have to maintain this good neighbor policy and be available to your mate at all times. There will be occasions when your spouse will feel lonely and want to unburden him- or herself, when your guidance and wisdom will be needed. There will be times of crisis, when you will be called upon to give of yourself and extend love and support.

This good neighbor policy also places a responsibility on husbands and wives to exercise discernment and wisdom in choosing their place of residence.

Dawn and Howie were a hardworking young couple with good values who were saving to buy their first home. They knew exactly what they wanted. The house had to be large enough to accommodate a growing family, with a spacious backyard for children to play, and the community had to have schools that offered quality education. They found their dream house and hired an engineer to go over it with a fine-tooth comb. The wiring, plumbing, heating, air-conditioning, and structure were all carefully examined, and when the engineer pronounced the house in excellent condition, they happily called their lawyer and gave him the green light to close.

What Dawn and Howie failed to check, however, was the sort of neighbors they would have. Their dream house turned out to be a nightmare. Their neighbors were a fast, high-living crowd who loved to party. Dawn became infatuated with the man living next door. Her marriage ended in divorce, and the children for whom she and Howie had bought the house were never born.

Some people might argue, of course, that the fact that Dawn succumbed to temptation indicated that her marriage was already troubled, that the fault was not so much with her neighbor as with her relationship with her husband. That may sound good in theory, but very often I have discovered that even in the best of marriages, there are moments when spouses become vulnerable, when they ask themselves, How could I ever have married him/her? If, at such a moment, a charming, dashing neighbor comes knocking on the door and makes you feel loved and understood, you can very easily fall into a trap from which it's difficult to extricate yourself—a moment of indiscretion for which you pay for a lifetime. Time and again, I have seen this happen—strong, good people compromising their values, and waking up too late. On the other hand, the converse can also be true: people with shaky marriages being influenced by neighbors who regard marriage and family as sacrosanct. When they observe their neighbors living in harmony and relating to each other with kindness and consideration, then they want the same thing for themselves.

When husband and wife are good neighbors, they recognize that as much as they love each other, they also have to respect the other's privacy and sense when the spouse needs to be alone, when even conversation can be burdensome. Good neighbors know that it is proper to knock before opening a door; so, too, husbands and wives must be sensitive to each other's moods. In a marriage, these considerations are especially important. Yesterday, the couple had their own space, but now, every nook and cranny must be shared. Although this can be wonderful, it can also be suffocating.

Lori, a young newlywed, came to consult me. She was distraught and convinced that her husband no longer loved her.

"Why would you imagine such a thing?" I asked.

"He doesn't communicate. He just doesn't open up. I know something is wrong."

"Do you try to talk to him?" I asked.

"Sure, as soon as he comes home from work, I ask him about his day—you know, I make small talk—but instead of answering, he buries his head in a newspaper or goes into the den to watch TV.

When I sit down next to him, he ignores my presence. Our marriage is falling apart. I can feel it. We should be going for counseling, but he doesn't want to go. I just don't know what to do," Lori said.

"Before assuming the worst, let's try the simple and easy way."

I told Lori about something that had happened to me a few weeks earlier. "My washing machine wasn't working, so I put in a call for service ASAP. The mechanic came, took a look at the machine, and said, 'Ma'am, it's not plugged in.' You can't imagine how foolish I felt and how annoyed I was with myself for not checking such a simple thing before sounding the alarm.

"Similarly, Lori, you may be jumping to conclusions, imagining major problems where none exist, so let's first make sure everything is 'plugged in.' It might just be that when you speak, your timing is off. There's no energy. Some men are so tense when they get home from work that they need a breather to unwind. They need their own space. Your husband may be the type who, after a full day's work, needs time to clear his head and just doesn't want to talk, so why don't you try the same conversation later in the evening, after he is more relaxed, after he has read his paper and watched the news on TV. Perhaps over a cup of coffee or while taking a walk he will be more open." I told Lori that every couple has to find their own method through which an ambience is created and communication becomes possible.

The advice was simple enough, but it worked. In our crisis-oriented society, we are so programmed to expect trouble in our marriages that we automatically assume that there are difficulties where none exist. Sometimes the solution can be as easy as switching gears.

Switching gears is not just an option but a prerequisite for a happy husband-wife relationship. Monotony is anathema to marital bliss, and because of that, marriage can become a "catch-22" situation, for the very accessibility of one's spouse can reduce the most intimate relationship to the mundane. Many responsible people have embarked upon paths of folly and sacrificed their families in pursuit of the novel, the illicit, and the romantic.

The Torah regards the love between husband and wife as sacrosanct. Intimacy is holy, and G-d Himself joins husband and wife in their love. Precisely because of that, the Torah recognizes that there are times when husband and wife must each be given their space, when all physical contact must come to a halt, so that when the couple reunite, they may reexperience the joy of their wedding night.

Interestingly enough, we find that very often marriage counselors recommend that couples whose marriages appear to be going stale, temporarily abstain from intimacy or take separate vacations in order to reinvigorate their relationship. This self-imposed separation usually does not work, however. For any discipline to be meaningful and lasting, a higher authority is required, and that is the beauty of our Torah laws, which bring sanctity to the institution of marriage.

It was not by accident that G-d created human beings in such a way that of all His creations, they are the only ones who in intimacy face each other, reinforcing the fact that they unite in total knowledge and love rather than just physical pleasure. Since intimacy is meant to be more than a physical act, Jewish marriage laws encourage husband and wife to bond in a nonphysical way as well. Thus, in accordance with Jewish law, for approximately two weeks every month (corresponding to a woman's monthly cycle, and seven clean days afterward, culminating with *mikveh*[1]), husband and wife refrain from physical contact. During this time, they are obliged to

---

[1]Ritualarium: a pool of natural rainwater, symbolic of the primordial waters of creation. Through immersion in these waters, accompanied by the recitation of special prayers, the woman invites G-d to bless her most intimate martial relationship.

relate to each other as "good neighbors"—always there for each other, enjoying each other's company, sharing thoughts, bonding spiritually, but at the same time, respecting each other's privacy.

Our commandments have been given to us by G-d and we need no other reason for their observance. Nevertheless, we derive innumerable benefits from upholding them. Anything physical, if overindulged in, loses its attraction; thus, if you love ice cream and eat it three times a day for a long time, you will become sick of it. Paradoxically, the more one limits physical pleasure, the more one comes to enjoy and cherish it. And so, to protect the marital relationship, G-d has prescribed boundaries through which this most intimate physical act becomes elevated and holy, setting a delicate balance to protect husband and wife from the malaise of monotony.

Intimacy in the Torah is called knowledge. Adam *knew* his wife, Eve (Genesis 4:1). At first glance, it may seem somewhat odd that such a physical act should be referred to as knowledge, but as I pointed out, intimacy between husband and wife is not only physical; it is the fusion of souls, a total oneness encompassing mind, heart, and spirit. This total oneness can best be realized when the cerebral and the spiritual are allowed to emerge independent of the physical, for when intimacy takes place after such a separation, the spiritual acts upon the physical, creating a true fusion of body and soul—husband and wife becoming one.

# EIGHT

# BE YOUR OWN ADVOCATE

I was speaking in Jerusalem, and after my program I stayed on to answer questions and talk to people one-on-one. Among the many who approached me was Michelle, a striking blond, who was visiting from New York. "It's strange that I should meet you here," she said. "For the longest time, I had been planning to come to see you in Manhattan, but somehow it never materialized, so when I saw the newspaper announcement, I said, This time I must go."

"Well, I'm glad you did."

"I've heard that you make great matches. I've come close to marrying a few times but never quite made it. Can you help me?"

"Why don't you come to Hineni in New York?" I suggested. "We have many terrific eligible guys, and I'll be happy to try to make an introduction." But even as I spoke, I spotted a tall, handsome man waiting in line to talk to me. I motioned to him to approach and asked point-blank, "Are you single?"

"As a matter of fact, I am," he said, somewhat taken aback by my directness.

"Good. I want you to meet Michelle. I think that the two of you should get to know each other. Why don't you go over to the refreshment area and have a cup of coffee together?"

"I can't believe this," Michelle said, laughing. "Rebbetzin, you're absolutely the best!" And that is how Gary and Michelle met.

They hit if off right away. Michelle was scheduled to return to the States, but she changed her flight in order to travel back with Gary the following week. Gary was divorced and the father of two grown daughters, ages twenty and twenty-three. He lived in Manhattan, owned a thriving business, and was active in many charities. About six months passed, and I had all but forgotten the incident when one morning I received a call from Michelle.

"Rebbetzin, I have good news. Gary and I are engaged, and you are the one who started it all. How can we ever thank you? We are so grateful! You must come to our wedding."

I was, of course, thrilled. What are the chances of something like this happening? G-d's ways are wondrous. He sent Gary and Michelle from New York to my program in Jerusalem. They stood in line, a few feet apart, and I had the privilege of introducing them. I happily accepted the invitation to their wedding and looked forward to seeing them again.

The ceremony was a small, private affair with only family and close friends present, but afterward there was a large reception at a hotel. I met the parents from both sides, as well as Gary's two daughters, who, I sensed, weren't all that happy to be there. I wasn't overly concerned, however. Experience has taught me that, whereas parents rejoice at their children's weddings, you can hardly expect the children to have the same reaction. In time, things usually work out and they all adjust.

After the wedding, I didn't hear from Gary and Michelle for some time, and I assumed that they were busy with their new life. Then one day I received a call from Michelle. She sounded terrible. "Rebbetzin, I need to talk to you. Can I come over?"

When Michelle walked into my office, her eyes were puffy and red. As soon as I put my arms around her, she broke down and wept. "What's going on?" I asked.

"Oh, Rebbetzin, Gary and I are having lots of problems."

"Tell me about it."

"I wish I could, but there's nothing specific that I can define. It's just that things are not good between us. We're not communicating. Sometimes, days go by and he hardly speaks. When he looks at me, there is such disdain in his eyes."

"Have you tried to get to the bottom of it?"

"It's complicated, Rebbetzin, and I don't want to rock the boat. I'm certain that his daughters are no help. As hard as I try to befriend them, I know they don't like me."

"Was anything said, or are you just surmising this?"

Michelle thought for a moment. "There's nothing that I can put my finger on," she admitted, "but sometimes you just *feel* things. And to be honest, Rebbetzin, I'm afraid that if I say something, Gary will resent it and things will get worse. There's really no one I can trust to talk to except Audrey. She manages his office and is one of his closest friends. Thank G-d we hit it off and she's trying to help me."

"What does she suggest?"

"Well, she thinks I should say nothing and give it some time. She told me that one of the reasons Gary walked out on Gloria, his first wife, was that she was overbearing and always on his case. I did try to make an appointment to see Gary's therapist. I thought he might be able to give me some insights, but when I called him, he said it would be a conflict of interest to see me, and the only way he'd speak to me would be if Gary signed a release, but I couldn't have Gary know that I called. What do I do, Rebbetzin? I don't want this marriage to fall apart. I love him so much, but after what Audrey told me, I'm afraid of losing him. He walked out on his first wife, and he could do it again—and this time he'd have a cheering squad of his daughters to goad him on."

"Sometimes," I agreed, "it's wise to wait and pretend that you don't see or hear anything, but I don't like things to fester for such a long period. Our sages teach that if you wish to overcome a negative trait and are able to do so for forty days, you can be reasonably assured that you have mastered the problem. But the converse is also true. If Gary has a mad-on, is not communicating, and forty days pass, that, too, can become habit-forming. After a while, he won't even know why he is angry, but he will continue to be angry because that has become his lifestyle, so I think you should take the bull by the horns, sit him down, and have a heart-to-heart. Nothing confrontational, mind you—more *sad* than *mad*. Tell him you love him, are deeply committed to your marriage, and are prepared to do whatever it takes to make it work."

"I was planning to do just that, Rebbetzin, but Audrey advised me against it. She said that if I wished, she'd feel him out for me, and that would be safer."

"I wouldn't discuss this with Audrey at all."

"Oh, Rebbetzin, it's not like that. She's sincere and is trying to help. Besides, she's much older than Gary and was genuinely happy when we got married."

"I'm not casting aspersions on her motivations. She may very well be sincere, but I'm not an advocate of going through third parties. I prefer the direct approach. Bypass Audrey, bypass the therapist, and speak to Gary face-to-face. Sometimes the problem is just a simple misunderstanding that can easily be clarified through discussion. I once counseled a couple—let's call them Jamie and Jimmy—who almost split up over something silly, but thank G-d, they talked it out and realized that they were on the same page but reading different paragraphs. It's like two people going to the circus. One is fascinated by the acrobats, the animals performing incredible tricks, the clowns making everyone laugh, while the other sees only some 'crazies' jumping around, animals that are smelly and offensive, and clowns that are more silly than funny. Now they both went to the same circus and sat next to each other in the same row, but each came away with a different perception. I give you this example because life is often very much like a circus. The same experience can affect people differently.

"In the case of Jamie and Jimmy, direct and open conversation revealed a simple explanation for their anger. They traced their problem to a drive to their country home in Connecticut. They had headed out on Thursday afternoon, their car laden with groceries, luggage, tennis racquets, and golf clubs. Unfortunately, there was an accident on the road, and a trip that should have lasted forty-five minutes took three and a half hours. Jimmy was at the wheel, and as annoyed as could be. Jamie, sensing her husband's mood and knowing that he hadn't had dinner, decided that as soon as they arrived, she would surprise him by heating and serving his favorite dish, which she had prepared that morning in the city.

"As soon as they arrived, Jamie grabbed the cooler with the food and ran straight for the kitchen, leaving Jimmy to unload. Jimmy was furious! 'What does she think I am—her schlepper?' he muttered. As he was carrying their belongings from the car to the house, rain began to come down in buckets, and Jimmy became angrier with each step. To make things worse, when he finally got into the kitchen, he found Jamie on the phone. Jimmy never saw the beautiful table that Jamie had so lovingly prepared; and he didn't know that it wasn't a friend with whom Jamie was talking, but a cousin with a sick daughter who was crying out for help—so Jamie couldn't very well cut her off. The only thing that Jimmy saw was that his wife was chatting on the phone while he was left to shlep. Jamie, on the other hand, was deeply hurt that Jimmy was so unappreciative and never so much as acknowledged her efforts, never mind saying thanks.

"If real or imagined slights are allowed to fester, resentment builds until after a while you don't even remember why you're angry. So now do you see why it's so important to communicate? In every marriage there are highs and lows, and if the lows are not resolved, you get caught up in your own emotions. You keep fighting and bickering, even though you don't really know what you are fighting about. So even if you are not on the greatest of terms with Gary right now, it is important that you communicate, that you talk like *good neighbors*. Good neighbors share, without any intermediaries. They know how to prevent their relationships from becoming a circus."

"Well, this puts a whole new spin on things," Michelle said pensively. "Maybe something turned Gary off. I need to think about it."

"Let me tell you one more story about the importance of communicating directly. Do you remember when we met in Jerusalem this past summer?"

"How can I forget? That's when you introduced us."

"Well, I was coming from a Hineni Heritage Tour of Czechoslovakia, Bratislava, and Hungary. My great-grandfather, five generations back, Rabbi Osher Anshil HaLevi Jungreis, was renowned throughout Hungary as a miracle rabbi. People from all over came to him seeking cures for their ailments, and he helped them all. It was said that Elijah the Prophet himself revealed these cures to him, and he later recorded them in a special notebook. The last person to have that notebook in his possession was the grandfather of one of my cousins. He told me that, before his death, his father revealed that his father, who was the rabbi in a small village in Bratislava, had placed the notebook in a tin box and buried it in his backyard in order to keep it from falling into the hands of the Nazi invaders.

"Now, as long as we were going to Bratislava, I decided to visit that village to see if I could locate the tin box. My friend Barbara, who is the executive director of Hineni and always ready for an adventure, came up with the idea of obtaining a metal detector to facilitate the search and had soon located one at a mail-order house on the Internet.

"We were scheduled to travel by bus from Prague to Budapest via

Bratislava. The map showed that the village where my great-uncle had been the rabbi was on the way, so I gave our group a choice. They could travel directly from Bratislava to Budapest where I would meet up with them, or they could make a two-hour stopover with me in Zseliz. They were all intrigued and opted to accompany me, so we stopped at the local version of Home Depot to buy shovels for everyone and, thus armed, set off on our adventure.

"But there were many hurdles to overcome. How would I find the house? Before I left New York, my cousin suggested that I go to the mayor's office at the town hall, where the location of the rabbi's house would surely be recorded. Even if I found it, however, what guarantee would I have that its current occupants would permit me to comb their backyard with Barbara's metal detector and allow everyone to dig?

"So you can imagine how thrilled I was when, that evening, as we arrived at Bratislava's only kosher restaurant, we found the American consul having dinner there. Not only was he Jewish but he turned out to be a very eligible bachelor as well. We had many singles in our group, and on our bus there was always much kibitzing. One of the young women jokingly said to my son, 'Rabbi, this time I'm really ready to get married, even if it means finding someone in Bratislava!' So when we actually found a live candidate, we couldn't stop laughing, and the poor consul must have wondered what we were all giggling about!

"After we had enjoyed our light moment, I turned to him about serious business, explaining my mission and asking for his help. *Would* he, *could* he, call the town hall in Zseliz and let them know that I would be coming? Could he ask for their cooperation in locating the house where my great-uncle had lived? Could he request permission for me to dig? To my delight, he readily agreed to everything and promised to call me with the results first thing in the morning.

"All that I could say was 'Thank G-d! This was *basherte* (meant to be).' Now it would be smooth sailing. But my elation was short lived. Early in the morning, the consul did call, but with bad news. I'd better stay away from Zseliz, he told me. If I arrived there with a busload of people and tried to dig in someone's backyard, I could be arrested, and even if I found the notebook, I wouldn't be able to keep it, because it would be declared property of the state, and he went on to enlighten me on the workings of Bratislava bureaucracy. 'If, however, you are still determined to forge ahead with your plans,' he added, 'you must consult attorneys—I'll give you a list of names to call. They can apply on your behalf to government officials, who, after due process, *may* approve your request.'

"I was devastated. How could I have been so stupid? Why had I consulted a third party? Why did I have to talk so much? What do I do now? I remembered my father's teaching: when you have a problem, it's always best to go directly to the person in charge. So I decided to take my chances and off we drove to Zseliz. As our large tour bus wound its way through the quiet village, all eyes followed us. A tour bus probably hadn't stopped in Zseliz for years, if ever. I asked the group to stay on the bus so as not to call more attention to ourselves than necessary, and I went on to the town hall by myself. As it happened, the mayor was away, and the assistant mayor was out to lunch, but the clerk in charge very graciously told me that he knew exactly where the assistant mayor was and he'd be pleased to take me there. We didn't have to go far. As soon as we walked out of the building, we spotted her. When I told her of my mission, she was only too delighted to be of assistance. She invited me into her office and opened all the village records, and then called the former mayor, who had a better knowledge of the community's history, to identify the house.

"Back at the bus, our Hineni people were worried sick. Why was it taking so long? They couldn't understand what could be delaying me. So you can imagine their delight when they spied me happily marching toward them with the former mayor, the assistant mayor, and an entourage of village officials who all wanted to accompany me to the home of the elderly widow who now occupied what had once been my great-uncle's home. The house was a sight to behold—no electricity or plumbing, an earthen floor, and a few sticks of crude furniture. The backyard was much bigger than I had anticipated, with a large vegetable garden, flocks of chickens, ducks, and geese, and even some stray dogs and cats.

"The lady of the house was truly thrilled by our visit. In all her years, she had never known such excitement. Yes, of course she knew this had been the rabbi's house. Her father had told her many times that this had been the most Jewish of all the houses in the village. She had no problem with our combing the yard with the metal detector and digging wherever we wished. Unfortunately, Barbara had obtained this complicated equipment without ever actually mastering how it worked! She had just assumed that she would turn it on and, presto, it would find our treasure. We had a lot of mavens (experts) in the group, each proposing a different way of handling it, each suggesting a different spot at which to dig. The metal detector beeped without surcease, but the only things we rescued were rusty cans, nails, and lots of bottle caps.

"News of our presence spread like wildfire. A reporter from the local paper arrived to photograph the event, and the assistant mayor sent one of her minions back to the town hall so that they might present us with a memento of the pottery for which the village is renowned.

"The two hours set aside for our visit flew by. It was time to get back on the bus if we were to arrive in Budapest that day. Although we made many new friends, we didn't even make a dent in the huge backyard, and to complicate things, the widow informed us that her father had built an addition to the house, so for all we knew, the notebook could have been buried under the house itself.

"We never did find my great-grandfather's treasure, but I did learn a lesson that I now share with you," I told Michelle. "Don't get sidetracked by third parties. Don't let them intimidate you. Like Audrey, the American consul in Bratislava was kind and considerate. He had good intentions and he did try to help, but the answers he came back with only further complicated matters. So, if one of these days, please G-d, I go back to Zseliz to search once again for the notebook that was bequeathed to my great-grandfather by Elijah the Prophet, I can assure you that I will do so *without any intermediaries*. Although," I added, "I should qualify that—there is one intermediary who is indispensable, without whom we cannot maneuver, and that is G-d Himself. Instead of talking to Audrey, talk to Him. Prayer is our most powerful weapon, Michelle. Avail yourself of it."

"Oh, Rebbetzin, what does this have to do with prayer or with G-d? This is *Gary!*"

"What does this have to do with prayer or with G-d?" I repeated. "Michelle, you must be joking. Nothing, absolutely *nothing* exists that is not connected to Him. G-d can open Gary's heart; He can give you the words with which to reach him. He can show you the way to win over his daughters; He can even help you convince Gary to have a baby."

"How did you know that I wanted a baby?" Michelle asked, startled.

"How did I know? How could I *not* know? You are in your late thirties; you have a biological clock ticking away—of course you dream of holding a baby in your arms."

"But it's impossible, Rebbetzin. He'll never agree."

"With prayer, Michelle, nothing is impossible."

"I don't know. I lost my faith—not that I was ever religious, but it just doesn't seem fair to me. All these years, I've been a bridesmaid but never a bride. Finally, I get married and the only thing I get is heartache."

Michelle's reaction was typical. It never ceases to amaze me how people who readily admit that they have no religious commitment, at the first sign of frustration or trouble turn against G-d. How could G-d allow this to happen to me? they ask indignantly. But when things go well, it never occurs to them to ask, How is it that G-d granted me all these blessings? How is it that I am healthy while others are sick? How is it that I have a job when others are unemployed? People take the good things for granted—it's all coming to them—but the moment something goes wrong, they assail Him and ask, How could He have allowed this to happen to me?

I told Michelle about a vibrant, beautiful young woman who was stricken with cancer.

"'Rebbetzin,' she said to me, 'one day I would just like to breathe without the help of an oxygen tank.'

"Have you ever thought of thanking G-d for allowing you to breathe, Michelle? There is so much to be grateful for. Of course you have to pray."

"I did try praying in my own way," Michelle now told me, "but it didn't help."

"Forgive me, Michelle, but what does that mean? That you mumbled a few words like 'Please G-d, help me' as you were getting dressed or rushing off to work? Admittedly, that, too, is prayer, but if you had an important request to make of your boss, is that how you would go about it? If you want your prayers to have impact, you have to put your heart and soul into them and remain steadfast. You can't just pray once and say, 'Okay, G-d, now do Your thing. Prove that You heard me!' Just as anyone who wants to succeed knows that his or her success depends on commitment and perseverance, so it is with prayer. You must turn to Him again and again. The psalmist declared, 'Trust and pray unto the L-rd, strengthen your heart' (even if at first it appears that He doesn't answer you, nevertheless, you must continue to pray and trust in Him—Psalm 27). Another precondition for effective prayer is genuine belief that *prayer works.* But somehow, from our conversation, I have the impression that you really don't believe that. Have you ever studied the prayer book?" I asked.

"Studied the prayer book?" she repeated incredulously. "My grandmother had a prayer book that my mom gave me when she passed away, but I never thought of it as a book to be studied."

"It is a fascinating study," I told her. "Our prayer is a compendium of the words of King David, Moses, the patriarchs, the matriarchs, and our sages. The manner in which we pray was actually formulated by a woman, Chana, the prophetess. Using the prayer book is like having credit cards from your grandfathers who were multibillionaires. Who wouldn't want to use them?"

"I must admit that I never thought about it that way," Michelle said, and then she quickly added, "I hope that you won't take offense, but somehow, I always felt that people pray for one of two reasons—either they feel guilty about something they did or they are looking for a simplistic solution to their problems."

"You're not the only one who thinks that way, Michelle. Many others have fallen into the same trap. They regard themselves as too sophisticated to pray. As a result, they have given up on prayer, and although they may feel a need to speak to G-d, they no longer know how. Prayer is not for simpletons, nor is it a reflection of guilt (although at times it is that). Prayer is our most powerful tool, through which we can invite G-d into our lives, connect with Him, and actually influence Him."

"Influence G-d?" Michelle asked, puzzled.

"Yes," I answered, "prayer can do just that," and to better explain it, I asked her, "Who would not want to have the ear of the president? Isn't it ironic that we can have G-d's ear and yet spurn it? But if you truly want to understand a concept, the best way to do so is to trace it back to the very first time it is mentioned in the Torah; and the first person to have prayed was Adam."

"Well, doesn't that reinforce what I just said?" Michelle remarked. "I'm not that familiar with the Bible, but didn't Adam feel guilty after he ate the forbidden fruit in the Garden of Eden?"

"Not at all. Adam's first prayer had nothing to do with sin or guilt. As a matter of fact, after he rebelled against G-d's command, he refused to accept accountability and blamed his wife, 'The woman You gave me—*she* made me eat from it.'

"Adam uttered his first prayer as soon as he opened his eyes and beheld the universe. He prayed because he realized that survival wasn't possible without G-d's help, and that is the primary reason for prayer—that human beings should know that they must connect with their Creator. Contrary to what most people think, Adam wasn't born into a lush paradise. To be sure, the world had the potential to become that. G-d had put all the pieces in place. The seeds were in the ground, the trees and flowers were ready to bloom, the grass was ready to sprout, but the earth remained barren and forbidding because rain was missing. G-d intentionally withheld it because He wanted Adam to pray for it, and to this very moment in time, we continue to pray for rain. The Hebrew word for rain is *geshem*, and that is the word from which *goshmiut* (materialism) is derived. Every day, we pray for *geshem*—rain—thereby affirming that even our material attainments, which we delude ourselves into believing are the result of our own efforts and cunning, depend upon G-d's blessings.

"You asked why all these things are happening to you, Michelle. I am not G-d. I cannot tell you, but our history testifies that very often G-d places challenges and difficulties in our paths so that we might turn to Him. We see this pattern throughout our history. For example, our patriarchs and matriarchs were denied the blessing of children, and only after they prayed were they granted offspring. Just as a father wants his children to be in contact with him, so G-d desires our presence. The greatest pain that parents can experience is to have children who forget them and call only when they are in need or in trouble."

"My brother is like that," Michelle said, "so I can identify with it."

"Well, how do you suppose G-d feels when His children never call? Perhaps G-d sent you this problem, Michelle, so that you might come closer to Him. Instead of fighting it, embrace the challenge. Pray and grow and become stronger for it. Our trials and tribulations are very often messages to awaken us to come closer to G-d.

"For example, when G-d punished Adam and decreed that he live by the sweat of his brow, and when He told Eve that she would give birth through pain and suffering, He wasn't really punishing them. Rather, He made life difficult so that they might become aware of their vulnerability and call out to Him in prayer. Punishment was meted out only to the malevolent serpent, to whom G-d said, 'You shall crawl on your belly and dust shall be your food.'

"At first glance, that's not much of a punishment. The snake is the only creature that doesn't have to forage for its food. It actually wallows in it. It never has to look up. It never has to turn to G-d for help, but that's its punishment. When a father says, 'Don't bother me. Here's a credit card. I don't want to see your face,' it means that that father is angry and wishes to disassociate himself from his son. On the other hand, if he withholds the credit card and says, 'Come over, son, and we'll discuss your needs,' it means that the father cares and wants to be in contact with his child. Similarly, Michelle, G-d wants to be in contact with you."

Michelle *did* take my advice. She learned to pray and asked G-d for His guidance. She sat Gary down, took his hand in hers, and looked him straight in the eye. Unashamedly, she told him that she was committed to his happiness and making their marriage a success. And miraculously, it *worked!* They cleared up the nonsense that had separated them, for in retrospect, most conflicts are nonsense. When people look back upon their lives and examine the causes of their anger, the source of their dissension, they most often conclude that it was all foolishness. They realize that they placed relationships in jeopardy for naught.

People look for all sorts of sophisticated solutions for their problems when often the answer is a simple, direct approach. Turn to G-d in prayer, then turn to the person that you want to reach; speak from your heart, be *sad,* not *mad,* and not only will you succeed, but you might just discover that your relationship will become stronger for the experience and your marriage more solid and stable. There is a timeless teaching, "Words that emanate from the heart must enter another heart," and above all, there is an even more powerful teaching, "Prayers that emanate from the heart reach the Heavenly Throne," and if you have that, that's all the help you will need.

# NINE

# GROWING TOGETHER— GROWING APART

R ichard Mansfield dropped in at our High Holiday services at the Pierre Hotel in Manhattan and was blown away. "Nothing short of a spiritual explosion," he said, describing his feelings. "Next year, this is where Kate and I will be worshiping," he promised.

Richard, an architect who was highly respected in his field, had just started attending our classes. "Why don't you invite Kate to join us," I would tell him, to which he always responded, "She works long hours, she's very busy," and since Kate was a trial attorney, I could accept that.

The year passed very quickly. The High Holidays were once again upon us, and I reminded Richard of his promise.

"Thanks for bringing up the subject, because I will need help with this one. Could you speak to Kate?" And he went on to tell me that, for the longest time now, there had been tension between them. "Don't get me wrong," he quickly added. "We love each other, and there's no talk of divorce or anything like that, but Kate is so resentful of my involvement in religion that it has driven a wedge between us."

"What's her objection?" I asked.

"Well, for one thing, she feels that I'm no longer the person she married—and it's true! Fourteen years ago I was totally secular, but coming to Torah classes has opened up a whole new world for me, and I really think that she's afraid of that world. She has some distorted ideas from her feminist school days that women in Judaism are stifled and treated as second-class citizens."

"I didn't think that was much of an issue anymore," I told him. "Somehow, I was under the impression that the feminist movement had peaked and women were now into marriage and family, and if they are into their careers, it's a means of earning a livelihood rather than an ideological statement."

"That may be statistically correct, but in our home Kate still has this attitude. I enjoy the Sabbath, I enjoy going to synagogue, and I would like to take my children along, but she fights me, so I thought that you, as a woman who is out there, could clarify things for her. As for the High Holy Days, she refuses even to consider the idea of participating in a traditional service. Kate has all these issues about religion being patriarchal and chauvinistic, and I really don't have the answers. Would you call her?" he pleaded.

I promised Richard to give Kate a ring at the first opportunity, even though I could never fully relate to the issue of feminism being in conflict with Judaism. From my father and grandfathers, I saw nothing but the greatest respect extended to women. If my mother happened to be temporarily occupied in the kitchen while we sat around the Sabbath table, my father would bring all discussion to a halt. "Wait until Mommy is at the table," he would say. If we asked my father's permission for something, his spontaneous response was "We have to ask Mommy," just as Abraham was told by G-d to listen to the voice of Sarah. The love and esteem in which my father held my mother remained constant throughout his life. Even in his last years, when painful terminal illness racked his body, this love remained his priority. I visited him daily, if only for a few minutes. When I entered the house, I would automatically rush to his bed-side, but even as I approached, he would say, "Go to Mommy first." Only when he was satisfied that I had spent sufficient time talking to my mother did he permit me to sit down next to him.

This profound respect for women that I witnessed at home was reinforced by Torah studies. Early on, I learned that women were the prime movers of the world, the inspiration of our nation, so I always felt secure and confident in my femininity. I never considered that my brothers, who had to get up at the crack of dawn to rush to synagogue, don phylacteries, and pray with a minyan (a quorum of ten men required for prayer), were superior in their service of G-d. I felt content to pray at my own pace and designate my own private time and place for my conversations with G-d. The Torah enabled me to appreciate that gender differences were made so that we might realize our potential and contribute our own unique talents for the greater good of the world. G-d created the world as a sym-phony, endowing each of His creations with its own unique instru-ment. To demand that every instrument be identical would be disastrous. The trombone cannot be a flute, a violin cannot be a cello; each must play its own part so that the world may function in harmony. This same rule applies in nature. The apple tree cannot be interchanged with the grapevine, nor a blade of grass with the oak. G-d's grand design is fulfilled only when each creation faithfully carries out its appointed calling, so I realized that my own self-actualization could be best achieved if I learned to play my own instrument and no one else's. Nevertheless, having interacted over the years with many feminists, and having witnessed the exploita-tion of women in our secular society, I understood where Kate was coming from, even if her premises vis-à-vis Judaism were all wrong.

In a culture that for centuries relegated women to a secondary position, in which they had to battle for equality not only in the workplace but in every other sphere of society, it is easy to believe that these same inequities hold true in Judaism as well. The great majority of women have never studied Torah. They have no clue as to what the traditional position on feminism may be. They fight a battle where there is no battle to be fought, and worse, where any gain is in essence a loss, for it compromises the uniqueness with which G-d endowed the female. Instead of exploring their femininity, they pursue masculinity, and in the process lose their identities and are left more frustrated than ever before.

Ironically, despite all the strides that have been made by the women's movement, wife abuse, child abuse, broken homes, custody problems, and just plain misery continue. It's not talesim (prayer shawls proscribed for men) that contemporary women need, but the wisdom to understand the power of their own womanhood.

It was with these thoughts in mind that, a few days later, I called Kate. As expected, she told me outright that she didn't think there was much point to our meeting, and then she added, "I hope you won't mind my saying this, but I have difficulty understanding how a woman of your capabilities can accept the inferior position that religion assigns to you."

I refused to be drawn into a debate over the phone. When I was a young girl, one of the lessons that my father taught me was that all discussions of a serious nature are best conducted face-to-face, "where people see you and you see them. A smile, a kind look makes all the difference and can soften even the sharpest words." So I turned the conversation to her and asked how she managed to juggle the roles of trial attorney, mother, and wife so successfully. By the end of our talk, she had agreed to meet me for lunch. Something told me that, with Kate, I would be better advised to meet her in an informal setting rather than at my office.

Kate arrived at the restaurant late, apologizing that she had been delayed in court. She was an attractive brunette in her early forties, exuding a confidence that bordered on arrogance. Once we had ordered, she got right down to business. "I'd like to make a few points clear," she said. "I agreed to this meeting only to please Richard. He's been after me to talk to you, but honestly, like I said on the phone, there's nothing that you can say that will convince me that Judaism is not patriarchal and chauvinistic, because it is."

"Well, that's being open-minded," I quipped.

Kate laughed. "I just like to be up front, and I'm not going to allow this religion thing to come between Richard and me."

"I couldn't agree with you more. Religion should never come between you; rather, it should unite you. But it appears that it has become a divisive force in your marriage; otherwise, we wouldn't be sitting here."

"I'm very resentful of what's happening," she said, pointedly ignoring my reference to religion being a force for unity. "When I married Richard, he was a secular, normal person, and now he's on his way to becoming one of those religious fanatics—and that wasn't part of the deal!"

"I don't know of any marriage ceremony in which a deal is made not to grow."

"Are you being sarcastic?" Kate cut in.

"Not at all," I assured her. "I mean it sincerely. In marriage we make a commitment to remain loyal and faithful, but nowhere is a deal made not to grow, not to develop, not to expand our spiritual horizons. Let's be honest—isn't that what Richard is doing?

"As for fanaticism," I continued, "experience has taught me that to most people, a fanatic is someone who doesn't agree with their views, whereas someone who does agree is regarded as open-minded and enlightened. But please, Kate," I said, looking her straight in the eyes, "I'm not happy with the way our conversation is going, so instead of exchanging barbs, why don't we start with your telling me what your issues are, why you think Judaism is a male-chauvinist religion? Perhaps there are some things that I can clarify."

"Well, it's obvious, isn't it? Historically, it's patriarchal; ritually, it's sexist; and in relationships, women are expected to be servile. I don't mean to be disrespectful to the memory of your husband, but even your title, 'Rebbetzin,' (which is conferred on the wife of a rabbi), bothers me. Isn't that just an extension of him? Don't you find it compromising? I mean, you've accomplished so much—don't you think you should have your *own* identity?"

"But, Kate, I do. Do you know what gave me the greatest sense of fulfillment in my marriage? That, yes, I became an extension of my husband, that we not only shared a life but shared our dreams and our visions as well. We were soul mates in every sense, and so I carried and continue to carry my title 'Rebbetzin' with pride. And this relationship was not unique to us. Thousands of years ago, Abraham and Sarah forged this same partnership and joined forces to disseminate the word of G-d. If I may, I think that your own relationship with Richard would become much more meaningful if you had something bigger than the two of you to unite you. When husbands and wives have a spiritual communality, their marriage becomes so much more rewarding and their bonding so much stronger."

"But why should the woman be the one to submerge her identity? Why shouldn't the husband renounce his?" Kate argued.

"You have it all wrong. No one has to renounce anything. In a sense, husbands and wives are like *good neighbors,* with each having his or her own space but nevertheless united by a common goal that is greater than them. As for your questioning why husbands don't take on the identities of their wives, they do. Let me tell you a story about a great rabbi who lived in Jerusalem. One day, shortly after the death of his wife, he was returning to his home by taxi. As the cab reached his corner, the driver turned to him and asked, 'Where is your home?' The rabbi didn't answer. The driver, thinking that he hadn't heard, repeated his question, 'Where is your home?' But still the rabbi didn't respond. Finally, the rabbi took a deep breath and said to the driver, 'From the day that my wife died, I no longer have a home—a house, yes; a street, yes; but not a home.'

"What the rabbi was expressing was not just some sentimental words but a profound teaching from the Talmud. A man's *wife* is his *home.* So you see, Kate, the great men of our people were not embarrassed to concede that their very homes were synonymous with their wives.

"When referring to the husband-wife partnership, the Talmud teaches us that a man's character traits are totally dependent on those of his wife. To illustrate, it points to a righteous couple who, after many years of marriage, were still childless. Although they cared deeply for each other, they nevertheless decided to part in the hope that in a new marriage their luck would turn and G-d would bless them with children. As things happened, the compassionate, lovely wife married a mean-spirited, angry man, but succeeded in turning him into a kind, considerate person. The husband, on the other hand, who was known for his goodness, married a nasty, self-ish woman, and tragically, through her influence, he, too, became nasty and selfish. So you see, Kate, our religious literature teaches that the power of women is so great that it is men who become extensions of their wives. What it amounts to is that a good woman makes a good man, and a bad woman makes a bad man."

"Are you implying that I'm a bad influence?" Kate challenged.

"I'm not implying anything," I told her. "I'm telling you openly that you, as a woman, as Richard's wife and the mother of his chil-dren, have the greatest power to influence his life, so instead of fighting him, join him in partnership and elevate him and your mar-riage to another level."

"My issues remain," Kate insisted, "and you didn't really address them. I still see Judaism as patriarchal and chauvinistic, an influence that would stifle my marriage rather than elevate it," Kate said coldly. And as she spoke, I could very well imagine her cross-examining a witness.

"I'm happy to discuss your issues," I responded, "but this time, let me be the one to say 'I hope you won't take offense,' because I have to tell you that you are misinformed on every count. I'm certain you're familiar with the old joke about the husband who says, 'I make all the major decisions in my house. It is I who decide whether the U.N., the Congress, and the President are right or wrong. My wife makes the minor decisions. It is she who decides everything that pertains to our children, to our family, and to our home.'

"In a sense, that's applicable to the matriarchs. It was Sarah who decided that Abraham should marry Hagar, and later, it was she who decided that Hagar and Ishmael should go. It was Rebecca who determined to which of her sons Isaac would give the blessing; it was Rachel and Leah who decided who Jacob was to marry, and later, when our forebears sojourned in Egypt, it was in the merit of the righteous women that they were redeemed. Still later, when they fashioned the golden calf in the desert, it was the women who refused to participate, and when the moment to enter the promised land arrived, the men lost heart, but the women remained steadfast. Perhaps even more telling, at Sinai G-d instructed Moses to speak to the women first. I could go on and on, but let me sum it up by telling you that even as we had prophets and kings, we had prophetesses and queens, judges, and even a female general, Deborah, who led our nation to victory—hardly a religion that has an antifemale bias, would you say?"

"Maybe that's true historically," Kate conceded, "but what about all those laws that are biased against women?"

"I hate to disappoint you," I said, "but we don't have any laws like that. There is no distinction between the sexes in terms of religious responsibility. Women, no less than men, are obligated to observe the commandments. There are however, certain time-bound commandments from which women are exempt—"

"Oh, that's a cop-out," Kate interrupted.

"On the contrary, it's an affirmation of a woman's superior role—caring for children."

"Oh, come on, Rebbetzin. You're telling me that that's not a cop-out?"

"No, Kate, it's not. Of all our discussions, this one is probably the most important. There is absolutely nothing to compare to the mitzvah of raising children properly. And note, I said *mitzvah*, because raising children is not just an avocation but is the fulfillment of G-d's will. Let me tell you a wonderful story that illustrates this teaching. One Yom Kippur night, the holiest time in the year, an eminent Hasidic rebbe was on his way to conduct services when he passed a house from which he heard a baby crying unrelentingly. The rebbe went to investigate and discovered that the mother had gone off to synagogue and left the child alone in the house. Now the rebbe had a decision to make. Should he go to his waiting congregation, or should he stay with the crying child? The rebbe opted to stay with the child, and that, Kate, sums it all up—that's our attitude toward children, and that is why women are exempt from all laws that are time-bound, even if it means not attending services. If you think about it, you have to admit that the world would be a whole lot better if these laws were our imperatives today. It's no secret that many of the ills of our society can be directly traced to children growing up without the loving care of their mothers."

"Are you pointing a finger at *me*?" Kate asked testily.

"Not at all," I assured her. "I am pointing, however, at our society and at our culture, which has placed children on the back burner and self-fulfillment right up front."

I told Kate about a young medical student I'd met when I spoke at the University of Texas at Austin. Through the generosity and vision of some very special people, we had obtained a grant that enabled us to distribute my book, *The Committed Life*, as a gift to college students following my lectures. Hundreds of young people lined up, and I wrote a message to each. By the time I'd finished, it was very late, and Barbara, who always accompanies me on these trips, whispered that if we were to catch some sleep, we'd better get going, because before we knew it, we'd have to be at the airport for our 6:00 A.M. flight.

From the corner of my eye, I spotted Vickie. She had an expression on her face that said "issues." "Are you waiting to talk to me?" I asked, and I heard Barbara mutter under her breath, "Now we're in for the whole night!"

"I've been waiting," Vickie said, "because I wanted some privacy. I have a problem, and I'd like to have your spin on it." She related that her mother, a judge who was politically and socially active, was never at home. "My sister and I were raised by housekeepers, and some of them were really awful. I remember my mother going away with my father and locking up her jewelry and cash, saying that 'You can't trust the help, they all steal'—but she entrusted *us* to them. Anyway, about eight years ago, Hazel came to work for us, and she was the best thing that could have happened to my sister and me. She was a really kind person, and she loved us and we loved her. But last year she fell, and she sued my parents. They became very upset, because she hadn't been seriously injured and had instituted the suit just to make some money. Anyway, she no longer works for us, but I still feel very close to her. I call her regularly and visit whenever I can. My mother found out and became very upset. She feels that my being in contact with Hazel is a conflict of interest, so I was just wondering what your opinion on this is."

"I have never forgotten that story, Kate. It reflects the tragedy of

American family life. When a young person asks, To whom do I owe my allegiance, to my mother or to the housekeeper? then something is terribly wrong. We have sacrificed our children on the altar of self-fulfillment, and we are now paying the price. We are reaping the harvest of dysfunctional families. So yes, Kate, the Torah exempts women from all time-bound commandments because nothing is to interfere with our highest calling, the raising of children. Self-fulfillment," I went on to explain, "can be realized only one way, and that is by doing that which is *right*."

"What about you?" Kate challenged. "Weren't you always working?"

"Yes, I did work, and I still do, but it's not the work, it's how we prioritize our time. Traditionally, our women have always been out there. As a matter of fact, among the attributes that King Solomon ascribed to the ideal wife was her business acumen. Many women today manage to support their families and raise beautiful children at the same time. It's tricky, but it can be done if you bear in mind that your children must remain your priority.

"As for my own life, like anyone else I struggled to maintain a proper balance. When my children were small, I worked from my home and taught from my kitchen and den, and when I accepted a speaking engagement, either my husband or my mother were there to stay with the children. When I traveled out of the country, I did so only in the summer months when the children were off at camp. My husband and I never left the children for any extended time. For example, after the Six-Day War, when Jerusalem was liberated, we wanted more than anything to be at the Holy Wall. Our children were small, our youngest still in diapers; my mother offered to take care of them, but no, we took them with us. We were a family, and the children knew that they were our priority. No matter what, children come first, and if you live by these rules, your marriage will become more solidified and your relationship with your spouse more meaningful."

"Okay, I can buy that. And you are right. Our world would look a whole lot better if there were more mothers keeping an eye on their children. To be sure, I have my own conflicts with it," Kate conceded. But ever the trial attorney, she put me on the witness stand again.

"If what you say is true, and there is no bias against women, why can't they be counted in a minyan? After all, there are many women who do not have child-care concerns. How can you justify that? A guy who doesn't give a damn about Judaism counts and you don't, Rebbetzin? It's downright insulting!"

"I'm not at all insulted," I assured her. "In fact, I'm complimented that I'm left out."

"Complimented?" she echoed sarcastically. "That's another thing I can't stand—not only are women excluded, but then they adopt a servile attitude and accept this *exclusion* as their divine destiny."

"Do you know how the entire concept of minyan came about?" I asked her.

"Sure," Kate replied, "some male chauvinist cooked it up."

"Not quite. It's a totally different story. But before I even share it with you, as long as you brought up the subject, do you know who in our history is responsible for all the laws pertaining to prayer? A woman by the name of Chana. Chana was barren, and she prayed for the gift of a child. Her supplications were so powerful that they shook the heavens—G-d granted her wish, and she became the mother of Samuel the Prophet. It is from her that our sages learned how to formulate prayer. There are many more stories that I could tell you, but let me get back to your question.

"Minyan has its roots in the Torah. When our people were about to enter the promised land, they started to agitate. There was murmuring and rumbling. They requested permission from Moses to scout out the land. Behind their rebellion were hidden agendas. Some of them had become comfortable with life in the desert—

manna falling from heaven, not having to worry about earning a livelihood. Others were fearful of losing their tribal positions, because once they were settled in their own land, a kingdom would be established. And still others simply lacked faith. Moses tried reverse psychology. 'Go right ahead—spy out the land,' he said, thinking that if he raised no objections to their going, they would calm down and renounce their plans, or, in the worst-case scenario, even if they decided to go, once they saw the land, they would fall in love with it. Twelve leaders were appointed, one for each tribe, but only two of them, Joshua and Caleb, passed the test and returned with a positive report. The other *ten*, although conceding that it was 'a land of milk and honey,' also added the word *but*, and with that *but* they negated everything. The biblical word for 'but' is *efes*, which literally means 'zero,' teaching us that *but* is a polite way of saying no. It is like a man who wants to terminate a relationship saying 'I love you, *but* . . .' Similarly, the ten spies praised the land, but added *but*, and with that *but* invalidated their reports and infused the hearts of the people with fear.

"In vain did Joshua and Caleb try to imbue the nation with courage. In vain did they try to tell the people to have faith. A movement arose to return to Egypt, and only the women remained loyal. All those rebellious men died in the desert, and only the women, and of course, Joshua and Caleb, were privileged to enter the promised land. The minyan, a gathering of ten men in sanctification of G-d's name, is a form of *tikun* (rectification) for that desecration in the desert, but we women did not need that rectification.

"Life is one big *tikun*, Kate," I went on to explain. "No matter in what position or place we find ourselves, we must endeavor to improve the world, to heal the mistakes of the past. So, for example, when we light Sabbath candles, we rectify the sin of Eve who extinguished the sacred light when she rebelled against the command of G-d."

"That sin of Eve," Kate cut in. "That's another one of those things that ticks me off! It has branded women throughout the centuries."

"Maybe in the secular world, but not in the Torah world. *Tikun* is not being branded; rather, it is going to another level in spiritual growth. G-d in His infinite mercy has shown us how to convert our failings into something beautiful and positive. Do you know where the name Eve comes from?"

"I really don't," Kate answered. "Outside of Sunday school, I never really studied the Bible."

"Then let me tell you. It was Adam who named her, and it happened after G-d confronted him with his sin. The name that Adam gave his wife was Chava, which means 'mother of all life,' implying that they would start all over again—that she was a source of inspiration for creating a new and better world. So you see, Kate, the name does not reflect sin, but faith, trust, and confidence. Unfortunately, however, this inspirational teaching of Adam was lost in translation. Instead of Chava, 'the mother of all life,' she was called Eve, which is etymologically related to 'evil.' Just think about that. No other biblical figure has had his or her name so misconstrued in translation, and that should tell you something about the secular world's attitude toward women."

"But there are other areas in which there are inequities," Kate persisted, not willing to give in.

"Such as?" I asked.

"Well, like men and women having to sit separately in traditional synagogues."

"There is a simple answer to that, too," I told her. "Prayer requires enormous spiritual concentration, which in and of itself is difficult enough, but much more so in mixed company. The magnetism of women is so powerful that it is not realistic to expect a man to concentrate upon G-d in their presence. The separation during prayer is not so much to separate the women from the men as it is to separate the men from the women. For example, there are synagogues in which one-way mirrors are used as a partition, giving the women a total view of the men's section but blocking the women from the men's view.

"But you know what, Kate," I said, deciding to take the bull by the horns, "you and I can sit here for hours, and every time I answer a question, you will come up with another one, because you really don't want to hear the answers—the issues that you mention are not really *your* issues. It's not the patriarchs or minyans that keep you awake at night. Something else is bothering you. When religion becomes the battlefield in a marriage, it is usually a smokescreen for deeper conflicts, and I wish you would share them with me. Perhaps we could brainstorm and find some solutions."

Kate didn't answer, but her eyes told me that I had touched a sensitive nerve, so I went on and asked whether she felt threatened by Richard's new life, whether their relationship was not all that she would like it to be, whether over the years they had drifted apart and she feared that Richard's new interest would further separate them.

"Yes, I *am* concerned about this religion thing coming between us," she admitted, "and if you recall, I told you this up front. Maybe our marriage is not all that great, but whose is? In the past, we used to go out on Friday nights—to a movie, dinner, shopping—just *out*. Now Richard won't even do that. I work hard. By the time the weekend comes, I need to unwind, but Richard is totally insensitive to my needs, so of course I'm concerned. Besides, we need some private time together. Don't get me wrong," she hastened to add. "We love each other, but like everyone else, we have some problems. Now he wants me to sit in the kitchen and make chicken soup!"

I was struck by the irony of it all. Here was Kate, a bright Ivy League graduate with an impressive career, yet so misguided about her personal life, trying to salvage her marriage through superficial activities and fighting desperately against the one thing that could cement her relationship with her husband and invest it with a higher purpose.

"Listen to me, Kate," I said, "it may sound trite, but that chicken soup, that *Shabbos* that Richard is asking for, really works. *Shabbos* is designed not only for connecting with G-d but also for bonding with our mates and our families. It's not a Friday night out, it's not a movie, a ball game, or a shopping expedition that you need. What you need is a *Shabbos* night *in* that will connect you. When husband and wife have something meaningful to share with each other, their relationship is enhanced and solidified. When you sit around your *Shabbos* table in the glow of the Sabbath candlelight, singing songs, exchanging ideas, and relating with warmth and love, that is exactly what will happen. At the Sabbath table, every husband sings an ode to his wife proclaiming that not only is she his inspiration, his source of wisdom and success, but that she is his home, his blessing, his very life. I realize that there is nothing that I can say, Kate, that can convince you of this, so why don't you and Richard come with the children for *Shabbos*—experience the magic for yourself. Try it, you have nothing to lose."

Kate took me up on my invitation. The rest is history. Today, she makes chicken soup for *Shabbos*, not only for her family but for a host of guests that I send her way.

# PART FOUR

# PROJECTING
# THE FUTURE

Be not as the bird who sees the corn
but not the net.

*Rabbi Yehuda Ben Tibbon*

*(Medieval Torah Sage, Spain, 1120–1190)*

# TEN

# THE HAZARDS OF DIVORCE

R abbi Shimon, the fourth disciple of Rabbi Yochanan, recommended that a person should strive to *foresee the future.* Now, obviously, he couldn't have been referring to prophetic vision, because that is a gift given by G-d and has no bearing on character development. Nor could he have been thinking of someone with 20/20 vision. Rather, Rabbi Shimon was suggesting that, in all situations, we should attempt to foresee the consequences of our actions. In a game of chess, it is necessary to think before making a move. So, too, in life, before speaking, before acting, we should take a few moments to consider the results that might ensue.

To most people, a foolish person is someone who lacks wisdom, perception, and understanding, but in our Torah language, we have a different way of defining a fool. One of the Hebrew words for fool is *pessy,* derived from the word *peesom* (suddenly). When people act impulsively, without forethought, chances are that they will act foolishly and come to regret their words and deeds.

Our sages teach that "A man doesn't sin unless a moment of foolishness overcomes him . . ." Unfortunately, for some people these moments of foolishness can last days, weeks, months, years, even a lifetime. Their *foolishness* can be so all-pervasive that they resent all attempts at reason, and will turn a deaf ear to even the most cogent arguments. People engrossed in their errant pursuits will find many rationales to justify their stance and convince themselves that they have been victimized, that no one understands them or cares about their needs, and even if you were to point out their faults to them, it would be of no avail, for in their foolishness, the picture that you paint is reflective of someone else and could not possibly be applicable to them. Already, at the beginning of time, this was a dilemma that plagued human beings. When Cain and Abel brought their individual offerings to G-d, Abel's gift was accepted but Cain's was rejected, for Abel gave the best of his possessions while Cain offered his leftovers. However, instead of acknowledging and regretting his miserliness, Cain became bitter and infuriated.

"Why are you angry? Why has your face fallen?" G-d asked him. "Surely, if you improve, you shall be forgiven . . ." (Genesis 4:6).

Cain does not respond to G-d's challenge, but in the very next verse he has a conversation with his brother, Abel, and then proceeds to kill him. The text does not indicate what Cain said, but there is a teaching that Cain repeated G-d's admonition to Abel and suggested that it was meant for him! Far-fetched? Not really. How many of us react in this very same manner? We read a stirring book, hear powerful words, listen to a lecture, or receive words of admonishment, and our immediate reaction is: my wife, my husband, my sister, my brother, my neighbor should hear this. This teaching is tailor-made for *them*. It will help *them* to change! Somehow, it never occurs to us that the message is really tailor-made for *us*—that it is *we* who must change, it is *we* who must stop to weigh, measure, and consider the long-range effects of our words and deeds. How different the history of humankind could have been had Cain stopped for a moment to think.

How many marriages, how many relationships could have been salvaged, how much pain could have been avoided, had people stopped to consider how their words and actions might affect their mates. Had they exercised a little more temperance, a little more discretion in their relationships, they could have avoided much pain. How sad it is that most of the suffering we experience we bring upon ourselves, and it is all because we fail to stop to think.

My father was very cautious with his words. He never spoke or acted impetuously. I can hear his sweet, gentle voice telling us, "What you don't say now, you can always say later, but once it escapes your lips, it's too late to take it back." If we argued, as children are wont to do, he would tell us to sleep on it and settle our differences in the *morning*. Of course, by morning, our anger would have dissipated, and that's exactly the lesson my father hoped we would learn.

My father's wisdom, like all his teachings, had its roots in the Torah. When our forebears were sojourning in the desert, on their way to the promised land, Korach, a cousin of Moses, fomented a rebellion against him. Despite the fact that Korach was enormously wealthy and powerful (or perhaps precisely because of it), he coveted Moses' and Aaron's position. He went from tent to tent, lobbied like a professional politician, and gathered an impressive following for his insurrection. Moses, the loyal shepherd of Israel, whose entire life was one of dedication and service to his people, was devastated when confronted by Korach's perfidy.

Moses, the Torah testifies, was the humblest of all men. He had no personal agenda, and it was with great reluctance that he accepted his role of leadership. He loved his people unconditionally and served them with his entire heart and soul. And now, these very same people were accusing him of personal ambition and nepotism. How could he possibly respond to such charges? Instead of arguing, Moses simply said, "*Morning*—wait until *morning*, and we'll settle it then." Unfortunately, the jealousy of Korach and company was so intense that even the morning sun could not banish it from their hearts. Korach and his followers remained intractable and unrepentant to the very end.

Moses' call for forbearance, however, did not go altogether unheeded. The morning light did bring illumination to Korach's children, who not only expressed remorse but composed psalms that are recited to this very moment in time. On Rosh Hashana, when we are about to fulfill the sacred command of sounding the shofar (ram's horn) and are called upon to reflect on our lives, it is the psalm of the sons of Korach that we chant.

When troubled couples consult me and one of the spouses is bent upon divorce, I have often succeeded in forestalling disaster simply by prevailing upon them to *wait until the morning*. There is always the hope that, if we can buy some more time, they will perceive their folly and reconsider their decision. Mel Cooper was a case in point.

Mel's wife, Nancy, came to see me with a heavy heart. After fifteen years of marriage, she had discovered that her husband was involved with another woman. She had difficulty talking about it, and every few minutes she would break down in tears.

"Do you want to stay in the marriage?" I asked as gently as I could.

"Do I want to stay in the marriage?" she echoed. "Oh, Rebbetzin, I'm so hurt that I can't even look at him, but in a strange way, I guess I still love him. I can't just forget all the good years we had, and then, too, I'm a mother. There are three beautiful children involved, aged eleven, nine, and six, who love their daddy. I have to think about them as well, don't I?"

"Of course you do," I agreed. "They are your priority. But tell me, how does your husband feel about the children?"

"G-d only knows what is going on in Mel's mind. Of course he loves the children, but look at what he's doing."

"Did you confront him?"

"I sure did and, initially, he swore by everything holy that I was imagining things. He tried to convince me that Sue, the woman he is seeing, was just a colleague from his office and that his relationship with her was strictly business. So I believed it—not because I believed it in my heart, but because I *wanted* to believe it, if you know what I mean. But there were telltale signs that kept cropping up, and then there were reports that I was getting from friends and people in his office. Rebbetzin, every report was like a knife in my heart. Anyway, about six months ago, the whole thing blew up—he couldn't deny it any longer, and I was forced to face the facts. As much as I suspected it, it's different when you know things with certitude. The pain was too awful to bear, but what could I do? I wanted to save our marriage, so I suggested that we go for counseling."

"Did Mel agree?"

"Oh yes, but he only went along with me to ease his conscience, so he could pat himself on the back and say 'I tried.' Truth be told, Rebbetzin, his heart was never in it. All the sessions were just a waste of time and money."

"If you feel I'm intruding, please say so, but can I ask what you discussed at those sessions?"

"I have no problem sharing with you, but there was nothing all that much said."

"Still, try to give me an example," I persisted.

"Well, at every session Mel made his hearts-and-flowers speech: he's sorry to be doing this to me; I'm a very good woman—a good mother to his children—and deserve someone better; but this is something beyond his control. He claimed that over the years we had grown apart, that he no longer felt connected to me, and that we no longer had anything in common."

"What did the marriage counselor suggest?"

"Oh, the usual palliatives—that we spend more time together, take walks, leave the kids with my parents and go away for a weekend, the whole *shpiel.*"

"Did you follow through?"

"Sure, but it was a wasted effort. He was just going through the motions. Like I said, his heart and mind were just not in it. Even when we were away, he was constantly on the phone, telling me that he had business to take care of, but most of the time, he was talking to *her*. Oh, Rebbetzin," Nancy wept, "I don't know what to do. My friends tell me that divorce is my only solution, but when I think about it, I can't help but feel that *the solution can end up being worse than the problem*. What is my life, if not my family? I have a cousin who went through a divorce four years ago, and her children still haven't recovered. Whenever they are with her, they cry for their father, and whenever they are with their father, they cry for their mother. Their schoolwork has suffered and they have developed all kinds of psychological and emotional problems. The entire family has become one big mess. My cousin discussed it with her therapist, and he told her that that's one of the bitter results of divorce, and if children are to feel a sense of wholeness, they need *both parents* at their side. I dread what all this could do to *my* children. I don't want to see them scarred or damaged. I don't want them to become just another statistic. I'm ready to do anything to save my marriage. I'm even ready to swallow my pride, forgive, and forget. Will you help me, Rebbetzin?"

My heart went out to Nancy. She was a sweet and unassuming young woman who wanted nothing more out of life than to keep her family together. "Of course I will try to help," I assured her, "but the track record on these things is not very encouraging. Husbands who become involved with other women are not easily retrieved. But tell me," I asked, "is there anyone in his family or among his friends who has challenged him and told him that what he is doing is wrong?"

"Not really," came Nancy's pathetic reply. "He is successful, so people are intimidated by him, and that includes his family and friends. But in all fairness, I guess some of them do believe that if he's not happy, he should get out and make a new life for himself. Many of them have done the same."

"Would Mel be open to talking with me?" I asked.

"Probably not. Like I told you, as far as he's concerned, he's done his bit. He's through with counseling and it's highly unlikely that he would agree to see a rebbetzin, but when I read your book *The Committed Life*, you had some great stories about people changing, so it occurred to me that maybe it could happen to my family as well. Maybe you could reach him."

"That's a tall order," I said. "Once people make up their minds, it's almost impossible to change them."

Nancy's face fell.

"I don't want you to take this as a refusal. I didn't say *impossible*— I said *almost* impossible. I can assure you that I will try. Divorce is a tragedy, especially when there are children involved, so of course I would want to help you."

"Thank you for saying that," Nancy said with a sigh of relief, "because for a while I thought I was crazy. Everyone has been telling me that I should just say good-bye and move on."

"People talk too much and much too irresponsibly. They don't realize how damaging their advice can be." I thought about all the couples I have known who confided to me that if they had to do it all over again, they would never go for a divorce. They were goaded on by so-called well-intentioned friends who encouraged them to think of their own happiness to the exclusion of all else. Too late they discovered that when they split their family into two, they also lost their happiness.

But to Nancy I said, "I will certainly call him, but please don't get your hopes too high, because chances are, he'll refuse to see me."

True to my expectations, when I called Mel, I was given a cold reception. "There's nothing much to discuss," he told me. "Nancy and I both agree that our marriage has fallen apart. It's unfortunate, but that's life."

"Mel," I said, "and I hope you don't mind that I'm calling you by your first name, but since I met Nancy, I feel close to your family. You say that 'that's life,' but it doesn't have to be. Life is what you choose to make it. So before you make your decision final, let's talk."

After some sharp exchanges, Mel reluctantly agreed to come by my office, but he warned me that his schedule was very tight and he would have only a few minutes to spare.

Mel Cooper turned out to be exactly as I had imagined—tall, handsome, and self-assured. "I really think that this is a waste of time," he announced as he walked into my office. "There is nothing that you can tell me that I haven't heard before. I tried my best, but it's just not going anywhere."

"How long have you been married?"

"Fifteen years."

"And all fifteen years have been equally unhappy?"

"I was very young when we were married," he said brusquely. "I really didn't know what I was doing—and sure, we did have some good times, but something was missing from the very beginning."

"When did you realize that something was missing?"

"I told you, from the very beginning. I probably sensed it even when we were dating," Mel said, with annoyance in his voice.

Mel's protestations rang a familiar bell. Over the years, I have discovered that whenever people are involved in a triangle, there is always a reluctance to admit to infatuation and folly, so they justify their stance by saying that their marriage was never good to start with. However, I didn't voice any of those thoughts to Mel. Nevertheless, he must have picked up on them because he said, "I don't know what Nancy told you, but if you're alluding to Sue, this has nothing to do with her. We're just good friends. She's a very accomplished lawyer in my firm and we work well together. There's nothing more to it than that."

"Look, Mel," I said, deciding to be direct, "let's put our cards on the table. You and I have a choice. We can be in denial and talk in circles, or we can be forthright and discuss this situation honestly. I have no hidden agenda. My only interest is to help you and your family, so can I be quite open with you?"

"Be my guest," he said with a shrug.

"Somehow, you don't sound like you really mean that."

Mel stiffened. "What do you want me to say?" he demanded. "That I will enjoy listening to being preached at?"

"No, Mel, I don't anticipate that you would enjoy that, but please know that it is not my intent to preach at you. Rather, I'm crying with you."

"Crying with me, *crying* with me? You *can't* be crying with me, Rebbetzin, because *I'm* not crying. There's nothing to cry about!"

"Not only am *I* crying, Mel, but it is written that when husband and wife divorce, even the altar weeps. And I'm not being melodramatic—I'm just quoting the Talmud. It is written that the reason the altar weeps is that it was upon the altar that sacrifices were brought, so the altar weeps as if to say, This marriage could have been saved had husband and wife made a little effort and offered sacrifices. Listen to me, Mel. I'm speaking to you from my heart. I'm a little bit older than you. I've seen and gone through a lot in my lifetime. We all make mistakes, but some mistakes can be very costly—and can never be rectified. Too late do we discover that we've destroyed that which is most precious in our lives."

"Hold on! I'm not destroying anyone. Nancy and I are just not getting along, so we're getting a divorce. Half of America is divorced. What's the big deal? I'm no expert, but I understand that even in the Torah there are provisions for divorce."

"That's true. Half of America *is* divorced, and half of America is on medication and in need of psychological help. There are many damaged people out there carrying deep scars from their parents' divorces. As for the Torah, yes, it does make provisions for divorce, but before issuing a bill of divorcement, we have to do everything humanly possible to avoid that disaster—and in situations like yours, divorce would be regarded as pure disaster. You're married to a good woman. She is the mother of your children, and despite everything, she loves you and is committed to your marriage. If you could in all honesty say that Nancy is an abusive wife or mother, and is unwilling to work out your conflicts or respond to your needs, then you could perhaps justify divorce. But what is your justification here? An office romance?"

"I resent that," Mel cut in, seething with anger. "This is *not* about an office romance. Besides, I never said that Nancy wasn't a good woman, but we no longer have anything in common. We just grew apart."

"Come on, Mel. Let's talk straight. Deep down, you know that if there is any one female on this planet with whom you have *anything* in common it is surely Nancy. Can there be a greater commonality than the children you had together? Can there be a greater sense of fulfillment than watching them grow?"

"Let's not exaggerate, Rebbetzin. We'll still have the kids in common. We'll still watch them grow. It will just be done differently—they'll have two homes."

"Two homes, Mel, is no home. Children need *one* home, *one* set of parents. Children do not like to be transients—one home here, one home there, this holiday with mom, that holiday with dad. Who's going to pay for this? Who's responsible for that? Daddy's girlfriend, mommy's boyfriend? And then, before you know it, you will have a bar mitzvah. Don't you think that your son is entitled to have both parents at his side?"

"What do you mean?" Mel protested. "Of course we will be there. Divorce won't change that."

"Sure, you with Sue, and Nancy with a date—and the poor kid in the middle. You know better than that. You know what is the most precious gift that parents can give to their children—that they love each other. When children see parents interacting in a warm, loving way, they grow up strong and confident."

"I told you, Nancy and I have grown apart. I have no feeling for her anymore."

"I would suggest to you, Mel, that if not for Sue entering your life, this conversation wouldn't be taking place and you wouldn't have these feelings."

"I think that this has gone far enough!" Mel said. "How many times do I have to tell you that this has nothing to do with Sue. We're just good friends and work well together. She understands me—she's a remarkable woman."

"I know you told me that, Mel, but I also told you that I'm going to be honest and tell it like it is. I have no reason to doubt that you and Sue work well together and that she understands you, but I'm equally certain that you are making the mistake of your life. You are allowing your passion to cloud your judgment."

"That's it!" Mel exclaimed angrily, making a move to leave. "You just don't understand."

"Mel," I said. "Please sit down and let's finish the conversation. G-d forbid, it's not my intention to hurt or insult you, but lives are at stake, so we have to talk honestly. In a marriage it's very easy for a relationship to crumble. The everyday nitty-gritty is not very romantic. Undoubtedly, there have been times when Nancy was impatient with you, when you felt that she was dumping on you, when she was irritable and even nasty. Sue, on the other hand, is always charming. You go out for lunch or dinner—for *business*, of course. She has the time and the patience to listen to you; she compliments you and makes you feel good about yourself—so of course she is *remarkable*. She's *not your wife*. She doesn't have to deal with the problems of your household. She doesn't have to run to the doctor with the kids. She doesn't have to go to their school and worry about their progress; she doesn't have to get involved in their quarrels or chauffeur them to their tutors. She doesn't have to pay bills and keep the house in order, so of course your relationship with her is different. But the moment you marry Sue, the moment she becomes *your wife,* the very same problems will erupt, except worse, because you'll also have to deal with your scarred children, your injured ex-wife, and your own messed-up life. And that realization will be so painful that nothing on earth will compensate for it.

"Let's face it, Mel. There's no such thing as taking a woman out for lunch, for dinner, traveling with her on business trips, and writing it off as *friendship*. Your relationship with Sue is, to say the least, *inappropriate*—and that's putting it mildly. You really must terminate it immediately, Mel, not only for the sake of Nancy and your children, but for your own sake, because at the end of the day, there is such a thing as decency and morality."

"Are you suggesting that I'm not decent or moral?" Mel challenged indignantly.

"On the contrary, I believe that you are *very* decent and moral, but I *am* suggesting that the *situation* you've got yourself into is not decent or moral, and that if you continue on your present course, you're headed for a collision. Please don't think that I'm being judgmental. It's a tough world out there, and there, but for the grace of G-d, goes any one of us. There are so many pulls, so many seductions, and so many voices. Values have become blurred. Almost anything and everything can be justified. It's easy to get trapped; it's easy to delude yourself into thinking that you are doing the right thing by pursuing your own happiness. But in your heart, you know that you can't build your happiness by destroying those who are near and dear to you. You'll never have peace that way."

"I know plenty of people who are divorced and they're happy," Mel snapped.

"You just *think* that they're happy. No one really knows what's going on in someone else's home, and especially in someone else's heart. People make mistakes, and then they're stuck with them. They put up a good front because they are loathe to admit that they blew it, but inside they are full of regrets and pain, although I'll grant you that there are couples who are in intolerable, abusive marriages, and to them divorce is not only justifiable, but a necessity and spells release—but thank G-d, that is not your situation."

I went on to explain to Mel the teachings of Rabbi Yossi, who advised that the most important character trait for a man to develop is *foreseeing the future,* visualizing how his words and deeds will affect others. "Close your eyes for a minute, Mel, and try to picture your eleven-year-old David, your nine-year-old Gabriella, and your six-year-old Debbie. Try to envision what this divorce will do to them. Then, close your eyes again and visualize Nancy. Now, there's one *remarkable* woman. After all she's gone through, she still loves you. Yes, she's deeply hurt, but she still has feelings for you, and that's an incredible gift. Don't throw it away. There are precious few things in life that really count, and family is right up there. Don't lose it. I know that, initially, the going will be tough, but I'm here to help you."

"Wait a minute! What are you helping me with? I haven't agreed to anything!"

"I know you haven't, but you asked me earlier if I was suggesting that you're not decent or moral, and if you remember, I told you that, on the contrary, I thought *you* were, but the *situation* in which you are involved isn't. I know that in your heart of hearts you realize that this relationship is wrong, but you have become so deeply enmeshed that you don't know how to extricate yourself. I also know that you are suffering, because there is no pain as excruciating as *neshama* pain."

"*Neshama* pain? What's that?" Mel asked.

"*Neshama* is a Hebrew word for soul. It is related to the word *nisheema*, which means 'breath.' When G-d created man, He *breathed* into him, and that breath of G-d is the soul of man. You can mess up your mind, your heart, but you can never mess up your soul—*that remains pure forever. When you do something that's against the law of G-d,* the *neshama* hurts—that's *neshama* pain, and it is agonizing."

"I don't know. I see plenty of rotten people walking around doing horrible things, and they don't look to me like they're having— what did you call it—*neshama pains.*"

"Some people, Mel, have layers and layers of soot and grime covering their *neshamas*, and after a while, it's difficult for them to feel anything. One of our sages explained this in the following manner: The first time you commit a wrong, you are revolted at what you have done; the second time, it's no longer so shocking or painful. The third time, not only do you not see anything wrong, but you actually develop a philosophy that transforms your sin into a virtue."

"What makes you think that I'm not one of those people? Maybe I also see nothing wrong with what I'm doing."

"If that were the case, you would have walked out of this office a long time ago. You may have wanted to, and you actually did get up to leave on several occasions, but despite everything, you are still sitting in that chair, and when I spoke about your children, I saw something more."

"What did you see?"

"Your eyes became moist, Mel, and behind moist eyes are strong *neshamas*."

"Don't lay a guilt trip on me," Mel protested.

"Guilt is a beautiful gift. As long as you feel guilty, it means that your *neshama* is alive and well. It's when you no longer feel pangs of conscience, when you can abandon and hurt your family and feel no remorse—that's when your *neshama* is in danger. It's like being anorexic. Healthy people feel hunger pangs, but anorexics have no desire for food. When they say they're not hungry, they really mean it. They can't eat. Their stomachs have shut down. So if it makes you feel guilty—that's good! What do you say, Mel? Let me help you; you won't be able to do this alone."

"Well, what do you suggest?" Mel asked reluctantly, and then quickly added, "Mind you, I'm not agreeing to anything."

"The first thing you'll have to do is call upon all your connections and find Sue another job. She can't remain in your firm. You can't be in contact with her."

"Oh, come on, Rebbetzin, isn't that taking things a bit too far?" Mel objected.

"Too far? I don't think it's far enough! Do you know what Joseph did when he found himself in a similar situation?"

"Joseph who?" Mel asked, puzzled.

"Joseph from the Bible, of course."

"You must be joking. Are you expecting me, living in the twenty-first century, to relate to someone from the Bible?"

"Absolutely," I answered. "Just because you can go on the Internet and fly around the world, do you think you have a better understanding of life than Joseph had? I can assure you that, if you'd only listen, you'd discover that Joseph has more to say to you than anyone in this century. Why do you suppose the Bible is replete with stories about our ancestors? So that we might learn from their lives. It is written, 'Whatever happened to our forefathers is a sign for us, the children.' Joseph's story could be the story of any man struggling to control temptation. Here he was, abandoned by his brothers and all alone in Egypt, a strange, hostile land. The Bible testifies that he was incredibly handsome and charismatic, and the wife of his Egyptian master fell in love with him. She tried every which way to seduce him, but Joseph consistently rebuffed her.

"Then, one day, on an Egyptian holiday when everyone had gone off to worship their idols, she feigned illness. She knew that Joseph, the Jew, would remain at home and saw this as the perfect opportunity to seduce him. Cunningly, she made her move and grabbed Joseph's jacket. Without a moment's hesitation, Joseph ran for his life, leaving her holding the jacket in her hands."

"Ran for his life?" Mel scoffed.

"Yes, Mel, he ran for his life, because passion is a fire that consumes."

"Oh, come on."

"Like I said, I would never wish to hurt you, Mel, but you are a prime example. You, too, have been consumed by this fire. Take a good look at your life and at what this relationship has done to you, and to your family. Joseph understood that in the face of temptation, a man must run—it takes just a split second of weakness to give in, and you end up paying for the rest of your life. Just look at our society. Many prominent men have been toppled by a *split second* of weakness. You can't be smarter than Joseph, Mel. Run for your life. Free yourself from this affair and sever all ties with Sue. And you will be doing her a favor as well. Let her start a new life and not take away another woman's husband."

For what appeared to be a long time, Mel was silent, and then he said, "I'm no Joseph, Rebbetzin. I'm not that righteous."

"That's true," I agreed, "but it's also true that you are his descendant, and you carry a spark of his spiritual genes. If he was capable of such heroic discipline, you, too, are capable of it. You need only make the attempt. Like I said, it's going to be tough, real tough, and that's why I offered to help you. I'll introduce you to my sons. They are wonderful rabbis. They will teach you how to pray and they will study Torah with you. This will serve to strengthen your resolve and nurture your *neshama*, because above all, it is G-d's help that you will need."

"I don't know," Mel said doubtfully. "I'll have to think about it. All this religious stuff, it's just not me."

"It's not religious stuff at all," I said. "It's your *neshama* yearning for G-d. There's nothing as fulfilling, as elevating, as knowing you have done that which is *right*. A serene and peaceful conscience has no price."

It was rough going. Mel had many ups and downs, but in the end, he made it. He terminated his relationship with Sue and returned to his family. Recently, I had the privilege of participating in the bar mitzvah of his son, and when I saw him and Nancy beaming with joy as David gave a dissertation on the Torah portion of the week, my own heart was filled with joy as well. The words from our morning prayer came to mind: "My G-d, the soul *(neshama)* that You placed within me is pure. You created it, You fashioned it, You breathed it into me—You safeguarded it within me . . ."

What a wonderful gift the *neshama* is—it grants us all a second chance.

# ELEVEN

# COMMUNICATING
# WITHOUT HURTING

Peter and Maxine Gold were referred to me by the rabbi who had married them. Their marriage was in serious trouble, and they were contemplating divorce.

"For years I have been dreaming of marriage, but not this," Maxine said bitterly. "For this I didn't have to get married."

"Unfortunately, the script doesn't always play out as we anticipate," I told her. "Only in fairy tales do couples live happily ever after. In real life, maintaining a good marriage takes hard work and sacrifice, so if you're going through some rough times, it's quite normal."

"Normal!" Maxine exclaimed. "Is it normal to have a husband who finds fault with everything you do but can't accept a suggestion that sometimes he might be the one who's wrong? Is that normal?"

"I find fault?" Peter cut in. "Boy, that's a new twist on things. I wouldn't have brought this up at all, but as long as she did, let me tell you, Rebbetzin, that no one can nag like my wife. Believe me, I've tried, but the only thing I hear from her is constant complaint."

"Rebbetzin, if I complain, it's because I'm subjected to verbal abuse," Maxine shot back.

"Abuse!" Peter exclaimed.

"Yes, abuse!" Maxine retorted, tears filling her eyes. "He doesn't realize it, but he's arrogant, inconsiderate, and irritating."

"You see what I mean?" Peter asked. "She speaks to me in a nasty tone of voice, labels me inconsiderate and irritating, and then reverses it and says that I'm the one who's abusive. Give me one reason why I should put up with it. I can get out of this marriage and lead a normal life. I don't need this."

"So, go," Maxine said. "You think you're frightening me? I don't need this either."

Listening to Maxine and Peter, I felt like I was watching a boxing match. Seldom had I encountered such hostility in a couple. "Let's try to calm down," I told them. "Don't invite the Satan into your lives."

"The Satan!" Maxine exclaimed startled.

"Yes, the Satan," I said. "Contrary to popular belief, the Satan is not some malevolent being with a tail, horns, and a pitchfork. Rather, it is an evil spirit that we evoke when we articulate negative thoughts. Therefore, our sages caution us never to wish misfortune upon ourselves lest it come true. How often have you heard people say 'I wish I were dead'—when for the same effort, they could wish that everything would be well. Thoughts can become self-fulfilling prophecy, so you have to be very cautious about the energies you generate. Let me tell you a great story to illustrate. We had a brilliant, wise lady in our history. Her name was Bruriah, and she was married to the eminent sage Rabbi Meir. Unfortunately, they had a miserable, contentious neighbor who caused them no end of grief. One day when the neighbor was particularly obnoxious, Rabbi Meir couldn't take it anymore and prayed that G-d would punish him. Overhearing her husband's prayer, Bruriah quickly interrupted and said, 'Rabbi Meir, instead of praying that G-d will punish him, why don't you pray that G-d will give him a kind, understanding heart?'

"Similarly, instead of wishing for divorce, wish that you could find a way to salvage your marriage. Instead of painful jibes and cutting remarks, find words that will stimulate growth and love, and instead of destroying, pray for G-d to show you the way to rebuild. Divorce is a last resort and should be considered only after all other avenues have been explored and exhausted. But the way you are going about this, you are making divorce your *first* resort, so let's stop the recriminations and accusations and use this opportunity for mending and healing."

"I don't know if that's in the cards," Peter commented dryly.

"Our sages teach that 'Every man is led on the path he chooses to follow' (Talmud), so it *is* in the cards, Peter, if you will it. Besides, isn't that why you came to see me?"

"Well, yes, but . . ." Peter left the words hanging.

"But what?" I pressed. "There are no buts. You just have to make up your mind that that's the path you will follow. Let me ask you: If you had a problem with one of your children, would you abandon the child or would you try to seek help? Why should your marriage be any less important? From what I've seen in the last few minutes, you don't know how to communicate with each other without hurting, and that's fixable."

"Fixable?" Maxine repeated. "To do that, Peter would have to take a vow of silence!"

"Hold it," I said. "Let's try to implement this right here and now, and refrain from sarcasm. Maxine, you could simply have said, 'I would be so grateful if that could happen' or 'That's what I've been hoping for.' Words like that would inspire Peter to try, but by saying that he would have to take a vow of silence, you declared him incapable of change. You simply must unlearn this negative way of speaking."

"You may be right, Rebbetzin, but if you had to go through what I do, you would realize how hopeless it all is."

"Nothing is hopeless, Maxine, if people want to change, and the very fact that you are both here tells me that you desire to overcome this painful situation, so let's start all over again. Why don't you tell me what sets you off on a typical day?"

Maxine thought for a moment and then said, "This may sound petty—I feel silly even relating it, but to me it was very hurtful."

"In a relationship," I assured her, "nothing is petty. Sometimes a sting can be more harmful than a bite, so tell me about it."

"Well, take what happened this morning. I was late for work, trying to get out, and I couldn't find my keys. Instead of helping me, Peter just stood there watching me with an expression on his face that shouted *She is a real case!* And mind you, I was prepared to handle it had he left it at that, but he made some real snide remarks and started to lecture me."

"I certainly did *not* do that!" Peter cut in. "I never said a word to you; I was just muttering to myself."

"Sure, you never said a word to me, you were only muttering. Rebbetzin, do you know what he was muttering, making certain that I heard every word?" Maxine began mimicking his voice: "'I never saw someone who is such a mess, so disorganized. I don't know why this·has to happen every morning. I'm sick and tired of telling her to put things away.' And he went on and on! By the time I got to work, I was a total wreck!"

"But what I said was true," Peter interjected. "Maxine has many good qualities, but she's hopelessly disorganized. I must have told her at least a dozen times to get her act together, but she just doesn't get it. And on top of it all, she's so darn sensitive that she overreacts to everything."

"Whether it's true or not is beside the point," I said. "Not everything that is true should be said, and it's not only what you say, but the manner in which you say it that is critical. 'Life and death are in the tongue' (Proverbs 18:1)—words can kill. As for overreacting, my husband used to tell a story about a man who went for a physical. The doctor told him that he had a hernia and would require surgery. 'But I wouldn't worry about it,' the doctor was quick to add. To which the man responded, 'I wouldn't worry about it either, doctor, if it was *your* hernia!'

"It's easy to remain calm and collected when someone else's hernia is being operated on, but when it's *your* hernia, then you shout 'Ouch!'—then you overreact."

"I don't know that that analogy stands. We're not talking about an operation, and for heaven's sake, she got upset before I even said anything."

"Every confrontation is an operation. Words can cut even more sharply than a surgeon's scalpel, and eyes can pierce like a needle." I told Peter and Maxine about the teaching of Rabbi Shimon, who recommended that before speaking, acting, or giving a look, we project the impact that our words, deeds, and facial expressions will have. "And when in doubt," I said, "it is best to remain silent. This is the key to good communication, which is essential to every marriage."

"So what am I supposed to do? Swallow everything?" Peter asked.

"I didn't say that, but I did say that you have to project, which means that you have to stop and consider: If I say this, how will Maxine understand it, and more important, will I be making things better or worse? Perhaps I should rephrase my words in a nonjudgmental manner?"

"It's pretty sad if you have to weigh and measure everything you say to your wife."

"On the contrary, whose feelings should you be more concerned with? Those of strangers? Precisely because she *is* your wife, your most precious asset, you would want to protect her."

"But if I'm never frank, how will she ever understand?" Peter persisted.

"Certainly not by destroying her self-esteem or by treating her like a nonentity."

"I don't think I was doing that," Peter said, annoyed.

"I'm certain that was not your intention, but I do think that's how you came across."

Peter wasn't buying it, so I suggested that we replay the scenario. "Maxine was late for work. She was turning the apartment upside down, frantically searching for her keys. From what you told me, this was not the first time this had happened, but that is all the more reason to think she was in distress. At that point, Peter, do you honestly think that she needed someone to tell her that she is disorganized? When you are down, you don't need anyone to remind you that you are down. Do you know what Maxine could have used? A kind voice saying 'Let me help you.'

"But instead, she heard you muttering and looking at her with daggers in your eyes, and to make matters worse, you spoke about her in the third person, as if she wasn't there. How do you suppose that made her feel? Had you addressed her directly and offered to help, it would have made all the difference in the world."

"Oh, I don't know about that," Peter answered. "I don't think it would have made a difference at all."

"Good communication is the key to a happy marriage, but if you cannot express yourselves without inflicting pain, you will destroy not only your marriage but yourselves as well. All the anger that you project will rebound to you. We are commanded not to curse the deaf (Leviticus 19:14). At first glance, it may be difficult to understand this concern for the deaf. After all, they can't hear you. But it is not only the hurt that you inflict on others but the debasement of your own self that the Torah is concerned with, for ultimately, it is the one who indulges in meanness who becomes morally damaged.

I realize that you didn't mean to hurt each other, but that's how you came across, and it is how you are perceived that counts. Peter, no one wants to hear him- or herself being described as inept or referred to in the third person. When you were muttering 'She did this' and 'She did that,' you cut Maxine to the quick.

"The Torah teaches that one of the ways through which affection is communicated is to lovingly repeat someone's name. The converse is also true. When you dislike someone, you can't bear to mention that person's name and will refer to the person impersonally as he or she. A name reflects a relationship, but when that relationship deteriorates, then the name is associated with bitterness, and that's the message that Maxine got from you. When G-d called upon the prophets and the patriarchs, He always did so by addressing them by name, and when He charged them with their mission, He repeated their names as a sign of love—'Moses, Moses,' 'Abraham, Abraham.'

"Had you referred to Maxine by her name, had you said, 'Maxine, let me help you,' it wouldn't have been so hurtful."

"I hear what you are saying," Peter said, "but I don't know if it's applicable in our case. I mean, I can just hear myself saying 'Maxine, Maxine' and Maxine never getting her act together!"

"You see, Rebbetzin! You see how condescending and arrogant he is?"

"There she goes again with her name-calling."

"That's not true!" Maxine retorted. "I never called you names."

"Really? So what was all this about? Didn't you just say that I'm arrogant and condescending? And how about the time I picked up the phone and heard you telling Lauren that you had the dubious pleasure of being married to an arrogant——."

"If you're going to bring that up, why don't you tell the whole story?" Maxine said, her voice taut with anger. "We were out to dinner with our friends Lauren and Matthew. I gave my order to the waiter and in front of everyone Peter said, 'You shouldn't be eating that. You've gained too much weight.'

"I didn't react," Maxine continued. "I didn't want to make a scene, so I tried to ignore his remark. Wouldn't you imagine that he would take the hint? Not a chance! He wouldn't let go. He went on and on about my weight and my lack of control, so can you blame me if I vented to Lauren?"

"If you want to speak about that evening," Peter retorted, "then do me a favor and tell the story like it really happened. How you knocked me and said that I have no taste and that if you didn't put my suit, shirt, and tie together, I'd go to work looking like a disaster."

"Well, you *would!*" Maxine snapped.

"Time out!" I said, "Do you realize what you are doing? If you were watching yourselves on a soap opera, you would say, 'That's a really nasty couple! Why do they insist on hurting each other?' And Peter," I added, "I don't want to belabor the point, but you complained about Maxine's *overreacting.* Has it occurred to you that you may be guilty of the same fault? You could easily have turned that remark around and said, 'That's right! I'm the luckiest guy in the world. I have a great wife who takes care of me and puts out my clothing every morning.'"

Maxine and Peter were silent, and for the first time that evening, I sensed that they were ready to listen. I told them how we can learn to administer criticism from our biblical giants. Take Jacob, for example. He was very cautious in criticizing his children and censured only their *actions,* "Cursed be their tempers" (Genesis 49:7), he declared, regarding Simon and Levi, but he never condemned their *persons,* and he immediately embraced them, teaching us that criticism should be followed by warm, loving words. The Talmud sums it all up, "With the left [weaker] hand you punish, and with the right [stronger hand] you draw near." Perhaps even more significant, Jacob showed his sons how to convert their negative traits (their tempers) into something beautiful and positive (fervor and zeal), and he assigned them to positions in which those traits would serve them well—Levi to the priesthood and Simon to teaching children.

"Were you to follow Jacob's example, Peter," I went on, "instead of branding Maxine as disorganized and out of control, you would tell her that the way she *does* things is disorganized, and you would show her how she might become more efficient. You might say something like, 'Maxine, I don't like to see you go to work so stressed out. Let me get you an organizer for your keys and whatever else you need so that your mornings won't be so harried and tense.' And, Maxine, instead of labeling Peter as arrogant and inconsiderate, had you said, 'I know that you would never want to cause me grief, but the manner in which you speak to me, *your tone of voice,* comes off sounding arrogant and condescending, and that hurts!' it would have been okay. But even this type of constructive criticism should be used sparingly, because, after a while, it becomes ineffective, very much like overdosing with antibiotics—you develop an immunity to them.

"As for the scene in the restaurant, that was totally inexcusable. You never poke fun or take potshots at anyone, *especially your mate,* and especially not in front of others."

"Oh, come on, Rebbetzin," Peter broke in, "let's not take everything so seriously. I was just kidding."

"Jokes of this sort can be very damaging and embarrassing. I don't know if you are aware of this, but shaming someone in public is akin to murder."

"Isn't that stretching things a bit? *Murder?* I was only talking—I mean, you have to have a sense of humor. I would *never* put Maxine down in public. Only Lauren and Matthew were there, and they are our closest friends!"

"It makes no difference whether they are close or not. As soon as something is aired in front of someone else, it becomes public. Parts of our laws of modesty enjoin us not to discuss our private affairs with others—and this includes friends and family. If you have a problem and feel the need to talk to someone, consult a professional. Keep your conflicts within the four walls of your home, because, once they are shared with others, they won't allow you to forget it."

"Just for the record, Rebbetzin," Peter said defensively, "it wasn't I who started the diet discussion. Maxine herself said she had gained a lot of weight and knew that she looked fat, and now, all of a sudden, it's all my fault."

"That may be," I agreed. "People don't mind tagging *themselves* with uncomplimentary names, but just let someone else do it and sparks fly. There must have been times when you also called yourself a fool, an idiot, and yet, if someone else had referred to you that way, you would have been outraged and ready for a major battle. What do you think Maxine wanted you to say when she complained about her weight?" I asked Peter.

Peter shrugged noncommittally.

"Well, that was one occasion on which she would have been thrilled to have you disagree. If you had said something like, 'What are you talking about, Maxine? You look great!' it would have been perfect. The last thing she wanted to hear from you was that she was right, that she needed to go on a diet. And to make things worse, you said it in front of others. Regarding conversation, the Torah cites two big no-nos: one is *loshen hora* and the other is *onas devarim*. *Loshen hora* is a generic Hebrew term that encompasses all negative talk about others, and *onas devarim* are words that are painful, mocking, and insulting. We are forbidden to speak *loshen hora* not only about others but also about ourselves."

I then told them a story about one of the greatest rabbis in modern times, Rabbi Israel Mayer HaCohen, better known as the *Chofetz Chaim* ('Seek Life'), from the title of his monumental book. He lived in Radin, a small shtetl in Poland. One day as he was walking down the street a stranger approached him. "Excuse me, I'm new in town. Could you direct me to the home of the renowned sage, the righteous Chofetz Chaim?"

"He's not a sage and he's not righteous," the Chofetz Chaim protested on hearing this description of himself. Whereupon the man became furious and lashed out at him.

"How dare you speak disparagingly about such a *tzaddik* (holy man)?" And the man punched him.

Without uttering a word, the Chofetz Chaim returned home.

A short time later, there was a knock on his door. When the stranger saw the man that he had hit standing there, he gave out an anguished cry. "Can you ever forgive me?" he begged.

"No, you must forgive me," the Chofetz Chaim responded. "You have taught me an important lesson. Not only are we not permitted to speak *loshen hora* about someone else, but we are also forbidden to speak negatively about ourselves."

"So you see, Maxine, you were wrong to put yourself down! After all, if you knock yourself, you can hardly blame others for picking up on it. 'If I'm not for myself, who will be for me?' is the teaching of the great Rabbi Hillel. It's not divorce that you require, but a new way of communicating, which, in essence, is the old way, the way of our ancestors. So what do you say? Are you willing to learn?"

Both Maxine and Peter nodded their assent.

I went on to explain to them that we have two primary expressions for criticism—*tochacha* and *mussar*. "Let's talk about *tochacha* first, and I'll get to *mussar* a little later. Literally translated, *tochacha* means to *prove*, to *demonstrate*, meaning that, instead of criticizing, we have to *demonstrate*—hold up a mirror and allow the person to see for *himself* where he went wrong. Let me give you a simple illustration. If your friend has a stain on her clothing, you might say, 'Your dress is filthy,' or you could use the *tochacha* method. Point to the stain and allow her to come to that realization herself. There's a vast difference between these two approaches. In the first scenario, the person may feel insulted, even attacked: She said my dress is filthy. She must think I'm a slob. On the other hand, the *tochacha* method does not label; it invites the person to make the judgment call for him- or herself."

"Funny," Peter commented, "I went to Hebrew school, I read the Bible. I never saw that anywhere."

"Unfortunately," I told him, "this holds true not only for you but for an entire generation that grew up ignorant of the wisdom hidden in the Torah. Actually, we learned this method of admonishment from Joseph, who was sold into bondage by his brethren. Twenty-two years later, we find him in the position of viceroy of Egypt. There was famine in the land of Canaan, and Joseph knew that his brothers would eventually have to travel to Egypt to purchase provisions, so he ordered his soldiers to be on the lookout for them. Sure enough, they came, and Joseph ordered them arrested on trumped-up charges of espionage. Brought into Joseph's presence, and unaware of his identity, the brothers stood before him seeking mercy. Now, Joseph certainly could have had a lot to say to his brothers. If anyone had the right to criticize and admonish them, it was he. If you were in Joseph's place," I asked, "what would *you* have said?"

"I would have given it to them!" Peter declared.

"And then what?"

"I don't know, but I sure would have given it to them!"

"Peter," I said, "let me remind you of the advice of Rabbi Shimon—that we must try to project the *consequences of our words and actions.* If Joseph had 'given it' to his brothers, how would that have helped to *reunite the family?*"

"I don't know," Peter said, "but it would have given me immense satisfaction."

"True, when you 'give it to someone' you do feel a cathartic release, but that's only momentary, and then a new group of realities set in, making starting afresh so much more complicated. So instead of 'giving it' to his brothers, Joseph used the *tochacha* method and revealed himself by saying, '*I am Joseph. Is my father still alive?*' And with those words, he totally demolished them. They could not find their voices and collapsed in fear.

"You might, of course, wonder what was so earthshaking in Joseph's declaration and question. If you study his words carefully, you will realize that what he said was *tochacha* in its purest form. Instead of taking his brothers to task, Joseph simply said 'I am Joseph'—implying: My dreams, which you attributed to delusions of grandeur, were fulfilled. G-d *did* make me king, and He *did* send you to bow down before me. But notice that *nowhere did Joseph actually say those words.* That declaration, 'I am Joseph,' was sufficient—he allowed his brothers to surmise the rest. And his question, 'Is *my* father (rather than *our* father) still alive?' cut to the core of the issue, for it suggested that they had not conducted themselves as sons should, else how could they have sold their brother into bondage, dipped his coat in blood, and led their elderly father to believe that he was dead? How could sons inflict such terrible pain upon their father? But again, Joseph never said those words. Rather, with his terse question, 'Is *my* father still alive?' he invited his brothers to judge themselves.

"On the Day of Judgment, *tochacha* is the method through which G-d will admonish us. He will not argue, but He will simply cause our lives to pass before us so that we may see for ourselves where we went wrong. Thus, the person who claims that he or she lacked the wherewithal to give charity might see a flashback of him- or herself vacationing in the south of France or purchasing an expensive piece of jewelry. The point being that, to be effective, admonishment must act as a mirror, and it can never be accomplished through painful jokes, shouting, cynical remarks, or name-calling. Such tactics can only result in secondary problems that lead to further resentment and alienation."

"But, Rebbetzin, you can't always hold up a mirror. We don't have the wisdom of Joseph, nor do we have the sensitivity or the humility of the brothers to pick up on such subtleties," Maxine protested.

"Well, if you can't hold up that mirror, it's best to remain silent, because your words will only serve to generate anger and bitterness. They can easily be misinterpreted as a personal attack rather than as a desire to help. Under such circumstances, not only will the original problem not be rectified, but the secondary problem, resulting from your criticism, will now become larger than life. So before speaking you must always consider, Will my words inspire the person to change or will they evoke resentment? If the latter seems likely, then, indeed, it is best to remain silent. As for not having the wisdom or the sensitivity of Joseph and his brothers, it's true that we don't, but G-d doesn't expect us to be *them*. He just wants us to learn from their lives and fulfill our *own* potential. Why do you suppose the Bible is replete with stories? Not to entertain us, but rather so that we might learn from them. There is no life situation for which you cannot find a precedent in the Bible."

"In a normal relationship, shouldn't there be room for criticism?" Peter asked.

"There should be, and there is," I said. "The best way, however, is to criticize without criticizing."

"Now, you've lost me!"

"Well, let me tell you about my husband. We had been married for more than forty years when cancer claimed his life. Throughout that period, I never heard a harsh word escape his lips. As a matter of fact, I cannot really recall his criticizing me. He had a gentle way of saying things that was far more effective than any criticism, and of course, he would never have dreamed of uttering a word that might embarrass me. This lesson was absorbed by our children, who live by it in their own married lives.

"My daughter Slovie married a young man from Brazil, and during the first year of their marriage, Mendy's business demanded that they spend a great deal of time in São Paulo. It was difficult for Slovie to be so far from her family and friends, and the hardship was compounded by the culture shock of living in Brazil.

"Well, one Sunday they were driving to an important engagement when suddenly, while passing through a primitive village in the midst of a tropical rainstorm, their car stopped dead. Mendy soon realized that he had forgotten to fill the gas tank.

"Even under normal circumstances, a wife would be hard put to remain calm, but stuck in no-man's land in pre–cell phone days with no service station in sight, in a country in which the crime rate was high and kidnapping commonplace, no one would have blamed Slovie if she had lost it. My husband's teaching, however, stood her in good stead: Slovie not only refrained from harsh words but told Mendy not to worry, saying, 'There must be a reason why all this is happening.' The seeds planted by my husband had borne fruit.

"Back in the States some years later, she and her husband were planning to take their children to Disney World. They were scheduled to take an 11:00 A.M. flight, but somehow Slovie misread the ticket and thought the plane was leaving at 1:00 P.M. They arrived at the airport only to discover that they had missed their flight and, worse, that all other flights to that destination were fully booked. The vacation that they had planned never materialized, but no one became argumentative, no one pointed an accusatory finger to lay blame. It makes no sense to castigate someone who has made a mistake—he or she feels bad enough without having it rubbed in.

"So you see, Peter, sometimes less is more. There are situations, however, in which the Torah not only gives us license to criticize but actually demands that we do so. 'You shall surely rebuke your fellow' (Leviticus 19:17).

"And our sages explain that, if necessary, one must do so even one hundred times. But like everything in the Bible, this teaching requires interpretation. The word *rebuke* is repeated twice in the text, reminding us that before we criticize others, we must first criticize ourselves, *examine our own motives* and be certain that we have no hidden agenda."

"What kind of hidden agenda could there be?"

"You'd be surprised," I said. "Very often we snap at someone, not because of what the person did or said, but because we are in a foul mood. Sometimes we harbor resentments for past slights and lash out, and sometimes we feel antagonistic toward in-laws, relatives, and friends, and seize the opportunity to vent. In other words, our behavior can be camouflaged by all sorts of smoke screens, some of which are complex and rooted in childhood—a need to control, a need to put down—so you see, there can be myriad hidden agendas. If, on the other hand, after sincere soul searching, we determine that we are free of bias, then we can proceed to the next step, which states, 'You shall not bear sin against the person you are rebuking,' which means that we must be careful not to cause anyone distress with our words."

"But didn't you say that criticism by its very nature is painful?" Peter protested.

"True," I agreed. "So you have to become creative. There are several ways in which you can do this. You can include yourself in the criticism. For example, Peter, you might say to Maxine, 'I also had problems getting organized and on schedule.' That way, you will take some of the bite out of your remarks and she won't feel like a loser. Or you might try the method of Aaron, the High Priest, who admonished through love. If Aaron came across a person who was guilty of some wrong, he embraced him, and that embrace motivated him to strive to be worthy of Aaron's love and teachings. My own father criticized us with this very method. If my siblings or I didn't behave, my father would admonish us by saying, 'My precious lights, this type of conduct is not appropriate for you.' And immediately, his words would put us back on track. When my father referred to us as 'precious lights,' he wasn't just calling us by endearing names. Rather, he was reminding us of our higher mission.

"This type of criticism is called *mussar*, which is derived from the Hebrew word *mesorah* (tradition) or *mesira* (to transmit), meaning that criticism—*mussar*—is most effective when it emanates from a higher authority, for that is a value system that cannot be refuted. One of the reasons that there is so much discord in family life is not only that people no longer know how to communicate, but also that there is no higher authority to resolve their conflicts and help them monitor their relationships. It would be very helpful if you could study Torah together, and we could arrange that for you. Additionally, I'm going to give you an assignment."

"I didn't anticipate getting homework," Peter laughed.

"Life is one big school and we are never free of homework," I said, choosing to take his remark seriously. "I would like you to put up a sign in your house, LIFE AND DEATH ARE IN THE TONGUE. Then, take a tape recorder and tape all your conversations. Next week, bring the tapes and we'll analyze them. You will hear yourselves, look in *that mirror*, and see where you went wrong."

Peter and Maxine did come back the following week, but their tapes were free of insults.

"What happened?" I asked.

"You won't believe it, Rebbetzin," Maxine said, laughing, "but every time Peter started to say something nasty, I pointed the tape recorder at him and it worked like magic. It changed the entire tenor of his conversation—it's like he recalled everything that we had discussed."

"That tape recorder looked like a gun!" Peter laughed.

"Well, when you pointed it at me, I also felt that it was a gun," Maxine admitted.

"Good," I said, "that was my intention. You both need that discipline. When we are aware that our words are being recorded, we measure them very carefully. For the time being you will need a tape recorder, but eventually you will internalize this way of communicating and you will have a peaceful home."

It didn't happen overnight, but today Peter and Maxine have a beautiful family life, and they would be hard put to believe that they had ever considered divorce.

# TWELVE

# WHEN YOU WIN,
# SOMETIMES YOU LOSE

Barbara tore her Achilles tendon. Fortunately for us, there are some very fine physicians and surgeons among the membership of our Hineni Young Leadership, so we had no difficulty getting an immediate appointment. I have discovered that, nowadays, waiting in a doctor's office is an altogether new experience. Certain things, of course, never change. The room is crowded, the wait is long, and then there are the unpredictables: the emergencies, the patients who come for routine examinations that turn out to be not-so-routine after all. These are givens in any doctor's office, but what is new, and most irritating to me, is that those who are waiting become prisoners of cell-phone conversations from which there is no escape.

When Barbara and I entered the waiting room, there wasn't a seat to be had. Since she had a foot injury, a chair was quickly brought for her, and a few minutes later, a seat opened up for me next to a fashionably dressed woman who appeared to be in her late thirties. I seated myself next to her and reached into my bag for my book of psalms. I try to be very conscious of time. Perhaps it stems from my childhood, when my father and mother would say to me in Yiddish, "Time is a gift, there is much to be done—don't sit with empty hands."

In any event, I never leave my house without my book of psalms. Psalms are wonderful—each one stands independently, so no matter where you are and no matter how limited your time, you can recite them, if even for only a few moments. But this time I had great difficulty concentrating, because as much as I didn't want to be, I was subjected to the cell-phone conversation of the woman seated next to me. I have come to the conclusion that cell phones are a mixed blessing, more often negative than positive. Somehow, we managed very well before they became available. Emergencies waited; when people went out to dinner, they actually talked to one another; when they took a walk, they had time to meditate; but nowadays, they're on their cell phones. Even when I lecture, and the chairperson very clearly requests that all cell phones and beepers be shut off, people just don't get it. Invariably, there is someone in the audience whose phone rings—always, it seems, when I am in the middle of a sensitive story. I have seen this cell-phone affliction mar wedding ceremonies and funeral eulogies, and I even encountered it when I was enveloped in prayer in front of the Holy Wall in Jerusalem. I stood there with my eyes closed, talking to G-d, savoring every second, only to have the intensity of the moment destroyed by the jarring ring or the silly jingle of a cell phone. In all these instances, however, I had the option to move on and find another place for myself. In this doctor's waiting room, there was no escape from the strident voice of the woman sitting next to me.

"I've had it," I heard her say to the person she had called. "If he thinks he can get away with dumping the kids on me while he's running around with his girlfriend, he has another thought coming! Two weeks ago, when he had them for the weekend, he called to tell me that he wanted to bring them back early. Right away I figured that he was up to something, so I said, 'No way! I have plans of my own.'

"Well, would you believe the nerve of that creep? Despite every-thing that I said, he dropped them off. I wasn't home, so the kids were left alone in the house for the entire day! I called my lawyer and had him send a letter to him. You'd think that he would have learned his lesson, but not him. This past week, Presidents Week-end, he called again to tell me that he wanted to bring the kids back early. 'No way,' I said, and just to make sure he wouldn't pull another fast one, I had taken the garage opener away from the kids. I never give them the key—for all I know he could make a copy—and with all that, he still dropped them off early. I wasn't home, so would you believe it, he left them standing on the street and told them to knock on my neighbor's door! I was so furious that I called up his girlfriend and told her what he really was. She thinks he's some poor misunderstood nice guy, but he's rotten through and through. I told her he's a confirmed gambler, a liar, and a cheat, that he'd do to her what he did to me. When he found out that I'd called her, he went nuts and threatened me. I told him to go to hell, that I'd take him to court. The kids heard it all, but I don't care. I've had it. I've made up my mind I'm not going to pro-tect him anymore."

The person at the other end must have cheered her on, because without even pausing to catch her breath, she continued. "I figured you'd be proud of me—and you know what? I don't care what it takes, this time he's going to get what's coming to him! I'm going to win."

When she finally hung up, she began searching her Palm Pilot for another number, and as she did so, she noticed me sitting next to her. "Don't I know you from somewhere? Didn't I see you on TV or something?" she asked.

"I teach the Bible on cable every Sunday. Maybe that's where you saw me."

"No, I don't think so. I never saw that program, but I know I saw you somewhere. What's your name again?"

As I introduced myself, I wondered whether I should pursue this conversation and comment on what I had just overheard or whether she would consider me meddlesome. In contrast to popular culture, which advocates minding your own business, our tradition teaches that we *are* our brothers' and sisters' keepers and that we have a responsibility to get involved. There is a caveat, though. Our sages warn that if we are reasonably assured that our words are going to be resented, then it is best that we remain silent. I debated all this in my mind. Maybe, I said to myself, it was meant to be that the only empty seat in the waiting room was next to her. Maybe I was meant to be privy to her conversation—after all, there are no coincidences in life. So I decided to tread lightly and make small talk. She politely responded by telling me that her name was Sandy Berenson; she was divorced and the mother of two children.

"Forgive me," I told her, "but I couldn't help overhearing your conversation. I'm sorry that you're having such a hard time. It must be difficult to be a single mom."

"It's tough, but I'm managing."

"How old are your children?" I asked.

"Andrew is ten and Karen is seven."

"It must be rough on them."

"It sure is. When it's my ex's turn to take them, they stay at his girlfriend's house, and there isn't too much room there. The kids have to sleep on a sofa in the living room, and last time, one of them ended up sleeping on the floor."

I looked at her and wondered, How do I begin to explain to her that more than sleeping on the sofa or even on the floor, it's being in their father's girlfriend's apartment that's a problem.

"Can't you request that he not take the children there?" I asked. "I mean, it's not exactly healthy for them to be in the apartment of their father's girlfriend."

"Oh, they know everything. Kids these days are very smart. Besides, why should I protect them? They might as well know who he is."

"For one simple reason—he's their father."

"He sure doesn't act like a father."

"Then that's all the more reason for you to pretend that he does."

"Oh, come on, that's not reality."

"Tell me, what is reality?"

"That I'm divorced and my ex is a selfish bum!"

"That's *your* reality, but if your children are to survive, it cannot be theirs. Despite the divorce, they need a father that they can respect. Don't destroy it for them. I told you that I teach the Bible. Well, let me share with you a story that I think has bearing on your situation."

"Don't tell me that even in the Bible there were husbands like Roger."

"The Bible, Sandy, has a teaching and a solution for every situation. That's why it is the Bible—the living Word of G-d. Of course you know the story of Noah. After the flood, when he finally emerged from the ark, it is written that he had a craving for wine, so he planted a vineyard and became drunk. In his inebriated state, he uncovered himself. One of his sons, Ham, came upon his father, leered at his nakedness, and debased him. Ham went on to relate the incident to his two brothers, Shem and Yafet, but they did not follow his example. Shem prevailed upon Yafet to safeguard their father's honor. They took a garment, draped it on both their shoulders, and walked backward into their father's tent with their faces averted to cover his shame. And that, Sandy, is the only logical response for children when they are confronted by their father's nakedness."

"I don't know," Sandy said. "I think it's more honest to tell it like it is."

"This is not a question of honesty. This is a matter of protecting your children from emotional and spiritual damage. When young people are encouraged to go on talk shows and tell all, or write books denigrating their parents, do you know who stands to lose the most? They, the children. Ham told it all and was cursed. Children need an image of their parents that they can respect, but if that image is replaced by one that is depraved and shameful, then their future is bleak.

"On the other hand, Shem and Yafet, who refused to look at their father in his disgrace, were able to retain their respect for their parent and, by extension, their own self-respect, and were blessed."

"I hear you, but I'm not convinced. Kids today are very savvy. You can't expect them to close their eyes."

"That's true," I agreed, "if you rub their noses in it, but if you allow them to look away, they will be grateful. Children don't want to be drawn into their parents' ugly fights or sleazy affairs. The fifth commandment, which requires that we honor our parents, was proclaimed by G-d more for the sake of children than for their parents. In order for children to develop into strong, confident, morally healthy adults, honoring parents is a prerequisite. Parents, however, have a responsibility to live their lives in such a way that the fulfillment of that commandment becomes possible."

"Well, Roger sure doesn't fit that bill."

"That may be true," I said. "Roger may not, but your children deserve to have a father they can honor, and you should help them along the way."

"I don't know. I'm not religious. All that Bible stuff was written for another age. I can't relate to it. Today, things are different and we have to use our own discretion."

"Let me tell you about using your own discretion." And with that, I related an allegory about two monarchs: King A and King B. The two men ruled neighboring kingdoms and were good friends.

One day, B said to A, "I will make you a wager that if you send me your ambassador, I'll get him to strip in front of my entire court."

"It will never happen."

"Are you ready to bet a hundred million rubles?"

"I certainly am."

And so it was that King A called in his ambassador and sent him off to B's kingdom, warning him to be on guard not to disrobe when he presented his credentials.

"How could His Majesty ever imagine that I would do such a thing?" the ambassador said, in shock. "Of course I would never do that," and off he went, leaving King A quite confident that his coffers would soon be one hundred million rubles richer.

When the ambassador presented himself at court, King B assailed him. "How could my friend have insulted me this way—sending me an ambassador who is a hunchback!"

"Your Highness, I'm not a hunchback," the ambassador protested, shocked.

"Oh, yes, you are," the king insisted, and no matter what the ambassador said, the king remained adamant. "I'm so positive about this," the king declared, "that I'm willing to bet a million rubles that you are indeed a hunchback."

"How can I convince you that I'm not?" the ambassador asked.

"Take off your shirt! Strip!" came the royal order.

The ambassador remembered his master's admonition: be on guard not to strip. *On the other hand,* he rationalized, *circumstances have changed. I think I'd better use my own discretion. If I bring my king a million rubles, he'll be so proud of me.* Thus convinced that he was acting properly, the ambassador stripped to prove that, indeed, he wasn't a hunchback. "You're right," King B said. "You win!" And he ordered his treasurer to present the ambassador with the million rubles.

When the ambassador returned to his homeland, he proudly reported to his sovereign, confident that he would be well rewarded for having acted so cleverly.

"Did my friend King B ask you to strip?" was the first question.

"Yes, Your Majesty, he did, but you'll be very proud of me. He accused me of being a hunchback and told me if I could prove that I'm not, he would present me with one million rubles. So of course I took him up on it, and now I'm very happy to present this money to Your Majesty."

"You fool!" King A cried out. "He bet you a million rubles that you are a hunchback, but I bet him a hundred million rubles that you wouldn't strip. You didn't win—you lost, and you lost big!"

"Similarly," I told Sandy, "when we deviate from the commandment of the King—the Almighty G-d—to honor our parents, and convince ourselves that what we are doing is correct, we discover too late that we lost more than we gained. You may think that you are doing the right thing by making your children see their father as he is. Perhaps you think that they will become stronger for the experience, but like the ambassador who lost a fortune, your children will, G-d forbid, lose their fortune—*parents that they can respect*. Make no mistake about it, Sandy, it's not only your husband who is being compromised, but you as well. When Andrew and Karen hear you cursing out their father, what impression do they get? What do you think goes through their minds? When you lock them out of the house, how does that make them feel about you? When they hear you on the phone, as I did, what message are they getting? Children need parents that they can respect. That is more important for their development than exercise, going to the gym, or even eating nourishing food. Granted, you can't very well control your former husband's aberrations and proclivities, but you *can* control your actions and your words. Precisely because you have a problem with Roger, you must intensify your efforts to present Andrew and Karen with at least some semblance of a parental image they can honor."

"I think I'm doing everything a mother can possibly do to be a good parent," Sandy protested, annoyed.

"I'm certain you are trying very hard, and perhaps I've come on too strong. After all, we don't even know each other, so please forgive me for being so frank, but maybe there was a reason that the only seat available was next to you. Maybe it was meant to be that I overhear your conversation and we share some thoughts. I'm certain that you don't see anything wrong with what you said, and many might agree with you. Our society prides itself on having evolved a new moral order, on having released itself from the puritanical tyranny of the past. We are open and free, but in our openness, we have lost our moral underpinnings and our souls. Everything has been affected—our value system, our conduct, even our manner of speech. Crude, vulgar language is not considered crude and vulgar anymore. I understand that you are upset, but your children shouldn't hear you speaking this way about their father. Remember the story I told you about the ambassador and the king. You can't defy the rules without paying an exorbitant price for it. I know that you have a problem with Bible stories, but nevertheless, I'll tell you another one.

"For centuries, our people were in bondage in Egypt. Now in the ancient world, Egypt was the most powerful and wealthy but also the most decadent of countries. You know how we managed to survive there with our morals intact? And mind you, we were a slave nation, stripped of all human dignity. Well, there was a simple secret to our survival—we never compromised our morality or our speech. There was no obscenity in our vocabulary and no promiscuity in our behavior. Our ancestors spoke the holy tongue, and the holy tongue has no curse words in it. You may consider this a small thing, but it is the small things in life that make a difference. The outside world can be degenerate, but as long as parents remain role models of decency and goodness, children will be immune to the ravages of their surroundings.

"My own experience as a young child in a concentration camp substantiates this. I have no doubt that one of the reasons I was able to survive the subhuman conditions of Bergen Belsen was because in my mind's eye I always had the image of my parents. The reality in Bergen Belsen was the savage Nazis and the SS, but *my* reality was my father and my mother, and that's what you have to try to do for your children, Sandy. Granted, Roger is not the role model they need, but that's all the more reason that you must strive to present them with some sort of image that they can hold on to."

"It's all well and good for you to say that," Sandy shot back, "but you don't know what I've been through. Roger's a real horror."

"You're right, I really don't know. No one can possibly know what someone else feels or experiences, and I understand your anger. I've lived through the divorces of many families. Under the best of circumstances, it's a nasty business, and yours seems to have been especially acrimonious. The harm that this has inflicted on your children is enormous. But, Sandy, the manner in which you and your former husband are relating to each other is compounding the damage. As difficult as it may be for you to control your hurt feelings, you should never take your anger at Roger out on your children. As it is, they are being shoved from pillar to post. They must feel battered, abandoned, and rootless. Think about it. What sort of message are they getting?"

"Well, what do you expect me to do?" she said. "Don't I have the right to a life of my own?"

"Of course you do, and your life, first and foremost, is that of a mother, because if with all that's going on you also lose your children and discover one day that they have become substance-abusers or delinquents, what will you have left? So, your priority should be to teach your children goodness and compassion, but I'm afraid that's not the message that comes through when they hear you speak about their father and see the things that you described in your telephone conversation."

"Well, I've had it," Sandy reiterated. "I have a strong case against him, and this time I'm going to win."

"Sometimes," I said, "like the ambassador in my story, when you win, you lose. What do you hope to gain? That your children spend more time in his girlfriend's apartment? That they see you drag their father to court or put him behind bars? That they hear gossip about him? That they find themselves locked out of their own home or consigned to the care of neighbors? Like I said, sometimes when you win, you lose—and in this case, you'd be losing big time!"

"So what am I supposed to do? Just take it and let him get away with everything?"

"No, I'm not telling you that you should just take it. There are certain areas where you should put your foot down. When your former husband takes the children, it should *not* be to his girl-friend's house. That's totally inappropriate, and for that you should put up a fight. Children deserve something more than that from parents. In your heart of hearts, you know that what's been taking place is wrong. That's why you called your friend—to validate what you did. So let me share with you a teaching that will keep you going.

"In our literature, we had an eminent sage who taught that one of the most important qualities for an individual to develop is the ability to see the future. This doesn't mean that he expected us to be Nostradamus—we don't believe in probing the future. We do what we have to do to the best of our ability, and after that we place our trust in G-d, so when the sage suggested that we attempt to foresee the future, he meant that we project the impact that our words and actions will have on the lives of others, and in your case, that means your children. Just think of that, and you will immediately realize what your priority should be."

"It's strange that you're speaking about projecting the future. Before our divorce, I used to project and I was so positive that I would be able to find a new, clean, good life, and now . . ." She paused, and her eyes told me of her terrible disappointment and pain.

"I know, Sandy. Many people embark upon the same course. Our society has glamorized divorce, making people think that they can be reborn and start all over again, but it doesn't happen that way. The old problems remain, albeit in different forms, and they become complicated by a new set of realities that are much more painful to deal with. I once heard a famous divorce lawyer say that a bad marriage is almost always better than a bad divorce, so of course you are hurting. You had both, a bad marriage and a bad divorce, but you know what? Let's do damage control. Let's fix what we can fix. Let me get to know your children. Let's see if we can impart a legacy to them and teach them values that will keep them anchored so that, with G-d's help, they don't repeat in their lives the misfortune that befell you."

We spoke a bit longer, and then the nurse appeared and called Sandy's name.

"Where do I find you?" she asked, as she got up to go. "I mean, I'm not promising anything, but just in case I want to call you."

And call she did. She came to see me with her children, and we embarked upon that course of damage control.

# PART FIVE

# A GOOD HEART

Man sees what his eyes behold.

But G-d sees the heart.

*The Book of Samuel*

# THIRTEEN

# A GOOD HEART

The last of the disciples to respond to Rabbi Yochanan's challenge was Rabbi Elazar Ben Arach. It was his belief that the most meaningful character trait for a human being to strive for is the development of a good heart, and it was this answer that Rabbi Yochanan preferred above all others. A *good heart*, Rabbi Yochanan felt, embodied all the qualities endorsed by all the other disciples. People who have a good heart will also have a good eye and will not be consumed by jealousy; they will be loving, kind friends and benevolent neighbors, and their sensitivity will enable them to project the impact of their words and deeds on others. Thus, all the virtues that were hitherto mentioned are encompassed in a good heart.

Rabbi Elazar Ben Arach's heart was so pure that, in describing him, Rabbi Yochanan said that if all the sages were on one side of a balance scale and Rabbi Elazar on the other, he would outweigh them all.

It was Rabbi Yochanan's sad fate to experience the pain of losing a son. Many came to offer him comfort, but none succeeded. It was only Rabbi Elazar, the man who cherished a good heart above all else, who was able to console him. You might wonder what the magical words of wisdom were that comforted Rabbi Yochanan. While the Mishna doesn't go into detail on the subject, I believe that I can tell you, because my husband was blessed with this very same ability. He, too, was able to offer consolation in situations in which there seemed to be no way to assuage suffering.

I have often told the story of his making a shiva call to comfort parents who had lost their one and only child in a tragic car accident. Sometime later, I met the bereaved father. He told me that my husband's visit had made all the difference in the world to him.

What words, I wondered, could provide balm for such painful wounds? I seized the opportunity and asked. "Could you share with me what exactly the rabbi said that you found so helpful?"

For a moment, he seemed taken aback by my question, so I explained that my husband was a very humble man who would never credit himself with anything, but for the sake of others, I wanted to know what were the words of consolation that were so meaningful. There was silence—he did not trust himself to speak. But then he regained his composure and said, "There were no words, Rebbetzin. Your rabbi just put his arms around me and wept with me."

One need not be a professional to offer such comfort. There is no school curriculum that teaches this subject. There is only one requirement—*a good heart* that totally identifies with another.

When my husband would return from a hospital visit, I always knew the nature of the ailment of the patient he had visited by the way he walked into the room. He literally took on the pain of the sick one. Our tradition teaches that when you properly fulfill the commandment of visiting the sick, you actually remove a portion of their illness. My husband did just that. I remember Jack, one of our congregants who was suffering from cancer, his body racked by agonizing pain. My husband would sit at his bedside, hold his hand, and sing in his soft sweet voice: "Do not fear My servant, Yaakov" (Jack's Hebrew name was Yaakov), and with that song, and with the strength that emanated from his hand, he lessened Jack's pain and eased his fears.

As difficult as it is to identify totally with a person's pain in his or her time of suffering, it is perhaps even more difficult to rejoice wholeheartedly with someone when you yourself have no special reason to rejoice. But my husband's good heart transcended that obstacle as well. Even when he was plagued by troubles and worry, he would dance at a wedding with gusto and zeal in celebration of the bride and groom. Often, people would tell me, "Rebbetzin, the rabbi shouldn't exert himself so. After all, he's not getting any younger." They didn't understand that it wasn't his feet that were carrying him, but his *good heart*.

Perhaps what attracted me to my husband as a young girl of eighteen was that I saw in him the same trait I had witnessed in my father—a *good heart*. One of the "souvenirs" with which my father was left after the concentration camps was a chronic foot problem that grew worse with each passing year. There were days when it was torture for him just to get about, but when it came to a wedding, the happiness he felt was so intense that it energized his feet and enabled him to dance. This held true not only for my father but for many others as well. Just watch the men dance at any Hasidic or traditional wedding. Suddenly, their circle will open and part like the Red Sea to make way for an elderly rabbi who, with great difficulty, makes his way to the dance floor and once there, somehow summons the energy to dance.

My husband's good heart was probably the key factor in making our marriage so very special. It was he who encouraged me in all my endeavors—my writing, my speaking, my work in outreach— and how proud he was to say, "I am the husband of Rebbetzin Esther Jungreis."

As our Hineni organization grew and won renown throughout the world, reporters and even some friends would ask if my husband resented my work. I always had difficulty relating to that question. "Resent?" I would ask. "Why would he resent it? He is the one who encouraged me. He's the one who would say, 'Go out there. You can make a difference in the world.' When he met people who did not know me, he would say, 'Oh, you must hear the rebbetzin speak. No one speaks like her,' and there was never even a twinge of jealousy in him." My husband's name was Meshulem, which in Hebrew means 'complete.' He was a *complete* man because he had a *good heart.*

Ann came to a Young Leadership class shortly after September 11. She was a beautiful, vivacious young woman who was starting to make a name for herself in the theater. "I'm ready," she said. "I'm really ready. I want to marry and settle down, and I've heard that you make great matches."

"We try," I said. "What sort of man are you looking for?"

"Oh, I don't know," she mused. "I guess I want everything."

"There's an old Yiddish proverb that has a great ring in the original. Loosely translated, it means, 'No one person has everything,' so forget that, but let's hope that when you meet Mr. Right, you'll *think* he has everything. But just so I know where you're coming from, tell me what you consider to be 'everything.'"

"Well, I'm looking for the Big Seven—looks, great personality, money, brains, athletic, fun, and successful."

"You may *think* that those are the Big Seven, but none of them amounts to anything. It's like looking at a bunch of zeros—if there's no digit in front of them, they still amount to zero, and I didn't see a digit in front of any of your sevens."

Ann was taken aback. "Rebbetzin, you've shattered my dream—what do you mean, *zero?*"

"Well, you forgot to include the one quality that is most important, and that is a *good heart.* Looks, money, brains are all meaningless. If goodness is missing, overnight that handsome face can become ugly, a brilliant mind can become just another instrument to make you miserable, and money can be just another means to control you. I'm glad you've decided to settle down, but try to figure out what you really want."

"Well, of course he has to have a good heart—that's a given."

"Unfortunately, Ann, that's not a given. That's the one quality that cannot be easily acquired. If he doesn't have looks, you can take him for a makeover; if he's not successful, you could try to motivate him; if he lacks education, you can inspire him to return to school; but if he doesn't have a good heart, what do you do? Where do you take him? Divorce court? Whether he will be a good husband or a good father is dependent solely on that good heart."

I told Ann that in our tradition a good heart is not an abstract concept. Rabbi Yochanan referred to Rabbi Elazar's good heart as "a spring flowing with ever-increasing force," which in and of itself is a phenomenon, for by logic, the pressure of the spring should diminish as the water gushes forth. But even as a spring increases in intensity, so a heart filled with goodness becomes stronger with each act of kindness.

People have various reasons for giving. Some have a need to gain recognition, others are riddled with feelings of inadequacy, and still others are plagued by guilt. Then there are those like Rabbi Elazar who are compared to a spring that is constantly flowing with increased energy. People like that actually suffer if they have no outlet for the goodness imbedded in their hearts. Even as a nursing mother feels uncomfortable when her breasts fill with milk, and finds relief only when she is able to nurse her child, so the individual whose heart is filled with kindness feels distressed when there is no outlet for his or her need to give.

Rabbi Elazar was a man of vast knowledge, and because of his *good heart* he had an insatiable desire to share his wisdom with others. Like the spring that increases in force, the more he taught, the sharper and more brilliant he became. When his master, Rabbi Yochanan, died, Rabbi Elazar's wife prevailed upon him to move away from the renowned Torah Academy at Yavneh and settle in a place where the climate was perfect and the comforts were many. Rabbi Elazar took his wife's advice, thinking that his disciples would follow him, but it didn't happen that way. Having no one to teach, he lost his great knowledge—the spring dried up, and it was only through the sincere prayers of his colleagues that G-d sent Elijah the Prophet to reteach him all that he had forgotten. More than comfort and a pleasant climate, we need an opportunity to give to others, and this holds equally true for husband-wife relationships. It's not luxuries that spouses need, but hearts that are always ready to listen and give.

I have a dear and most precious friend who, like Rabbi Elazar, has a heart that is a spring overflowing with goodness. Her entire life is one of *chesed*—loving-kindness, giving, teaching, and visiting the sick. Although she is plagued by her own illness and is in constant pain, she nevertheless transcends that pain and continues to give. When she is too ill to go out, she runs a hot line from her bedside and lends those in need the most amazing support laced with wisdom, kindness, and strength—and incredibly, her callers never suspect her pain. One day, she contracted a severe throat infection, and her doctors ordered complete voice rest. My friend could not bear the thought of a day going by without giving something back to the world, so she did a mailing for her Bikur Cholim group (Visiting the Sick Society) from her bed.

My friend, who was not given a Torah education, had probably never heard of the sad fate that befell Rabbi Elazar Ben Arach, but intuitively she knew that once you stop giving, you dry up. You lose your energy, you lose your wisdom, you lose your very life. This holds true in marriage as well. If husband and wife become narcissistic and self-focused, placing emphasis on self-realization rather than sacrifice and commitment, then the marriage will dry up, even as the spring of Rabbi Elazar. There are those who make the pursuit of happiness their life goal, and then there are those like my husband and my friend to whom *service with happiness becomes the goal.*

My beloved mother was also such a person. She literally lived to give. Nothing made her happier than to know that she was able to help someone. She was the paradigm of a rebbetzin, but she was lovingly called Mama by everyone, because that's exactly what she was, a mother to one and all. Her training started early. Her father was an eminent sage, the head of a great rabbinic academy in Hungary with myriad disciples, but I have been told that my mother contributed much to the popularity of my grandfather's yeshiva. She would get up every day at the crack of dawn, bake fresh bread and rolls, and serve a delicious hot breakfast to the students. To her dying day, she continued along that path; cooking and baking for the children in our yeshiva in Brooklyn were just some of her many deeds of *chesed*. My mother's name was Maryam, and as a young girl she was known as the *Gutte Maryam*, because goodness radiated from her. After her passing, during the shiva, we were visited by a very old talmudic scholar (a relative of my mother's through marriage) who told us that he had been privileged to participate in my mother's wedding. Although the stories about my mother are legion, he related a story that I had hitherto not heard. Just before the marriage ceremony, my mother disappeared. For a moment, there was total confusion and chaos—where could the bride be?

At Jewish weddings in Hungary, it was a tradition to invite all the poor of the community to participate in the festivities. My mother had left her bridal chair to serve them personally and to make certain that they felt welcome and were well taken care of.

When the Nazis occupied Hungary, they gathered the Jews from the provinces and herded them into ghettos in large cities. Szeged, where my father was the chief Orthodox rabbi, was the second largest city in the country and a major transport hub. Our apartment became the heart of the ghetto, and countless refugees were continually housed with us. I had always remembered our home as spacious, but when I returned to Hungary some fifteen years ago and visited the house where I was born, I was shocked to discover that it was only a three-room flat. It was my mother's warm heart and graciousness that expanded the walls of our little apartment into a home in which everyone felt welcome.

Among the many refugees brought to our ghetto were Jews from the shtetl of Zenta. In that transport was a young woman from a prominent family of sages who was expecting a baby. Her life was in jeopardy, since pregnant women were immediate candidates for deportation and death. My parents hid her, and when the birth was imminent my father converted our synagogue into a hospital for infectious diseases (temporarily making it off limits to the Nazis), and it was there that my mother delivered the woman's baby. My mother's faith infused us with courage. Her commitment to *chesed* was such that it overcame all our fears. She instructed my eleven-year-old brother to remove his yellow star and yarmulke and jump the ghetto wall to buy supplies for the baby. That baby today is a highly respected Hasidic rabbi in New York with an international following. When my mother passed away, he was the only nonfamily member who gave a eulogy. He related that his mother had often told him that she gave birth to him in a room filled with countless Torah scrolls. That image evoked painful memories. In my mind's eye, I once again saw the Gestapo cramming the Jewish refugees into our ghetto. They arrived hungry, exhausted, and frozen with terror, carrying the few belongings that the Nazis permitted them to take along. Some of the people managed to bring Torah scrolls wrapped in prayer shawls. Lovingly, my father placed them in the synagogue, and it was in the presence of those covered Torah scrolls that the baby was born. Those scrolls were consumed by fire, but not before their holy words entered the baby's heart, and today that baby has become a great rabbi, teaching Torah to his flock. It was my parents' loving-kindness—their *good hearts*—that made it all possible.

I tell these stories because ours is a generation that has very little spiritual stamina and inner resilience. At the slightest provocation, we fall apart and cave in, but if we took the cue from people like my parents, if instead of focusing on our own needs we concentrated on others, we could summon the strength to meet life's challenges.

Beth and David were not getting along. Sabbath was their worst time because, whereas they went to work and were involved in their jobs during the rest of the week, on Sabbath they had to confront each other. I recommended a simple solution—focus on others, invite guests for *Shabbos*—and it worked like a charm. In the presence of strangers, they both had to exercise restraint and hold their anger in abeyance, and in time, their anger dissipated.

Every marriage has its ups and downs, but when you allow your good heart to reign and open your home to guests, it becomes easier to maintain a warm, kind spirit. Instead of anger and cold silence, conversation and laughter will fill your house, and these positive energies will rebound to your relationship.

Actually, a good heart, the ability to extend loving-kindness, is part of our spiritual DNA, passed on to us by the patriarch Abraham. Abraham's passion and commitment to giving were such that his tent had openings on all sides so that wayfarers coming from every direction would find a warm welcome. He and Sarah offered all passersby free food and lodging. There was only one requirement—that their guest acknowledge G-d and thank Him for His many bounties. At the age of ninety-nine, the patriarch was commanded by G-d to circumcise himself. To relieve Abraham of the responsibility of serving guests during his period of recuperation, G-d sent a blistering heat wave to keep travelers from his door. But Abraham couldn't bear for a day to pass without being of service to others. He suffered more from his inability to give than from the physical pain of his circumcision, so he sat at the threshold of his tent searching for guests. Perhaps someone would come along to whom he could extend *loving-kindness*, someone he could invite into his tent (Genesis 18:1).

Suddenly, three angels disguised as nomads appeared. Abraham *ran* to greet them and joyously hastened to prepare a lavish banquet in their honor. How could Abraham, an old man recuperating from surgery, *run*, personally serve, and then escort his guests? Whence did he derive the strength? The answer can be found in the words of the prophet Isaiah: "Youth may weary and tire and young men may constantly falter, but those who place their trust in G-d will have renewed strength. They will grow wings like eagles; they will run and not grow tired; they will walk and not grow weary." Such is the reward of those who nurture a good heart.

You might, of course, question the plausibility of such a thing happening. Can an old, sick man really run? Do men grow wings like eagles? Can they run and not grow tired?

Yes, if you are truly committed, you just don't give up. You don't succumb to despondency, and you don't become tired.

Have you ever wondered why people become tired? Your automatic response might be "overwork," but work that is fulfilling never tires anyone. What *does* sap a person's energy is frustration and aggravation, or feelings of futility and uselessness, and if you live a self-focused existence, you are bound to experience much of that. The first man to complain of tiredness in the Torah was Esau, and this despite his being young and robust. His life was devoted to the hunt and to the pursuit of pleasure. He had no goal or higher purpose that would allow him to *grow wings;* his soul was empty and tired, and he sought relief through physical gratification, through taking rather than giving.

There are givers and there are takers—givers have an inner

resilience; takers are never satisfied. Marriages often fail because, after a while, husbands and wives get tired and become takers. There are so many frustrations, so many misunderstandings, so many hurts, it becomes easy to think divorce or to resign yourself to a humdrum existence.

Arlene was one of these tired housewives. She and her husband, Walter, had just drifted apart, but fortunately for them, Walter remained committed to their marriage and was not about to give up. He placed his own needs second and told Arlene point-blank: "I know we have problems, but I love you. I'm not going to allow this marriage to dissolve. Whatever has to be fixed, we'll fix. I'm committed to us staying together, and we *will*." Walter's commitment to give of himself awakened the goodness in Arlene's heart and she reciprocated in kind. Where yesterday they had found relief in escaping from their home, they now converted it into a place in which their own and their children's friends were welcome. I realize that this may sound jut a little too pat—but try it, it works. We are so accustomed to seeing our lives in a complex light that we fail to apply the simple time-tested solutions that have enabled our people to maintain tranquil homes from the beginning of time.

There are myriad little acts of *chesed* that can go a long way to generate a good heart and give us our much sought after happiness. You send an e-mail composed of just three words: I love you. Make a point of smiling at your mate. Express appreciation and empathy. Your spouse is sitting at his computer, and you ask, 'Can I get you a cup of coffee?' As you pass her chair, you lovingly touch her shoulder, just to let her know you care. These little gestures require no expenditure, no special energy, but they can change your life and fuel your good heart.

Is a good heart inborn? Is it genetic? Or can we develop it?

The Torah testifies that a good heart is not easily come by: "The heart of man is evil from his youth" (Genesis 8:21).

You might be offended by such a statement. After all, aren't children innocent and adorable? Yes, they are, but they are also selfish and self-focused. Early on, they have to be taught, "Don't kick," "Don't bite," "Say thank you," "Please," "Excuse me." A baby will not think, *My mommy had a rough day. I shouldn't wake her up.* When out on a shopping expedition, the toddler will not understand that it can't grab everything in sight. Children have to learn to give, to share, to be patient, to be generous and considerate of other people's feelings. "Let your brother, cousin, friends, play with your toys," "Offer them some of your candy"—all must be part of their educational process. As a child gets older, the stakes become higher, but the training must continue. It's an ongoing discipline in sacrifice and consideration for others. The child who masters this will attain a good heart.

We come into this world with clenched fists, as if to signal that we want to grab it all, but we die with our palms open, for we can't take anything with us but a good heart—that is, if we were fortunate enough to develop one.

Melanie and Bernie flew in from the West Coast. "We have a very serious concern," she announced, "and we felt it important enough to come to see you personally."

"Tell me how I may be of help to you," I said.

"It's about our daughter, Janie." Melanie turned to her husband, "Maybe you want to explain to the rebbetzin."

"No, no, go right ahead," he urged. And with that, Melanie plunged into her story.

"Janie lives here in Manhattan, and we feel very troubled about her. We'd like to see her married and settled, but she doesn't seem to be dating anyone."

"How long has she been living here?" I asked.

"It must be about four years now. In all this time, she hasn't met anyone, and that's what we're concerned about. She goes to work and does well, but she has no life."

"What does she do?"

"She's a systems analyst. She sits with those darn computers all day, and when she comes home, she's at it again, and that's her life."

"How old is she?"

"Thirty-six, and if she doesn't marry soon, who knows if she'll be able to have children."

"Well, I'd be happy to try to introduce her to someone, but obviously I can't do so from a distance. Can you get her to come to see me here at Hineni?"

"Not a chance. In fact, if she ever found out that we were here it would be disastrous."

"Well, how can I meet her? I can't make a recommendation without knowing her. Would she perhaps come for a Sabbath dinner?"

"I'm afraid not."

I looked at Melanie and Bernie and felt truly sorry for them. They appeared to be in their late sixties, an age at which most people are enjoying their grandchildren, and here they were trying to find a match or, at the very least, a date for their single daughter.

"Well, let's brainstorm," I said. "Do you have any other children who could perhaps motivate her to come? Or perhaps she has a good friend to whom you can speak in confidence to get her here," I said, turning to Bernie in an attempt to draw him into the conversation.

But it was Melanie who responded again. "We have one son. He's married and lives in Los Angeles, so that won't work, and we don't know her friends. She's a recluse—she doesn't have much of a social life."

"Was she always that way?" I asked.

"I'm afraid so, and *he* had a lot to do with it," Melanie answered, looking directly at Bernie.

"I figured this was coming," Bernie said. "She always blames me for everything."

"Not for everything, but he was never there for the children. He worked at his office until all hours of the night, so I could never entertain, and that's why the kids never developed any social skills."

"She could have entertained. She could have had people over; she just didn't want to, so she lays the blame on me. All of a sudden, it's all my fault. I'm tired of hearing it," Bernie said, his voice seething with anger.

The tension between them was embarrassing, but they were so caught up in their recriminations that they had lost all sense of propriety.

"Before we go any further, can I say something to the two of you?" Receiving no response, I continued. "I believe that it was *basherte*, meant to be, that you came to see me—not so much for Janie's sake as for your own. I understand that you are hurting for your daughter, but that doesn't mean you should hurt each other. Look at what you are doing: instead of applying yourselves to the problem, you are wasting your energy on attacking each other. So before we continue, try to communicate as husband and wife rather than as adversaries. One of the first things that I always tell husbands and wives is that it's not "he" and it's not "she"—it's *Bernie*, my *husband*, it's *Melanie*, my *wife*, and that's totally different from saying he or she, which renders you objects rather than people."

"*She* always does that!"

"*Melanie* always does that," I prodded, as gently as I could. "Try to say *Melanie*."

"All right," Bernie said sheepishly. "*Melanie*."

"But what I said is true. He was never home!"

"*Bernie* was never home," I once again corrected.

"I'm sorry. I'm so used to speaking that way—so, okay, *Bernie* was never home."

"Try to work on this, and also try to remember that you can't go backward. There is a teaching in the Talmud, 'What was, was,' meaning that what is in the past is over and done with, and every day presents an opportunity for a new beginning. Sure, you made mistakes raising your children—who hasn't? But if you become fixated on those mistakes, and keep blaming each other, then not only will you be unable to move ahead, but you will destroy what you *do* have—your marriage, your home—and that will certainly not help anyone. And Melanie," I said, turning to her, "forgive me, but you can hardly blame Bernie for Janie's habits and attitudes. I know many young people who are socially active and yet come from very antisocial homes, and the converse can also be true. But most important, remember that Bernie is your *husband*. When you think about him, you should do so with a good heart. If he stayed late at the office, he did so because at that time he felt it was the right thing to do and he wanted to maximize his income for your sake and the sake of the children. Certainly, it was not out of malice, so let's try to calm down and bear in mind that recriminations will not produce a husband for Janie."

"Rebbetzin, you don't understand. I'm so full of pain. Whenever I go to a wedding and see the bride walking down the aisle, I cry. People think I'm crying because I'm sentimental, which I am, but truth be told, I'm crying because I'm jealous. And *he*—excuse me, *Bernie*—refuses even to go to weddings. He finds them too upsetting."

"Well, why should I want to go? So that *she*—*Melanie*—should bend my ear with her complaints that it's all my fault? And to top it off, I have to extend a big *mazel tov* while my daughter doesn't even have a date. Why should I be a glutton for punishment?"

"You know what?" I told them. "I think I've discovered the reason that you're having such difficulty with Janie—you're going about this backward."

Melanie and Bernie gave me puzzled looks.

"Allow me to explain. In order to find a *shidduch* (marriage partner), you need G-d's help, and the two of you are doing everything to rebuff that help."

"How can you say that? Whenever I light candles, I ask G-d to help."

"That may be, but it seems to me that you are negating your prayers." I took a book of psalms off the shelf. "Have you ever studied the psalms?" I asked.

"Not really. We're not very religious people, you know. We go to temple on the High Holidays, and like I said, I light candles whenever I can, but that's about it."

"There's a beautiful psalm that I would like you to study that will open up a new world for you." I turned to Psalm 89 and read the third passage: "'For I said the world is built upon loving-kindness.' What do you think that means?" I asked them.

"You tell us," Bernie said.

"It is written in the Midrash: 'At the time of creation, the world was tottering like a chair with only three legs. But then G-d propped up the chair with a fourth leg, and that fourth leg was *chesed—loving-kindness.*'[1] Whenever it appears that your life is coming apart, that you are beset by what seem to be insoluble problems, then just emulate G-d and find that fourth leg—*loving-kindness*—and things will fall into place. This is a teaching that is reaffirmed throughout the Bible. The Torah opens with the letter *beit* (B) and concludes with the letter *lamed* (L), which in Hebrew spells 'heart.' It is a compassionate heart that G-d wants us to develop, and that is the essence of our commandments. Throughout the Torah, in every portion, the

---

[1] In the Mishna it is written that the world is supported by three pillars: Torah, Prayer, and Loving Kindness. However, in order for these three pillars to be effective, loving kindness must be at their root. Even kindness must be extended with kindness.

focus is on kindness. It is our mission here on earth—to extend that kindness and thereby emulate G-d."

"I really don't understand what this loving-kindness business has to do with our problem," Bernie said, "and with all due respect, Rebbetzin, I certainly don't understand what you are driving at when you say we have to emulate G-d."

"G-d *is* loving-kindness, and when we are kind to one another, we become godlike. Therefore, even as He is gracious and merciful, so *we* must endeavor to be gracious and merciful; even as He is compassionate and forgiving, so we must be compassionate and forgiving; even as He visits the sick and consoles the mourner and feeds the hungry, even as He rejoices with bride and groom, so we must do the same. Do you get the point?" I asked.

"I'm not sure what you mean."

"Well, ask yourself—have you rejoiced with bride and groom, or did you allow your heart to be filled with resentment and bitterness? By allowing jealousy to overtake you, you have actually shut the door on G-d."

"Well, that's a new one!" Melanie exclaimed, her voice betraying her irritation. "We flew into New York in the hope that you'd help us find someone for Janie, and now you're telling us that G-d won't help us because we are jealous when someone else gets married while our daughter sits home like a wallflower! We're only human, after all. How can we be happy for someone when our own hearts are breaking?"

"You're right," I agreed. "Undoubtedly, it's a tough call, but that's why G-d has charged us with the mission of developing a *good heart*. It's a challenge that we have to work on constantly. There are days when we do better, and there are days when we fail, but we have to keep trying, because that is our ultimate purpose in life—to develop a good heart. Let me show you just one more psalm."

I turned to Psalm 121:5. "'G-d is your shadow,'" I read, "meaning that the way in which we conduct ourselves is the way in which G-d will conduct Himself toward us. Therefore, if we rejoice for someone, then G-d will give us cause to rejoice as well. On the other hand, if we allow bitterness and jealousy to fill our hearts, then that, too, will rebound to us."

"Are you telling me that we should be happy for our friend's daughter when she gets married and forget about our own daughter sitting home alone?"

"I'm not telling you that you should forget about Janie, but, yes, I am telling you that you should be happy for your friend's daughter. Harboring jealousy will not get you anywhere and it will not help Janie, but it can do you much harm. It can turn you into an angry, bitter person and make you ill. King Solomon said that jealousy actually rots your bones, and our sages teach that 'it removes you from the world' because it deprives you of peace of mind and doesn't allow you to enjoy that which you *do* have. And worse, jealousy builds a wall between you and G-d and shuts the heavenly gates of compassion. There is a wonderful Yiddish word, *fargin*. It is difficult to translate because it has no English equivalent. There are two levels on which it can be understood. *Fargin* means that you are happy that someone else has that which you possess. There are people for whom this is difficult, because they have to be *more* successful, *more* popular, *more* attractive, and they cannot bear that *someone else* might equal them. The Golden Rule, 'Love thy neighbor as thyself,' doesn't really mean that we are expected to love others as we love ourselves (as a matter of fact, Jewish law mandates that saving our own lives takes precedence over saving someone else's), but it does mean that we should *fargin* our friends everything that we *fargin* ourselves. It follows, therefore, that the extent to which we love our neighbors depends upon the extent to which we want them to be blessed. People have a need to surpass others, to be superior to them. They never stop to consider how foolish they are. After all, why should it bother them that someone else has what they have? Will they lack anything as a result? Will it diminish them in any way? But jealousy has no logic or reason. It is a disease that consumes you and gives you no respite.

"Then there is another level of *fargin* that is directly applicable to your situation: to be happy for someone when he or she possesses that which your yourself lack (which admittedly for most people doesn't come easily)—this level of *fargin* is really proof of *a good heart*. So my advice to you is that you try to become *fargin*-ers."

"What exactly are you suggesting that we do?" Bernie asked skeptically.

"Simple—*fargin*, and remember that G-d is your shadow, and whatever you do, your shadow reflects. Create shadows of kindness so that He may respond to you with kindness."

Seeing the doubtful looks on their faces, I told them the story of Sally, who came to me with a similar problem some years ago. "Like Janie, Sally's daughter refused to socialize and buried herself in her work, so I advised Sally to volunteer for our Hineni match-making program. At first, Sally rejected my suggestion out of hand, saying it would be much too painful to work on matchmaking for others while her own daughter was sitting home alone. So I told her what I have told you, 'Create *shadows of chesed* and G-d will cre-ate a miracle for you.' Having no other options, Sally decided to give it a try—and guess what? Today she is the grandmother of two adorable little girls."

"But something bothers me," Melanie said. "Isn't what you're suggesting rather hypocritical? I mean, let's suppose that I followed your suggestion and volunteered to help make matches, and per-haps even sponsored events for young singles—even if I ran the gamut, I'd be doing it all for selfish reasons. I mean, G-d would know that I don't have loving-kindness in my heart, but an ulterior motive. Wouldn't that negate everything I did?"

"That's a valid point, and there's an answer to that as well." This time I referred them to the monumental work of Rabbi Chaim Luzzato, *Mesilas Yesharim* (the path of the righteous), in which he writes that *outward actions elicit inward emotions.* "It is easier," I went on, "to change your deeds, your behavior, than to change your thoughts and emotions. So start out with that which is within your reach, and eventually you will achieve that which was beyond your reach. You change your actions, your behavior pattern, and if you persevere and remain consistent, you will one day wake up and discover that *you have changed* as well. You are no longer that angry, jealous, bitter person. When you smile and say *mazel tov,* it's no longer an act—you really mean it. And that's how you develop a kind, compassionate heart, the barometer of which is to be a *fargin-*er, to rejoice for someone, even if you yourself lack the thing that he or she possesses. This same teaching has been substantiated throughout our rabbinic literature. And perhaps more important, if you do this, you will energize the goodness in your heart and that will infuse your marriage with new life and assure your own happiness. So what do you say?" I asked. "What do you have to lose? Let's start immediately."

"What would you like us to do?" Bernie asked.

"Well, let's recap: Start out by being kind to each other. Remember, 'my Bernie,' 'my Melanie,' 'my husband,' 'my wife.' No finger-pointing, no accusations. 'What was, was.' Every day is a new beginning, and bear in mind that the best thing you have is each other—don't destroy it! Learn to smile at each other. My father of blessed memory used to say, 'A smile is such an easy, wonderful way to create happiness. It doesn't cost anything. It doesn't take any time, and it enriches both the giver and the receiver.'

"When you get back home, volunteer to work with an organization that helps young people find their marriage partners, and if such an organization doesn't exist in your community, then hook up with us and we'll show you the way."

Bernie and Melanie wanted to know the many details involved in setting up such a program, and they returned home with a packet of information. As I suspected, there was nothing much doing in their community, so they started a program in conjunction with a local synagogue. Suddenly, they became very busy with other people's problems. They called in regularly for guidance, and some matches were actually made. But Janie's situation remained unchanged.

I was on a conference call with Bernie and Melanie, discussing a Chanukah program for singles.

"What's doing with Janie?" I asked.

"Nothing. I guess G-d is too busy for us," Melanie answered sarcastically. "We are doing everything you said. I'm even praying, but nothing is working. My friend Gladys was the only one in our bridge club besides me with an unmarried daughter, and this week her daughter got engaged. It's just not fair, Rebbetzin. I guess G-d doesn't hear my prayers."

"You're wrong, Melanie," I said. "Not only does G-d hear every prayer, but He hears every sigh, He sees every teardrop, He even listens to the unspoken words in your heart. But I think you are praying the wrong way."

"Here we go again. Don't tell me you're going to give me something else to do."

"No," I laughed. "I'm not going to give you something else to do. Just continue to reach out to others and pray. But you must pray the right way. Pray like a *fargin*-er."

"What does that mean?" Melanie asked.

"It's quite simple, nothing complicated. Instead of indulging your resentments, ask for G-d's mercy. Bear in mind that there is a world of difference between asking for His help and making a claim against Him. For example, if your son were to angrily confront you and say, 'How come you paid for a vacation for Janie and not for me? It's not fair. You always play favorites. She gets everything!' you would be annoyed because you know that there is a reason that you had to send Janie on that vacation, and you had hoped that his filial love would make him understand.

"Similarly, G-d has a plan for every person, and what our neighbor has in no way impinges on us. In helping us control our feelings of jealousy, our sages suggest that we consider a bird. Would we be jealous of it because it has wings? Even as a bird has no bearing upon our lives, so, too, what others have is irrelevant."

"That's far-fetched," Melanie interrupted. I mean, a *bird!*"

"It is," I agreed, "but that's exactly why our sages make that analogy. As far-fetched as a bird is to your life, that's how far-fetched jealousy of another person should be. Why should it bother you that Gladys's daughter got engaged? It's not like she's marrying the man who was destined for Janie. Say *mazel tov* to her with a full heart, without resentment, *fargin* her."

"As long as we're working on the *fargin*-er business," interjected Bernie, who until now had been silent, "maybe you'll tell Melanie to *fargin* me a little sleep. Every night she wakes me up and wants to know how I can sleep while Janie is all alone in New York!"

"Oh, please," Melanie said, "I certainly *fargin* you your sleep, but how can anyone go to sleep knowing that our poor girl has no one in her life?"

"Let me give both of you some good advice. *Fargin* yourselves some peace of mind and place your burdens upon G-d. Pray like a *fargin*-er, without jealousy in your heart, and if, despite yourself, these negative feelings overtake you, ask for G-d's help. Tell Him that you are ashamed of your jealousy, that you are struggling to fight it, and ask for His forgiveness and help."

"Allow me to give you one more tip regarding prayer: 'He who prays for the needs of his friend (before his own) is answered first' (Talmud). We learn this from the patriarch Abraham who prayed that King Abimelech and his wife be blessed with children, although he and Sarah were childless. It is written that immediately after Abraham's prayer, 'G-d remembered Sarah . . . and she conceived and gave birth' (Genesis, 21:1). So, as you run your programs for singles, pray on their behalf as well."

Almost a year after this conversation, Janie was called in as a consultant to a large brokerage firm, and it was there that she met her husband, Jack.

I first met the young couple at their engagement party. When I saw Jack, I couldn't help but smile. Jack was a regular at our Hineni functions. Janie had never wanted to come to see me, but we had made the *shidduch* after all!

# FOURTEEN

# THE POWER OF KIND WORDS

In his day, Sam Walker was a powerful man—the CEO of a large business and socially and politically influential. I had heard about him but never met him. Then one day, Caroline Walker, an attractive young woman in her late twenties, came to one of my classes. She was bright and spiritually hungry and took to Torah classes like a sponge to water. Often, she would tell me that she wished she could bring her father to one of our sessions. "It would do him so much good to study," she said, but somehow, Sam was always too busy and every appointment was pushed off. Then one day Caroline called, very upset: her father had suffered a stroke and had been hospitalized. His recovery was slow, and unfortunately, the stroke left him impaired. Gone was his booming voice, his speech became slurred, and his hands lay feebly in his lap. It was deeply painful for Caroline to see her once-agile, powerful father just lying there.

"Somehow, I always thought he was invincible," she told me in the midst of tears. "Other people could get sick, but not my father! I'm sorry that he never made it to a Torah class," she added, "but perhaps you would come to visit him, Rebbetzin. He can't communicate too well, but he does understand everything, and I think it would do him a world of good if you'd come. He's so down, so depressed."

When I visited Sam, I was impressed that even from his sickbed a certain presence emanated. I had no difficulty visualizing him as a major player, capable of making decisions and carrying them out. I also met Sam's wife, Beverly, a sophisticated woman in her sixties who was active in many charities dedicated to the arts. When I expressed my concern for Sam, I sensed a certain detachment, but then I thought to myself that I was reading into things. Maybe she was in denial, I thought. After all, not everyone is able to handle illness. I reminded myself that our sages enjoin us to give others the benefit of the doubt, so I was careful not to make any judgments.

Sometime later, Caroline asked to speak to me privately. "This is very difficult for me," she confided. "I really don't know how to say it without sounding critical of my mom, and I know that you're not supposed to speak *loshen hara* (negative talk about others), but I really need guidance. I don't quite know how to handle this. You know how difficult it is for my dad to articulate words—his speech is still not normal—but I do understand him, and he keeps asking for my mom. But she just doesn't go near him. I don't think she has sat at his bedside even once. When I tried to tell her that dad has been calling for her, her response was that she can't handle it, and that we should put him in a nursing home!

"Rebbetzin, I couldn't believe that my mother actually said that. I tried to reason with her by telling her that that would be a terribly cruel thing to do to Dad. After all, the poor man is no trouble to anyone. There are nurses around the clock to care for him, and the apartment is big enough so that they're not in her way. It's not like she has to do anything for him. But my mom got real upset with me and told me that I didn't understand—that it was easy for me to talk, because I have my own place and don't have to live with this and deal with it day in and day out. But for her, it's constant; it makes her depressed and she can't handle it anymore. To be honest, my parents didn't have the greatest of marriages. There was lots of stuff going on between them. Very often, my father was tough, but then again, so was my mother—but after all is said and done, he doesn't deserve to be treated this way. Everything that we have he provided, and to think that now, in his old age, he should be dumped like someone who is homeless. I can't bear the thought of it. I'm an only child, so there is no one to fight my mother on this except me."

"You shouldn't fight," I said. "It's not your place. You have to relate to your mother with respect. Just volunteer to help out, be around often, and assure her that she can call on you anytime to help."

"I did that, and Mom said that if I'm so anxious to keep him out of a nursing home, he should move in with me and I should take care of him. Believe me, I've thought of doing just that many times, but my apartment is much too small. It's gotten so that every time I go home, we end up in an altercation, so I thought that maybe you could talk to her—but please, don't tell her that I spoke to you about it."

I was somewhat taken aback by Caroline's story. Although I had sensed some coolness from Beverly toward Sam, never would I have imagined that things could be this bad. I told Caroline that I would make an attempt to speak to her mother, but since she wouldn't give me permission to reveal that I knew what was going on, it was questionable whether Beverly would tell me of her plan. Nevertheless, I promised to give it a try and scheduled a visit to Sam. The following week, when I arrived at their apartment, I found Beverly sitting in the den.

"This must be so difficult for you," I said. "I mean, to have a sick husband in the house."

"Yes, it is," she agreed.

"Perhaps," I suggested, "you would like to join our women's Torah seminars. In addition to its being a great learning experience, the women who attend will offer you a wonderful support group."

"It's not a support group that I need," she replied, with an edge of bitterness in her voice. "This apartment has become like a prison for me. I can't stand to see Sam like this. I find it very depressing."

"Depressing?" I said. "I agree that what has happened to Sam is very sad, but instead of being depressed, you have so much to thank G-d for. I think that you should be grateful that he is recovering—slowly, to be sure, but nevertheless recovering. You have the where-withal to provide for all his needs, and you have a daughter who is involved and cares. All those things are major pluses—blessings."

Beverly didn't respond, but her eyes told me that she wasn't impressed, so I said, "Let me tell you a story about an incredible woman whom I visited not long ago. The woman, let's call her Goldie, is the mother of a large family. Tragically, she suffered a stroke that left her almost totally paralyzed—unable to move or speak. The only part of her body that is unaffected is one eye. Now, *that's* cause for depression, wouldn't you say?"

Beverly nodded in assent, and I went on with my story. "Instead of giving in to depression, however, Goldie decided to use the one part of her body that still functions and build a life for herself with it. She taught herself to communicate with her one eye. When she blinks, her family and her nurse count and determine which letter of the alphabet she is referring to, and in this way, she spells out words.

"Her hospital bed is not hidden away in some bedroom on an upper floor but is just off the kitchen, in the center of the house, where she can see everyone and everyone can see her. I visited her and brought her a copy of my book. With blinks of her eye, which I could not follow, but which the nurse understood, she told me that she had already read my book and loved it, and she instructed the nurse to point to it resting on the shelf. I had heard about Goldie, but it's one thing to hear and something else to see with your own eyes, so when I actually saw her, I was awed. I expressed my amazement at her ability to communicate, and the nurse told me that she had even taught her, with that blink of an eye, how to prepare each of her children's favorite dishes!"

"That's touching," Beverly said, "but it doesn't solve my problem."

"That's true," I agreed. "Other people's burdens don't lessen yours, but they should help you put things into their proper perspective and inspire you to think about your own life. Here is a woman who has lost all movement in her body. The only thing she has left is the ability to wink an eye, but with the wink of that eye, she still runs her family. After hearing such a story, who are we to complain, let alone give in to depression. Besides," I told Beverly, "depression is pointless. It leads you down a dark road from which there is no escape."

Beverly was still unresponsive, so I continued. "Someone once told me that it's helpful to think of life like reading a book—when you come to a particularly difficult page, just turn it and move on. So why don't you turn the page, Beverly?"

"You can only turn the page when you finish reading it, but I can't get through this page," she snapped.

"I don't know about that," I told her. "I've read books in which I encountered a difficult page, but instead of getting stuck on that page or giving up on that book, I skipped some words and even paragraphs, and turned the page."

"You're losing me. I don't know what you mean. The only way I can see moving on is to have Sam put into a nursing home. That's where he really belongs, you know, but Caroline is fighting me on it."

"There's no need to take such a drastic step. What I meant when I said that you should skip the difficult passages is that you should analyze what bothers you about his illness and learn how to bypass it. Is it having the nurses in the house, or mealtime with Sam, or taking him for a walk in his wheelchair that you find so depressing? Tell me what it is and let's see how we can make it easier for you to turn that page."

"I might as well be open with you," Beverly said, with a determined look on her face. "Sam and I have been married for more than forty years and it hasn't been a particularly good marriage. It's true, Sam built a big business and made lots of money, and everyone envies me, but I paid a price for it. He was always very domineering. Wherever he wanted to go, I had to go, but he never came with me to any of the places that I enjoyed or were important to me. I've always been active in charities, but I had to go by myself to all the dinners and events and make excuses for Sam, which I found mortifying. And don't think I didn't hear people whispering about it behind my back.

"When he retired two years ago, I thought that at last we would go places and do things together, but nothing changed, except that he became grouchier and more demanding. For forty years I've had to put up with his idiosyncrasies and demands, and now, I have to deal with Caroline!"

"Thank G-d for that, Beverly."

"Thank G-d?" she repeated, looking at me uncomprehendingly.

"Yes, thank G-d, because it means that, with everything, you still have a family. True, for forty years you may have had to deal with someone who was domineering, but you had someone to deal with, and now that he is sick and can't communicate, you have Caroline—you are not alone. There is someone in your life who cares, even if you are not always in accord, and that's what having a family is all about. You know who are the people to be pitied?" I asked. "Those who have no one to make demands on them. Those who can come home in the middle of the night and there is no one to say, 'Where were you?'; those who do whatever they wish and there is no one to say, 'What are you doing to yourself?' So, yes, thank G-d, Beverly."

"I don't see it that way. This apartment looks like a hospital! I'm sick of it all. Frankly, I don't feel that I have any obligation to Sam. He was never a good husband. I considered divorce many times, but I stuck it out because, had I left, he would have seen to it that I got nothing! With his connections, he would have hired the best lawyers. I wouldn't have had a chance, but I have no love for him anymore. I don't feel any closeness to him. So why should I be saddled with him? Why shouldn't I enjoy the years that I have left?"

"Love? What's love, Beverly? When couples marry, our tradition requires that we bless them with the wish that they establish a *faithful home*, because that is the true meaning of love. Love is loyalty, love is commitment, not passion or butterflies in the stomach. In our self-indulgent, materialistic society, love has lost its meaning. The word has become so overused that it has lost its value. It's so easy to say 'I love you' and the next day to say 'I hate you. I'm serving you with papers.' You claim that you don't feel love, that you don't feel close. In the Hebrew language, the words for 'close' and 'sacrifice' are derived from one and the same root, teaching that if you want to feel love and closeness to someone, the key is *sacrifice*— giving of yourself.

"Sam needs you now, and you should be there for him because he is your husband, the father of your child, because it is the decent thing to do. And if you do it, you will find the love and closeness that is so painfully lacking in your life."

"But you don't understand. I have no feelings left for him at all. Throughout our married years, he always put me down, derided everything I said, trivialized the things I considered important. He would do this to me in front of Caroline and even strangers, so how can you expect me to sacrifice for him?"

"Beverly, we don't reach our senior years so that we may take revenge on our mates for real or imagined wrongs. I don't know what transpired between the two of you. I wasn't privy to it and I didn't know Sam when he was well, but life is about *forgiveness* and *kindness*. That's what having a good heart is all about. Every night, before we go to sleep, there is a bedtime prayer that we recite . . ."

I paused, reached into my bag for a prayer book, and asked Beverly to read the opening passage. But she was reluctant to even glance at the prayer book, so I read the words for her: "Master of the Universe, I hereby forgive anyone who angered or antagonized me, or who sinned against me; whether against my body, my property, my honor, or against anything of mine; whether he did so accidentally, willfully or carelessly, in this life, or in another life."

"Now you must admit, Beverly, that those are really powerful words, and if we are called upon to extend this forgiveness to strangers, how much more so should you forgive your husband, the father of your child? Don't allow bitterness to take over your life. More than hurting Sam, it will hurt you. It poisons your system and consigns you to a life of torment. Tap into the goodness in your heart and let it flow into your entire being. If you do that, it will bring you serenity and joy, a priceless gift that no amount of money can buy. Start with a simple act of kindness. Just once a day, sit down next to Sam and give him a few words of encouragement. Assure him that he's going to get better and that you are there for him. Do you know how tortured he must feel, lying there? And don't you think that if you suffered through a loveless marriage, he suffered as well? Try to imagine, just for a moment, how it must feel to be a prisoner of a body that is not capable of functioning. After all, his mind is agile—he understands and is aware of everything. Do you know what a few kind words of hope and encouragement from you can do for him? Our sages teach that G-d grants each and every one of us opportunities through which we can make a difference in the world and give people a new lease on life. You, Beverly, have been presented with the privilege of doing just that for your husband. Do it for him, do it for Caroline, do it for yourself— but most important, do it because it's the right thing to do. It will enable you to look back on your life without shame or regret."

"With all due respect, Rebbetzin," Beverly said, "aren't you exaggerating this a bit? I mean, let's say I follow your advice and I sit down next to Sam and say a few words to him. Are you telling me that that will save his life?"

"Yes, I'm saying just that. Before I leave, let me tell you one last story from my own experience. My brother-in-law, Rabbi Amram Jungreis of blessed memory, the only member of my husband's family to have survived the Holocaust, became the Chief Rabbi of Budapest after World War II. During the 1957 Hungarian revolution, he fled the country and settled in Israel. He was a very pious man, a great scholar, who devoted his entire life to Torah study. He even refused to have a phone in his home lest it divert him from his holy books. He had a one and only son who studied in a yeshiva in the holy city of Bnei Brak. It happened that one cold winter day, he suddenly decided to bring his son home, a most unusual decision because he was loathe to interrupt the boy's learning. He studied with his son the entire evening, and sometime around midnight he sent him to bed, while he remained at his desk, poring over his volumes of the Talmud. In the early hours of the morning, my sister-in-law went to look for him. She found him seated at his desk, a glass of tea that was still warm in front of him, and the Talmud opened to the words *I found it!* His soul had departed.

"That very same night, a cousin who was a renowned Hasidic rabbi had a dream in which he saw my father-in-law and grandfather-in-law dressed in flowing white garments. 'Take heed,' they exclaimed, 'a holy soul is joining us.' Deeply perturbed by the dream, he hastened to take a taxi to my brother-in-law's home to discuss it with him, only to discover that he had arrived just in time to deliver the eulogy. As you may know, Beverly, Jewish law dictates that burial should take place as soon as possible after death.

"My brother-in-law was buried in Bnei Brak, and one of my trips to Israel coincided with the anniversary of his death. It is deemed especially meritorious to visit a grave at such a time, so I decided to make the trip from Jerusalem. But finding a grave site at the cemetery in Bnei Brak was no simple matter. The tombstones are so close to one another that it is impossible to navigate, and to complicate matters, the stones are flat instead of perpendicular as in the States, making it necessary to view each and every inscription from up close. As hard as I tried, I couldn't find his grave. I was devastated. It was winter, the weather was cold and windy, and it was a fast day. I became sadder by the minute. Why couldn't I find his tombstone? I wondered. Had I made this trip for naught? From a distance, I noticed some Hasidic men praying. Dare I interrupt them and ask for their help? I debated the matter back and forth in my mind, but as the hour was late and I had to get back to Jerusalem, I took my chances. 'Excuse me,' I said, as I approached them. 'I'm looking for the resting place of Rabbi Amram Jungreis. Would anyone happen to know where it is?'

"No one seemed to know, but amazingly, they all volunteered to help and spread out to search. After some time had elapsed, without any success, I was ready to give up, and I said to myself, I'll pray right where I am, and ask the souls who are buried here to deliver a message to my brother-in-law. But just as I was about to do that, I heard one of the Hasidic young men call out, 'I found it! I found it!'

"Those words, 'I found it! I found it!' pierced my heart. As I rushed to the grave, all my pent-up emotions burst forth and I began to weep uncontrollably. Immersed in prayer, drenched in tears, I suddenly heard a kind voice behind me ask, 'Why are you crying so?'

"I looked up—it was an old Hasidic man with a long white beard. 'Don't worry,' he said. 'It's going to be good. You'll see. Everything will be good. There's no reason to be afraid. G-d will bless you.'

"I can't begin to tell you what those few words did for me," I told Beverly. "They brought such balm to my heart. They gave me such great comfort that, to this very day, they resonate in my mind. I tell you this, Beverly, because, yes, with a few words of encouragement and faith, you can save Sam's life. Think about it. If a stranger can have such impact, can you imagine what you can do for Sam? What do you say, Beverly? Shall we go to Sam's room together?"

She thought for a moment, rose from her chair, thanked me, and said, "I think I'll try to do this by myself—although I'm not sure if I can," she added.

"Of course you can. Like I said, just tap into the goodness that is in your heart." When I left their apartment, Beverly was still with Sam.

~~~~~

# FIFTEEN

# GROWING OLD TOGETHER IN DIGNITY

My Fridays are always pressured, but it is a pressure that I welcome with joy, because in its wake comes the holy Sabbath, when I enter a different time zone. It's strange, but no matter how early or late the Sabbath is ushered in, Fridays are always a battle against the clock. Cooking, baking, grocery shopping, responding to and making "Good *Shabbos*" calls—all have to be accomplished before that magic hour of candle-lighting.

I was at the supermarket doing my usual Friday shopping when I spotted Thelma and Herbie pushing a shopping cart down the aisle. Herb was a physician who had recently retired from his practice in internal medicine. As they came closer, I overheard Thelma say, "All these years I managed very well, and I don't need you to drive me crazy now to save a few pennies on a box of tissues! Why don't you go to the fruit and vegetable section and pick out some tomatoes? Just make sure that they're not bruised." Thelma sounded more like an exacerbated mother trying to keep her cantankerous little boy busy than a wife talking to her husband. As Herbie marched off on his mission, she noticed me standing in the aisle.

"Rebbetzin," she greeted me, "I'm so glad we met. I've been thinking of calling you, but somehow, I just never got around to it." She must have realized that I had overheard their conversation, because she went on to say, "I'm having such a hard time since Herbie retired. I can't even go to the supermarket without him following me. Can you imagine, a man of his education pinching pennies over a box of tissues. We had planned to move to Florida when he retired, but some unexpected problems came up, and things didn't work out as we had hoped, so here I am, stuck in the supermarket with him."

"There is a Yiddish saying," I told her, "based on a teaching from the Book of Proverbs. Loosely translated it says, 'Man proposes, G-d disposes.' We make all kinds of plans and things hardly ever work out as anticipated. That's life. There is always the unexpected. From one moment to another, we never know what can happen, but you know what, Thelma? G-d runs the world, and we have to believe that everything that occurs is for the best."

"I wish I could believe that there is something redeeming in our situation," Thelma replied, "but I don't see anything positive about it. All I can tell you is that Herbie's getting on my nerves. If we had only moved to Florida, it would have been okay. He would have been busy fishing or playing golf, the two things he loves to do."

"That's not always a solution. Recreation is all right when it's recreation, but not when it becomes a full-time occupation."

As I was speaking, Herbie joined us, carrying a bag of tomatoes. "How nice to see you, Rebbetzin. How *are* you?" he asked in a warm, friendly manner. We exchanged some small talk, then went our separate ways to finish our shopping. My heart went out to Thelma and Herbie. The "golden years" are not always so golden after all. But then I thought of all the lonely widows and widowers I know, and the many people who reach their senior years only to suffer from Alzheimer's and other forms of crippling mental and physical illnesses. So, thank G-d, I said to myself, Thelma and Herbie are healthy, and at least they have each other, even if they fight over the price of a box of tissues.

The Torah does not advocate retirement. We have to be active and constructively occupied throughout our lives. The Sabbath and the holidays provide all the rest that we require. Additionally, the sabbatical year (during which, every seventh year, we cease to labor) afforded us an opportunity for spiritual rejuvenation, as our entire nation immersed itself in the study of Torah. But that was in another time, another age. Today, at age sixty-five we are put out to pasture, and that, very often, causes more harm than good, for in our work-oriented culture, if we cease to work it follows that we will also ask, Who are we? What are we?

A few days after my encounter with Thelma, she *did* come to see me and poured out her heart. "What should I do, Rebbetzin? This retirement is the worst possible thing that could have happened to us. He's always underfoot, and not just in the supermarket. He gets involved in the running of my kitchen and is forever on my back. If I go into a room and open the blinds to let in some light, he follows me and closes them. If I raise the thermostat because it's cold, he lowers it, and in the summer when it's hot, he turns down the air-conditioning. I feel like I'm living in a tomb! Then he picked up this weird habit of closing the doors to all the rooms. If I open them, he tells me that we're wasting energy. His favorite pastime is going to discount variety stores and buying cut-rate paper cups from restaurants that are no longer in existence. Then he stores them in the garage and forgets about them, while I'm left with cups inscribed with *Dino's Diner* or some other crazy name. When I met you in the supermarket last week, I was lucky, because I was able to do all my shopping in one place. Usually, he makes me go from market to market to pick up all the 'specials.' In vain do I tell him that the gas and our time are worth more than the fifty cents we'll save on a

container of orange juice—he just doesn't get it. But his worst habit
is going through the garbage for recyclable bottles, cans, and newspapers and then storing them in his bedroom closet so I won't see
them. I literally have to sneak into his closet and throw everything
out just before the garbage is picked up. We don't have recycling in
our neighborhood, and it's gotten out of hand. I could go on and
on, Rebbetzin, but I think you get the picture."

"I certainly do, Thelma, and you're right—it shouldn't be this
way. Herbie is a wonderful man, bright and gifted, and this is not
how he should be spending his senior years. You cannot alter the
fact that he is retired—that's the reality of his life—but you can very
discreetly guide him to occupy his time with meaningful and fulfilling activities. As a doctor, he has so much to offer. He can volunteer
his services in health-care programs. If he likes young people, he
can become a mentor on a high school or university level, or if he
prefers to work with little ones, he can do tutorials and help children learn how to read. But most important, he should study. Just
as muscles that are not exercised become atrophied, so, too, do
minds that are not learning. I would suggest that the two of you
participate in our Torah study sessions. Then, instead of arguing
about the price of tissues, you will have something of substance to
discuss. There is an exciting world of wisdom out there that can fill
his every day and night. Do your homework behind the scenes: determine which of our classes might suit his interests, but allow him to
feel that he arrived at the decision to study of his own volition.

"In our society a man's value is equated with his productivity, his
ability to earn a livelihood," I told Thelma. "Therefore, retirement
can become very tricky. If not handled properly, Herbie can lose his
self-worth and feel that his life is over. Herbie must find something
meaningful to live for. Trailing after you in the supermarket is
annoying to you, but it's demoralizing for him and destructive to
your relationship."

"Tell me about it," Thelma commented dryly.

"Forgive me, I'm not saying all this because I want to upset you, G-d forbid, but the other day when we met in the supermarket, I couldn't help but overhear your conversation, and frankly, you were rough on him. I understand your irritation, but, still, you have to be careful not to demean him. He's going through a difficult transition. His ego is fragile and he can fall apart very easily. There is a pithy saying of a talmudic sage who complained that when he was young, he was dealt with as an adult, meaning that mature behavior beyond his years was demanded of him; but when he grew old, people related to him as though he were a child, which very often happens when one's spouse assumes the role of caretaker, or when children reverse roles and try to be a parent to their parents. Need I say more?"

"You're right, Rebbetzin. I have to be more careful, but when I'm with him, I just lose it. I don't know if I can control myself."

"Of course you can, Thelma. There is so much *goodness* in your heart. Let that goodness hold sway."

"I don't know if I have any goodness left in me," Thelma said, and broke down in tears.

"How can you say such a thing?" I said, putting my arms around her. "Your tears are proof positive that you are *all* goodness, and if you don't believe me, just ask your children and grandchildren. And speaking of them, they should be called in on this as well. They could be a tremendous source of support to Herbie."

"It's not so simple," Thelma answered.

"Why not?" I asked.

"Well, for one thing, my older daughter lives in Colorado. We see her only once or twice a year, and although the younger one lives in New Jersey, we don't get together all that much."

"I guess that's one of the downsides of our mobile society—our families are splintered. I understand that you can't visit your daughter in Colorado regularly, but there's no reason why you can't drive out to New Jersey and enjoy your grandchildren. I'm sure your daughter and son-in-law would welcome your presence. You could help the children with their homework, take them to the park—there are so many things that loving grandparents can do."

"It won't work, Rebbetzin," Thelma said matter-of-factly. "The children have their own lives. They're very busy with their friends, their sports—you know how kids are these days. They don't have time for a retired grandpa."

"But don't you have a relationship with them?" I asked.

"Well, what can I tell you, Rebbetzin. When they were little, Herb didn't have time, and now that he has time, they aren't interested."

How sad, I thought. We are a generation that had everything going for us, but we messed up and lost that which is most precious and meaningful in life—our families. But to Thelma I said, "I wouldn't write the grandchildren off so quickly. My experience with young people has shown that, no matter how old they are, they yearn for grandparents.

"During the early years of our Hineni movement," I told her, "cults were a serious threat, but with the help of G-d, I was able to retrieve countless young people from their clutches. It was one thing, however, for me to rescue these boys and girls from the cults, and something else again to keep them stable and anchored. It was no easy task, especially since cult leaders went in hot pursuit of their followers and were not about to let go. Well, do you know how I kept them anchored? I introduced them to my father.

"Now mind you, my father did not speak English and those kids did not speak Yiddish, but my father would look at them with such love in his eyes that he became their instant *zeide*—Grandpa.

"I remember Mark Goldman. He was a law student at Columbia, and he became a leader of a powerful cult. I had heard about the damaging effect he was having on many of our students, and I wanted to reach him, not only for his own sake, but for the sake of all the innocent young people that he was misleading. I called and invited him to Hineni.

"In those days, my classes were held in my father's synagogue in Brooklyn. Mark arrogantly accepted my invitation. He was positive that he would be able to prevail upon me to join his cult or, at the very least, embarrass me and put me in my place.

"The debate that he was planning never materialized. When he walked into the synagogue, I introduced him to Zeide. I hadn't told my father Mark's story, but with his penetrating eyes he immediately surmised what was going on. The pain that my father felt for this lost soul was so genuine that he began to cry. He took Mark into his arms and said in his broken English, 'Your name is Moishe—do you understand what that means, my son?' And Mark just melted into my father's arms.

"People asked me, 'How did you get him to come back so quickly? What arguments did you use?' All kinds of stories were circulated, but the simple truth is that his heart was reached through the tears and love of Zeide. It's been more than ten years since my father passed away. No one has been able to take his place, but his legacy endures. Our young people need *zeides*, so whenever possible I make 'matches' between seniors and searching youth, and what I find most rewarding about these connections is that both parties feel enriched and grateful.

"So, I wouldn't give up on those grandchildren, Thelma—they need you as much as you need them. You and Herbie can give them something that their parents can't. You can shower them with unconditional love and understanding. You can make them feel that they are the apples of your eye. You can tell them stories of how life once was. Kids love that."

I told Thelma of the very special relationship that my own husband enjoyed with our grandchildren. "When they were babies, they were always resting on his shoulder; as they got older, he took them on 'expeditions.' Nothing exotic, mind you: a visit to feed the ducks at the lake across the street from our home, digging in the backyard to explore the wonders of nature, picking flowers and enjoying their delicious scent, making arts-and-crafts projects, walking to the park, or telling stories. It's more than seven years since his passing, but ask my grandchildren and they can still recall every detail of the special time they shared with their Abba Zeide.

"With the older children, his relationship took on a different dimension. He always made himself available, offering them an open heart, a willing ear, a hug, a kiss, a blessing. I will never forget the Thursday afternoon when during a checkup my husband was told by his doctor that he had a growth in his colon that looked malignant and would require immediate consultation with an oncological surgeon. Never anticipating such news, my husband was alone when the doctor conveyed this information. I was teaching at Hineni in Manhattan, and he would never disrupt my class. When I finished my session, I called the house—there was no answer. Where could he be, I wondered? I called my daughter. Perhaps she would know where Abba was. Sure enough, he was at her house, teaching our grandson. Today, that grandson is an outstanding student of Torah and an incredibly kind young man of seventeen who, at the conclusion of every Sabbath, comes to my home to recite the farewell prayer for the holy day. He was only ten when his Abba Zeide was called from the heavens above, but he will tell you that those sessions with his grandfather are forever etched on his soul as they are on the souls of all our grandchildren. In my book *The Committed Life*, each of our grandchildren lovingly rendered their memories of Abba Zeide, and those are the things, Thelma, that make life worthwhile. So if you and Herbie missed out on all those years, don't throw in the towel and say, It's too late for me now. Make a concerted effort to salvage what was lost and start building a life between you and the children."

"I don't know if that's possible," Thelma said, with a tinge of sadness in her voice. "Certain things are just lost and cannot be recaptured."

"True," I said, "that which has passed cannot be retrieved, but if we will it, each period in our lives presents a new opportunity."

Thelma's expression told me that she wasn't convinced, so I presented her with a hypothetical situation. "Consider grandparents who are on vacation in some remote country and are attacked and killed by a gang of rebels. Ten years later, there is a revolution in the country. A new government takes over and it emerges that they weren't killed after all, but kidnapped, and now they are on their way home to rejoin their families.

"Are those grandparents to say, 'We lost the ten most important years in our grandchildren's lives. It's too late for us to connect with them now'? Or should they say, 'Precisely because we lost ten years, henceforth each day will be a gift. Our grandchildren will be our priority, and whatever it takes, we will get to know them and try to make up for those ten lost years'?

"Wouldn't it make sense, then, for you and Herbie also to apply this logic and regard this new stage in your life as an opportunity to bond with your family? Has it ever occurred to you that perhaps it was because of this that your Florida plans have been thwarted? Perhaps G-d in His mercy wanted you to experience the joy of grandchildren rather than the distractions of the golf course or fishing. Think about it, Thelma. It makes sense."

"What you are saying sounds beautiful. I wish it could be so simple. I wish it could work out for us, but I don't want to be a burden on our children."

I smiled to myself. Those words had a familiar ring. When my husband passed away, I had that very same fear. What do I do? Where should I go?

Each of my children begged me to move near him or her, but like Thelma, I was afraid of being a burden. In our society, there is so much talk about grandparents and in-laws infringing on the privacy of their children that people have actually become fearful of interacting as a family. I related all this to Thelma. I told her that just as her Florida plans came to naught, my decision was taken out of my hands. The house in which my husband and I had lived for more than forty years belonged to the congregation, and I was told that I would have to vacate it.

My daughter called. There was a small house on her block that had just gone up for sale. "It would be perfect for you, Eema," she said. "It would be so wonderful to have you just a few houses away. It would be so great for the children." It was with much trepidation that I made that move, but it was the best decision I could have made. Every day, I thank G-d for it. There is nothing as wonderful as being together with your children on the Sabbath and the holidays—to know that any minute one of the little ones could walk in just to say hello, grab a nosh, or borrow this or that. Early each Sabbath morning, my granddaughter comes by and we walk to synagogue together. How I cherish those walks. How I savor those conversations.

Fridays are very special. All the grandchildren stop by to wish me a good *Shabbos*. Just recently, my oldest granddaughter was married and she moved into the neighborhood, so she and her husband join us as well. As our *Shabbos* table expands, our joy increases. Would I exchange that for Florida? Never!

"So think about it, Thelma, and think again. Maybe, just maybe your inability to move to Florida is a blessing in disguise. Perhaps you should sell your house and move to New Jersey and start a new family life."

"Listening to you, Rebbetzin, I'm almost tempted to call a real estate agent and put our house on the market, but how much time can Herbie spend with the grandchildren? I mean, what would he be doing all day?"

"He would get a life for himself, Thelma. He would join a synagogue, attend classes, become active in organizations. There are so many wonderful, worthwhile causes in which he can become involved, and his medical background would make him such an asset in hospitals, in schools, in senior-citizen facilities. I can guarantee that, if he desires it, he can become busier than ever before. Additionally, you'll be close enough to the city so that if you want to go to a concert, visit a museum, or whatever sparks your interest, you'll be able to do that. But most important, you'll be near your child and your grandchildren."

For the longest time, Thelma was silent, mulling over my words. "Rebbetzin," she finally said, "I don't quite know how to put this, but when you described the relationship that prevailed between your father, husband, and grandchildren, I sensed such deep respect. I mean, your grandchildren seem to have revered them. But it's different for Herbie. He is not a rabbi—our grandchildren don't relate to us in the same way. Please don't get me wrong. They're good kids, but I don't know if it will work out."

"That's precisely why I suggested that you enroll in Torah study classes."

"Forgive me, but how's that going to help?" Thelma asked.

I answered her by relating a story of a modern-day sage who was traveling to Israel, accompanied by his grandson. The young boy hovered over his grandfather, bringing him drinks and food, adjusting his pillow, carefully attending to his every need, and addressing him in the third person: Would my grandfather like this or that? A passenger in an adjacent seat observed all this in fascination and, unable to hold back, asked, "Tell me, what is the magic that makes your grandson so respectful and attentive to you? I try hard, but my kids don't show this type of respect, either to me or to my elderly father."

"There's no magic to it," the sage responded. "It's all a matter of logic. We trace the most sacred moment in our history to the time when, more than thirty-three hundred years ago, G-d revealed Himself at Mount Sinai and gave the Torah. Because of that, we honor the generation that is closest to that hallowed time. But if you believe that human beings are the product of an evolutionary process, then obviously it is the newest link in the process—youth—that must be held in esteem."

The answer of the sage was not just a clever, witty teaching, but something that we see reinforced in our everyday lives. In the secular world, we regard every new generation as more advanced than the preceding one. This is reflected in our values, our mores, and the education of our children. For example, the textbooks that my grandchildren use are totally foreign to me, and by the time their children graduate, the latest textbooks will be foreign to them as well. Should the kids ask me for help with their homework, whether in math, biology, or chemistry, I would be at a total loss. Even the little ones outstrip me. They take to their computers like ducks to water while I struggle to master the basics. We have a fascination with whatever is the latest and the newest. The highest compliment that we can give someone is to say, "How young you look!" To be young is to be beautiful, clever, and with it. On the other hand, old age is associated with foolishness, forgetfulness, and even senility.

In contrast, in the Torah world, the young look to their elders for guidance. They are taught to seek their wisdom, to stand up for them in deference. "Remember the days of old, consider the years of many generations; ask your father and he will show you, your elders and grandfathers and they will tell it to you" (Deuteronomy 32:7).

The Hebrew word for elderly is *zaken*, which is an acronym for "he who has acquired wisdom," and it is that wisdom, going all the way back to Sinai, that our young are taught to venerate.

"So," I told Thelma, "you are right. My grandchildren *did* hold my father and my husband in great esteem and reverence because they were a step closer to that Divine wisdom, and that's precisely why I suggested that you and Herbie study, so that you, too, might have something to impart to your descendants."

"Oh, Rebbetzin, Herbie and I are too old to learn new tricks."

"I wouldn't say that. It's never too late. I will agree with you that maybe it's more difficult. The Mishna teaches that learning in your old age is like writing on a piece of paper that has been previously erased. Nevertheless, we can still write, and the writing is legible."

I told Thelma the story of George Hendricks, a graduate of Harvard who began to attend our Young Leadership classes when he was in his eighties. "He had no background in Torah study, but he had a thirst for knowledge that energized him. Every week, without fail, he would come to the class and sit among the young people, who all came to adore him. My sessions were held on Tuesday night, and on Wednesday he would attend my son's class as well. He developed such a great love for Torah that he printed visiting cards announcing our seminars and distributed them wherever he went. By the time he passed away at the age of eighty-nine, he had become a scholar in his own right, and was writing articles for Jewish newspapers and other publications. If George was able to accomplish this in his eighties, then Herbie can surely accomplish it. So instead of resenting old age, seize it and make it work for you. If you will it, they can become golden years after all."

There is a midrash that teaches that until the time of the patriarch Abraham, old age did not exist in the world. For example, Abraham and Isaac looked exactly alike, and no one was able to distinguish between the two, but Abraham realized that people have to know how to differentiate between fathers and sons, mothers and daughters, that the elderly must occupy a special place in society so that the young might come to them for guidance.

Abraham prayed for old age, and we pray for G-d to sustain us when we reach that time in life. On Yom Kippur, the holiest day of the year, when we open the holy ark, we beseech G-d not to cast us off in our old age when our strength fails us. When my father pronounced those words, he would openly weep. As a young child, I never quite understood the meaning of his tears, but today I, too, weep. G-d must have heard my father's prayers, because although in his old age his body was racked by illness, there was a serenity about him that proved that G-d did not forsake him. My father was grateful for every moment and every day. He had his Torah, his wisdom, his books to sustain him. They were his constant companions. My father had a most magnificent voice; it just penetrated your heart and soul. When he pronounced a blessing under the marriage canopy, his voice would ring through the wedding hall, and when he chanted the High Holy Day prayers, you felt the presence of angels in the synagogue.

Every year, I would send my children to my parents for the High Holy Days. I wanted them to have the experience of seeing their grandfather enveloped in prayer. I wanted them to hear his voice and see his glowing countenance. The years have passed. My children are now the rabbis and rebbetzins of our Hineni organization. It is they who now chant the prayers, but Zeide stands right there next to them, as does my husband and all those who preceded them going all the way back to our father, Abraham.

*Postscript:* After much discussion, Thelma and Herbie started to explore my suggestion. Initially, their daughter and son-in-law were somewhat taken aback. They had never thought that their Florida-bound parents would consider living in the community, but once they absorbed the idea they were delighted.

Thelma and Herbie found a modest house, and the process of integration started. They joined the many programs in study and outreach available in the community. As Herbie became comfortable in synagogue, he asked his grandsons if they would accompany him on the Sabbath. Today, they sit side by side, sharing prayers and thoughts that take them back to that moment at Sinai.

"A broken contrite heart, O G-d

Thou wilt not despise . . ."

*(Psalm 51)*

# HANG IN THERE

It was a muggy summer day and the heat was stifling as Barbara and I drove up to the Women's Correctional Institution to visit Wendy Tucker. Knowing that I would be limited in what I could take in with me, I decided to leave my handbag with Barbara and took only my I.D. and a prayer book that I planned to present to Wendy. As I made my way rather nervously to the gate, I wondered about her. I had never met her, nor did I know much about her apart from what Doris, her closest friend, had told me.

Wendy Tucker had been a physician with a successful practice. Her husband, Jack, was a civil engineer, and with their pooled income they lived very well. They had two teenage daughters, Nina and Monica, who attended private schools in Manhattan, and to all intents and purposes, they were the picture of a perfect family. Then, overnight, their lives were shattered as everything around them collapsed. Wendy fired a member of her staff, who in a fit of revenge made all sorts of allegations, and what had started out as an office altercation turned into a nasty Medicare scandal. Wendy was indicted, tried, convicted, and sentenced to two years in prison. Her public as well as her private life was in total ruin. Jack tried to stand by her, although the scandal placed a terrible strain on their marriage.

As for the girls, they were angry and refused to have anything to do with their mother. Wendy attempted suicide and was taken to the prison hospital. It was at that point that Doris approached me for help. Would I visit Wendy? Could I talk to her and give her some courage and hope?

I called Wendy's husband to confirm the story. He was overwhelmed and felt like someone had hit him over the head with a sledgehammer. In addition to his financial and legal problems, he was at a loss to understand how to deal with his daughters, who were acting out and failing in school. "We are living a nightmare," he said. "I'm trying my hardest, but it's tough—real tough. Do you know what it feels like to see her in prison? She doesn't belong there, Rebbetzin. She's a good lady. She was involved in so many charities and gave so much of herself, and with all that, she was always there for the girls and me. And now, look what's happened to us."

"Would you like me to visit her?" I asked.

"Oh, Rebbetzin, that would be an act of mercy. She's in such a deep depression. Whenever I go to see her, our conversations are more like monologues—me talking and Wendy staring into space. And after a while, I have nothing to say. What is there to say anyway that makes sense? I just hope our marriage survives this."

"You have to make sure that it does. That's what committed love is all about. Wendy may have made some mistakes—I really don't know the details and I don't want to know them—but I do know that she needs you now, and you have to be there for her unconditionally. This may sound trite," I added, "but hang in there. Time is a wonderful healer. With G-d's help, you and Wendy and the children will get through this. And if there's anything I can do to help, I'll be happy to try."

And that's how I found myself joining the dozens of people queuing up to visit family members and friends at the prison. I felt sick to my stomach. The entire atmosphere was so demoralizing. While I was being processed, I was told that I couldn't bring my prayer book with me but would have to give it to the prison chaplain who, in turn, would give it to Wendy.

As I passed from one area of the prison to the next, the iron gates clanged ominously behind me. Together with the others, I was escorted to a large holding area to await Wendy's coming. I looked around and felt uneasy. I wondered what Wendy was like, and then I was concerned as to what I could say that she would find inspiring and yet not condescending; strengthening, yet not preachy or syrupy. As I was mulling over these thoughts, Wendy appeared escorted by a guard. Her eyes were dark and lifeless, and she was thin to the point of looking anorexic, but I could see that in better days she must have been a beautiful woman. How tragic it is, I thought, what can happen to a person overnight. Beads of perspiration glistened on her forehead, and it hit me that, in contrast to the visiting area, there was probably no air-conditioning in the prison compound.

"Your friend Doris asked that I come to see you. I'm so glad to meet you," I said, trying to be as positive as possible.

"Under normal circumstances I would be happy to meet you as well," she said, "but this is not exactly a place to entertain guests."

'No, it's not," I agreed, "but before you know it, you'll be back home."

"I no longer have a home," she said bitterly.

"Of course you do. I spoke to your husband, Jack. He's worried about you."

Wendy didn't respond, and for a while we sat there in silence. And then she said, "He's a good man—he doesn't deserve this."

"Do you know, when I called Jack, he said exactly the same words to me about you—that you are a good lady, and that you don't deserve this. The two of you have something very powerful going for you—your love—and that's a mighty foundation stone upon which you can rebuild your lives."

"It's all words—doesn't mean a thing. My life is over, Rebbetzin," she said, and for the first time she looked me straight in the eyes. "Even if I get out of here on early release, which my lawyers think is a good possibility, I have nothing to go home to! My daughters refuse to talk to me, and my friends, with the exception of Doris, have all disappeared; my license to practice medicine has been suspended, so I can't go back to work; and Jack would be better off if I were dead. So tell me, what am I going home to?"

"Realistically," I agreed, "it doesn't look very good, but life is not always what it appears to be, and what seems like an impossible dream today may just become your reality tomorrow."

"Next you'll tell me to believe in miracles," she said sarcastically.

"As a matter of fact, that's exactly what I was going to say. Of course, I believe in miracles. The very fact that I'm here talking to you is a major miracle. As a child, I was in Bergen Belsen concentration camp. In that hellhole it wouldn't have been realistic to have imagined that I would even survive, much less build a new life in America and teach people about faith in G-d. To believe that that was possible, Wendy, would have taken a much greater stretch of the imagination than to believe that you will get out of here and rebuild your life together with your family."

"I'm sorry," Wendy said apologetically. "I didn't know your background."

"Let me tell you about the thoughts that my father taught me to focus on to keep me going. My father would tell us stories from our distant past when our forebears were enslaved in Egypt, when our children were bricked into the walls, when our newborn males were drowned in the Nile and the spirit of our people was broken by the constant sting of the lash.

"If, in those days, you had asked a citizen of ancient Egypt who would survive the centuries—the Jews or the Egyptians—he would have laughed at you. It was no contest: the Egyptians, of course. But today, ancient Egypt is gone, and we are here.

"This pattern has held throughout history. Centuries later, the great Babylonian empire ruled the world; they conquered our land, ransacked our Temple, destroyed Jerusalem, slaughtered our people, and took our remnants into exile. Were you to have posed the same question to the Babylonians, they, too, would have laughed; they, too, would have predicted our demise. But today, ancient Babylon is gone, and we are here.

"Let's skip the centuries to the era of the mighty Roman empire. They, too, conquered our land, torched our Temple, and laid waste to Jerusalem. They took our people to Rome in chains, sold them in the slave markets, and forced them to become gladiators, fodder for the lions. Were you to have posed the same question—who will survive the centuries, the Romans or the Jews?—you would have been considered deranged. But today ancient Rome is gone, and we are here.

"In Bergen Belsen, it was hard to believe that we, dressed in rags, fuel for the gas chambers and crematorium, would survive our Nazi masters. But my father would tell us, 'Just think of all your cousins throughout the centuries. Remember them and have faith. The Nazis, just like all the others, will soon be gone, and we will be here.'

"So, yes, Wendy," I said, "of course I believe in miracles. Just hang in there and you'll see."

"Rebbetzin, that's a beautiful story. It made me feel good to hear it, but it doesn't apply to me. My situation is different. Being in a concentration camp was not your *personal* scandal. You were the victim of man's evil, and you had your faith and your sense of self-worth to sustain you. When your father told you those stories, he imbued you with pride and dignity, and that's a power that no Nazi could have robbed you of. But with me . . ." Wendy's words hung in the air—and then in a voice that was barely audible, she whispered, "There is only *shame*."

I took Wendy's hand in mine. "It's true the circumstances are different," I said, "but what I wanted to establish is that miracles can and do occur—and something that appears impossible today can happen tomorrow. All is not lost. You have a lot going for you."

"Like what?" Wendy asked sardonically.

"Like when you said you feel *shame*."

Wendy looked at me incredulously, so I explained to her that the Talmud teaches that if a person is *ashamed* of his deeds and shows remorse, G-d pardons him.

"Rebbetzin, you are just trying to make me feel better about myself."

"That's true—I would like to be able to accomplish that, but don't think that the rabbis were just uttering sentimental pronouncements. There is logic to their teachings. Feelings of shame and contrition can inspire self-scrutiny, which in turn can convert nightmares into learning experiences. If you can find the strength to do that, Wendy, then, indeed, all is not lost, because you will emerge from here stronger and wiser."

"I don't have any strength left," Wendy said in a low voice. "The only thing I have is self-hate. I hate myself for my stupidity. I hate myself for what I did to my family, and the worst is that I can't blame anyone but myself."

"If you want G-d to forgive you, you have to forgive yourself," I said. "Although feelings of shame and contrition are assets if they become springboards for growth, they can also become debilitating if they turn into despair. It's up to you, Wendy. Those feelings of guilt that you describe can become either incentives or impediments. The choice is yours."

"Oh, Rebbetzin, the next thing I know, you'll find something good in this prison as well."

"That's not as far-fetched as you think, but let me explain why. When you said that you blame no one but yourself, you said something very courageous. Most people do just the opposite. They always manage to find someone or something to blame—factors that they claim are beyond their control. Such people never see themselves as they are, and therefore are incapable of change. They silence their consciences and lose the greatest gift with which G-d has endowed us—introspection, which leads to spiritual growth.

"King Solomon, in his Book of Ecclesiastes, described this sorry state when he said, 'G-d made men straight and they (men) sought out all forms of calculations'—meaning that G-d endowed us with pure souls, but we corrupted ourselves, and then to escape accountability, we advanced all kinds of rationalizations. This was the sin of Adam when, in the Garden of Eden, G-d questioned him about his having eaten the forbidden fruit. Instead of admitting his guilt, instead of saying, 'Forgive me, G-d, I am so ashamed,' he said, 'The woman You gave me, she made me eat from it!' And with those words, Adam lost paradise. But you, Wendy, have had the courage to say '*I'm ashamed. I can blame no one but myself.*' Those are powerful, life-transforming words, so if this awful place forced you to take a closer look at yourself, then all is not lost."

"It's lost with my daughters," Wendy said, fighting back tears.

"I'm not so sure about that. I'll grant you that the girls won't be easy; teenagers never are. But they'll calm down," I assured her.

"I don't know. They won't even take my calls."

"I'll tell you what," I said. "I will visit them, please G-d, next Tuesday at 5:00 P.M., before I teach my Young Leadership class. Let's agree that you will call. I'll be there to pick up the phone and connect you to them. But there's one thing you must do—pray and have faith."

"I don't know how to pray," Wendy said.

"You learn to pray by praying. Just start. I left a prayer book for you with the chaplain. Open it and talk to G-d from your heart. Tell Him how you feel—beg for His help and don't be afraid to cry in front of Him."

"I can't cry anymore. I have no tears left."

"Of course you do. I just saw them glistening in your eyes. Just let go and those tears will come forth, and you will feel such relief." I told Wendy that the prayer book included psalms and suggested that she look for Psalm 51:19: "The offerings of G-d are a broken spirit, a heart broken and crushed."

"When G-d sees your sincerity," I assured her, "He will accept your prayer and bring you healing."

We chatted a while longer and agreed that Wendy would call her home the following Tuesday. Before we knew it, visiting hour was over. As I walked back to the car, I had my own praying to do. "G-d," I pleaded, "give me the words to reach the girls so that their tortured mother may know some peace."

From the car I called Jack and asked if I could come over the following Tuesday at 5:00 P.M. I sensed that he was somewhat surprised, if not shocked.

"I appreciate your having visited Wendy," he said, "but I don't want to impose upon you."

"You won't be imposing," I said. "I'd like to meet your girls. I think we should talk."

"My girls—they're tough. They are very angry, and usually at that time of day they like to go to the gym."

"That's precisely why I'm calling. Ask them to make an exception on this one occasion."

The following Tuesday, when I rang their doorbell, I found Jack at his computer and the girls watching TV and munching potato chips. He greeted me warmly and apologized for the mess in the apartment. It was evident that there was no woman in the house.

"We had to let our housekeeper go," he explained.

Things must be pretty bad, I thought, if Jack can't tell his girls to clean up and put things in order. The girls' eyes were fixed on the TV screen and they grunted to acknowledge my presence.

"Monica, Nina, say hello to the rebbetzin," Jack now said. "She made a long trip to see us. Maybe you can turn off the TV so we can talk."

The girls didn't respond, so Jack picked up the remote and hit the power button.

"Dad, what are you doing," Monica whined. "You're making us miss the best part."

"I'm sorry," I said. "I'll try to make up for it. Perhaps what I have to tell you will be the best part."

The girls just stared at me, and I saw resentment in their eyes. "I'm bringing you regards from your mom," I continued. "She loves you very much."

"We really don't want to discuss her," Nina said.

"I have no intention of discussing your mom with you. It's not the place of children to discuss their parents. I'm merely stating a fact— your mom loves you, needs you, and I bring you regards from her."

"You have to understand," Jack interjected, "the girls have been very hurt."

"Of course I understand, but the girls also have to understand. Have you ever considered how your mother is hurting?" I asked them. "Have you ever thought about the suffering that she is undergoing?"

"Well, that was her doing!" Nina snapped.

"Don't be so quick to judge," I said. "We all make mistakes in life, and while it's happening, we don't necessarily realize that we are doing something wrong. It's only in retrospect that everything becomes clear."

"Yes, people make mistakes," Nina answered, "but this was not just a mistake. This was ignoring the law!"

"But how about you?" I challenged. "Aren't you also ignoring the law?"

"What do you mean?"

"Aren't you ignoring the commandment to honor your parents? Aren't you ignoring all the good things that your mother did for you? How about all the years that she nurtured you with her love, sat at your bedside when you were sick, comforted you when you were upset, took you shopping and got you the best and the finest? And how about the trips and the vacations? And how about the fact that, for nine months, she carried you under her heart, gave you life, watched over you? Is all that chopped liver?"

"Don't lay a guilt trip on us," Nina interrupted.

"Not at all. I'm just asking you to be honest and not commit a grievous wrong. It's just not honest to judge a person based on one bad incident in her life and dismiss everything else. And it's a grievous wrong for children to sit in judgment of their parents. The Ten Commandments require you to respect your mother and father and to remember that you are forever indebted to them. When I walked into this apartment, your dad apologized for all the mess in the house. If your mom were here, everything would have looked different, and for all those years everything did look different. Has that all been forgotten? Where is your love? Where is your loyalty? Where is your good heart? For heaven's sake, Nina, you're not talking about a stranger, you're talking about your mom!"

"The girls have really been having a very rough time," Jack once again interrupted, trying to break the tension in the room. "People are whispering behind their backs, excluding them from parties—it hasn't exactly been a picnic for them."

"I'm sure it hasn't," I agreed. Then I turned to the girls and asked, "Have you stopped to think about how it has been for your mom? People may be talking behind your backs, but your mother has to contend with inmates who curse her to her face and G-d knows what else. In prison she has no place to escape—she can't run to her room and hide under the covers. The only thing that can keep her going is your love, the knowledge that you are there, and the awareness that with every passing day, she is one step closer to seeing you again.

"As for those friends who whispered behind your back—ignore them. One of these days you will realize that all those so-called friends are not real friends. They don't give a hoot about you or your life. Believe me, they're not losing any sleep over you. But for your mom, every night and every waking minute is filled with one thought—and that is you!

"More than you are suffering, she is suffering; more than your life, it is her life that is ruined, not only because she is in that horrible place but, more important, because she is haunted by the thought of what this has done to you, and that is a pain that she cannot bear. She can deal with almost anything, but not that you are hurting because of her. Usually," I continued, "it's parents who give life to their children, but you have the unique opportunity to give life to your parent, so instead of judging, pray for your mother with all your heart. I brought you a prayer book and a book of psalms, and I left this exact same prayer book for your mother as well. Wouldn't it be special if you could make an arrangement that, at the same time of day or night, you'd be reciting the same psalms for one another? Can you imagine what that would do for her and you? Your souls would be connected in prayer, compassion, and love, and if G-d sees that, He, too, will join you in partnership, and there will be forgiveness, blessing, and the start of new life.

"Your mother doesn't want you to visit her—she doesn't want to subject you to that—but she does need to hear your voices, and she desperately needs to hear three powerful words from you, words that she has said to you myriad times, 'I love you.'

"I arranged for her to call here. As a matter of fact, her call is due any minute now."

As I spoke, I watched their eyes, hoping to see some sign of emotion, some feelings from their hearts. Finally I saw tears, and to their credit both Nina and Monica apologized and told me that they were ready to speak to their mom.

The phone rang. Wendy's voice sounded tentative and frightened.

"I met your girls," I told her, "and they're terrific. They miss you, Jack misses you, and this apartment misses you! It needs your feminine touch."

I handed the phone over to the girls and stepped out of the room to give them some privacy. I asked Jack to join me. "I know that you are trying to show the girls that you understand them, but you are going about it the wrong way. Support for the girls should not be at Wendy's expense. If your family is to make it, you will have to show them that you and Wendy are one, and that you love her unconditionally. Bring forth the goodness in their hearts by reminding them to focus on the many kindnesses with which their mother showered them all these years.

"One of the pillars of our faith is gratitude, and honoring parents is at the root of it. More than the gym, your girls need spiritual training so that they may face life free of anger, meanness, and bitterness. What Monica and Nina should remember from this terrible time in their lives is that your love for Wendy was so total and complete that it enabled the family to heal and start all over again. If they see that, then they, too, will be able to love and respect their parents."

I kept in touch with Wendy and her family throughout her incarceration. The girls started to attend my classes, and their attitude mellowed with each passing week. Wendy was released early for good behavior. It wasn't easy for the family to start over again, but life is all about growing, and in growth there is much struggle. And struggle, although often painful, is worthwhile, because it is through that struggle that we realize our potential. To be sure, Wendy made some costly mistakes, but she learned from them and emerged stronger and better for the experience. And that's what life is all about—converting darkness into light and hope. We need only hang in there and have faith in G-d.

# SEVENTEEN

# *SHTEIG*ING—GROWING STEP-BY-STEP

My grandson dorms in an out-of-town yeshiva and calls me every Friday to wish me a good *Shabbos*.

"So, how are you doing?" I ask.

"*Baruch HaShem*, thank G-d, I'm trying to shteig, Bubba" is his usual answer.

The Yiddish word *shteig* is difficult to translate, but it most aptly describes the purpose of life. To *shteig* means to be in a constant state of growth and development. To *shteig* is to understand that we never graduate, that as long as we are alive there's always something more to be done, something more to accomplish, something more to strive for in order to realize our mission in life. Often, I would suggest to the members of our Young Leadership that when they go on their blind dates or attend social functions and the perennial question "So, what do you do?" comes up, they should simply answer by saying, "I'm *shteig*ing," an answer that is bound to knock any questioner for a loop, and become a great conversation piece. My students have reported back to me that the *"shteig"* message has taken off like lightning and has become the new buzzword.

Some of them have even suggested that we start a "*Shteig*-ers Club" complete with T-shirts and buttons.

Our rituals, our ceremonies, our outlook on life are all affected by *shteiging*. When we complete the reading of one of the books of the Torah, the congregation is asked to rise and declare, "Be strong, be strong, and be strengthened." At first, it may be difficult to understand why it is that upon the conclusion of our studies such pronouncements are made. Surely, it would be more appropriate to express such wishes at the beginning of an endeavor—but there is a deep message therein. It is at the *completion* of a task that we need an infusion of strength, so that we may acknowledge that we must continue to *shteig*, for our task will first begin.

If we wish to describe a scholar in the Hebrew language, we refer to him as a *talmid chochem*, which, literally translated, means "a student of wisdom." And once again, the message of *shteiging* comes through. The true scholar remains a *student* throughout his life, striving to keep growing through learning.

Similarly, if spouses are to preserve the freshness of their relationship, they have to be constantly vigilant and search for new ways to *shteig* as husbands and wives. Unfortunately, once they marry, most people think that this is a chapter in their lives that has been signed, sealed, and delivered and will no longer require their attention. Little do they realize that the *real* work, the work of *shteiging*, is just beginning.

Ironically, most people will readily concede that success in any undertaking requires innovation, growth, and a willingness to change. Yet they fail to come to this same conclusion when it relates to their marriages. They slip into a humdrum existence that steadily deteriorates as their relationship erodes. Wistfully, they wonder what happened to "that man," "that woman" whom they dated and married. Where has he disappeared to? Why can't she change? Why can't he be more sensitive, more attentive, more attractive? The answer is simple—they ceased *shteiging*.

On occasion, I have challenged my classes to identify what they consider to be the most awesome miracle in the Bible. Many answers were forthcoming: the splitting of the Red Sea, manna falling from heaven, water gushing forth from rocks, the sun standing still for Joshua, Jonah surviving in the belly of the whale, Daniel in the lion's den, and more. However, none of these was the answer that I was seeking, for they were all acts performed by G-d, and for Him the miraculous is ordinary. There is nothing that He wills that cannot occur. Therefore, miracles can occur only in the human domain. When we transcend ourselves, when we overcome our frailties and master our passions, *that's* a miracle, and that miracle occurred when our forebears, a nation of slaves, degraded and brutalized for generations, were in seven short weeks transformed into a holy nation that stood at Sinai. Our exodus from Egypt was an event brought about by G-d, but it was our ancestors who wondrously removed Egypt from their hearts, and that is the miracle that should give us all pause, make us all ponder. How did our ancestors do it? How did a lowly nation evolve into a priestly kingdom in seven short weeks—a feat that others could not accomplish in centuries?

The answer is *shteiging*—growing and developing. From the moment that we left Egypt, the process commenced. We counted every day by shedding a fault, adopting a mitzvah, absorbing a gem of wisdom. Every day we *shteig*ed a little bit more, until the forty-ninth day when we stood at the foot of Mount Sinai totally transformed.

Rabbi Yisroel Salanter, the eminent sage and teacher of ethics, once said that the most powerful sound in the world is the sound of bad habits breaking and base character traits shattering. For forty-nine days following our departure from Egypt, mighty booms were heard in the desert. They were the sounds of our negative traits being crushed. That experience was forever etched upon our hearts, and to this moment in time, we continue to count, continue to grow, breaking the shackles that would inhibit us and stymie our growth. We are *shteiging*—growing and developing.

My husband, who was a master teacher with a knack for translating profound thoughts into lay terms, would often explain this concept with the following analogy: "If you were told to read the phone book and retain the names, addresses, and telephone numbers therein, you'd throw up your hands in frustration and rightly declare the task beyond human capacity. On the other hand, were you told to look for just *one* name, *one* address, *one* number at a time, you would do it effortlessly."

Similarly, if we were told to change, to alter ingrained habits, to temper personality traits, even if cerebrally and emotionally we understood the necessity of this, we would nevertheless feel overwhelmed, if not threatened, and give up before even trying. But were we told to make just *one* little change, shed *one* little nasty habit, take on just *one* little mitzvah, and do it *one* day at a time, we would readily accept the challenge, and that powerful boom, the sound of change and rebirth, would resonate within us.

The first person to have discovered this method of growth was Cain. The Midrash teaches that after he committed his heinous crime, he met his father, Adam.

"What was your judgment?" Adam asked.

"I repented and reconciled with G-d," Cain answered.

To which Adam responded in amazement, "I never knew of the awesome power of repentance."

At first glance, it is difficult to understand what exactly it was that Adam failed to comprehend. Certainly, he had a deeper knowledge of G-d's expectations of human beings than Cain did. Our sages teach, however, that what Adam learned from his son was that it is possible for us to embark on the path of change through *small but steady steps.*

A Hasidic rabbi once challenged his disciples: "Tell me," he said, "who is on a higher level—he who is on top of the ladder or he who is at the bottom?"

"He who is at the top," they all responded.

"No, my children," the rabbi answered. "The one who is at the bottom is on a higher level, because he strives to raise himself up. He is growing, and that's what life is all about."

It was with these thoughts in mind that I built my book around the teachings of the sages who identified the five most important traits through which we can grow. And if, after having read this book, you try to look at others with a *good eye*, or if after having some angry thoughts, you chide yourself and say, "I should really reevaluate this entire matter with a *good eye*," then I will have achieved my goal and feel amply rewarded, for once you start the process, you will continue to *shteig* and move on to become a *good friend*, a *good neighbor*, a person who *projects the future* and digs deeply to uncover that *good heart*, all qualities that will transform you into a good person, a good husband or wife.

If you follow this formula for growth, then you, too, even as our ancestors so long ago, will wake up one morning to the sound of that powerful boom and discover that you have changed—that you have re-created yourself.

# EIGHTEEN

# POSTSCRIPT:
# TIME TO GROW UP

W hen you finish writing a book, your feelings run the gamut, from excitement to trepidation. It's akin to giving birth to a child and waiting for the doctor to pronounce the baby healthy and well!

Such were my emotions when I sent my manuscript to Susan Friedland, my editor at HarperCollins. Soon afterward, she sent me a note. She found the book strong, well written, and inspiring. "But," she wrote, "all your stories convey success. Haven't you ever had any failures?" I realized that others might ask that very same question. How is it possible to reach people all the time? How is it possible always to succeed?

Well, the truth of the matter is that it's not possible, but there *is* a method that guarantees positive outcomes. When people call our Hineni office for an appointment regarding a personal matter, the only time spots available to them are after 9:30 P.M. on Tuesday or Thursday evenings. Most people complain. "Why such inconvenient, unsuitable hours? Why can't we see the rebbetzin at a *normal time* in the morning, afternoon, or early evening?" they ask. The answer is simple. Before I meet with anyone regarding a personal concern, that person must attend a Torah study session (which I conduct on Tuesday and Thursday evenings). It is Torah study, and not me, that brings about that miraculous change and makes happy endings possible. Admittedly, from time to time I have encountered cases in which participation in study sessions was well-nigh impossible, but even in those cases, I would preface my counseling with Torah study.

Just as a surgeon requires his scalpel if he is to perform a successful procedure, so I need my instrument if I am to penetrate the *neshama* (soul), and that instrument is Torah study. I discovered this method early on, at the inception of our Hineni organization. After my first Madison Square Garden rally in 1973, a family from Florida approached me about their daughter, who had become a leader of a Christian cult. Would I come down to Miami and speak to her? they asked.

As much as I wanted to help, I knew full well that whatever I might say would just bounce off her. She was programmed to shut out all ideas that challenged her beliefs, so I advised her parents to organize a gathering at which I could impart Torah and to make sure that she attended. Although she and her friends *did* come (ostensibly to pray for my soul), she refused to speak to me afterward, so I proceeded to her home and waited. When she walked in, I picked up on the teaching where I had left off, and in no time at all, she agreed to come with me back to New York, where she continued her journey through the pages of G-d's Book.

People asked what the magic words were that sparked this miraculous change. In vain did I tell them that there were no words. All it takes is opening the Book and allowing its wisdom to seep into the soul. Many have difficulty accepting this basic truth— it just sounds too simplistic. They might also argue that this response may be valid for those who are entrapped in cults and have a religious bent, but is hardly applicable to secular people with marital or personal problems.

To be sure, every situation is different. Nevertheless, there is a common denominator connecting all problems, and that is an inclination to *resist change*. We are creatures of habit, and once we become accustomed to a certain lifestyle, a certain way of thinking, we have difficulty letting go. Then, too, we can't bear to admit that we may have been wrong—that we have lived a lie—so we expend much energy and money in pursuit of solutions to our problems and ignore the thing that is readily available, free to all, and guaranteed by the test of time. Torah study is a *life-transforming* experience. It has an impact on our personalities; it inspires us to examine our lives, to restructure our relationships, and to see ourselves as G-d intended us to be: disciplined and in charge of our lives. There is nothing as exhilarating as the sense of freedom that comes with the knowledge that we are in control of our baser instincts and desires, that we can curb our tongues, hold our anger, and make changes in our lives. That is what results from Torah study if we allow it to penetrate our minds and hearts. So, yes, my stories have positive endings. However, that has nothing to do with me; it is a tribute to the Torah study that I advocate.

You might wonder how far into the night my counseling sessions last. After all, if I begin to see people at 9:30, and sometimes even later, it could very well happen that the sessions stretch into the early hours of the morning. In fact, they go very fast because, invariably, the Torah portion does the job.

"It's amazing," people comment as they enter my office, "it's like tonight's teaching was tailored specifically for me!" Whatever burdens people may carry, the Torah always sheds some light, making my task relatively simple. I need only help put the pieces together, point to the appropriate passages, and wrap it up. It is a totally non-threatening experience, for it is not I making the judgment call but a higher authority, to which both I and the person seeking guidance must subscribe. And so, in response to Susan's question, "Have you ever failed?" the answer is no, if they agreed to come to a Torah class and allowed the words to penetrate their hearts, but yes, if I couldn't convince them to do so. Such was the case with Marty Gibber.

Marty was tough, moody, and temperamental. Over the years he tried his hand at several businesses and wasn't particularly successful with any of them. His wife, Miriam, a sweet, shy woman, the mother of four little children, helped support the family by selling sweaters and costume jewelry from their home. One of her customers presented her with a copy of my book *The Committed Life*, and that is how she came to attend my classes. After one of the sessions, she came to my office to speak to me and related the sad saga of her marriage. Marty was verbally abusive and terrorized her and the children. But she was committed to the marriage and wouldn't consider divorce. She related that they had gone for counseling, but to no avail—Marty remained Marty, obstinate and unchanged. Would I speak to him?

When I called, Marty refused my invitation out of hand, and when I suggested that he attend one of my sessions, he laughed it off. That certainly was of no interest to him.

Then one day Miriam fell ill with a nagging cough that just wouldn't go away. She was treated for bronchitis, but no matter what medication she took, the cough did not abate. Soon enough, she discovered the reason. It wasn't bronchitis at all but a malignant spot on her lung.

Miriam was in shock, as were her family and friends. A nonsmoker who took good care of herself and exercised regularly, she was at a loss to understand whence this horrible disease had come. Things like that were not supposed to happen. It was a terrible tragedy. The prospect of a young woman dying prematurely is awful, but the thought of four small children being orphaned is enough to break anyone's heart. It was then, in the midst of this horrific nightmare, that Marty called me. The cancer took over Miriam's life. She had to stop working and concentrate on her chemo treatments, which left her drained and debilitated. She missed the classes that she had come to love and cherish, so I tried to visit her as often as I could to study with her as she rested on her sofa. She asked Marty to join us, and he didn't have the heart to refuse her. It was then, for the very first time, that Marty experienced Torah study— alas, too little, too late, for in six short months it was over.

I will never forget the funeral—the four little children clinging to one another and crying, "Mommy, Mommy," and Marty weeping like a baby. Apart from the officiating rabbi, the only person who spoke was Marty. His words touched everyone. "Miriam," he sobbed, "please forgive me. You were a perfect wife and I caused you much pain and grief. I was not worthy of you. Please forgive me—I love you."

Everyone in the chapel wept with Marty. It was a small gathering of relatives and friends, who to one degree or another were all aware of their troubled marriage. To see Marty get up in front of everyone and openly ask for forgiveness was overwhelming and took people's breath away. I prayed that Miriam heard him. How sad that he had never uttered those words while she was still alive and well. How sad that we have to experience pain and suffering in order to become wise. If only we could learn *before* tragedy strikes.

There was a magnetic, spellbinding preacher in the Jewish world known as the Maggid of Kelm. He lived in Lithuania in the nineteenth century. One day he challenged his congregation with an amazing question. "If, by some miracle, G-d allowed all those who are buried in the cemetery of Kelm to get up for half an hour, what do you think they would do? Where would they go? What would they say?" he asked.

Consider these questions, ponder them, and ask yourself, What would I do? Where would I go? What would I say if I had just half an hour in this world? And what if, instead of half an hour, you were told that your wife or your husband had just six months to live. How would you relate to her or him?

And what if they have more than six months? Does that give you license to act differently toward them?

When you study Torah, you learn to value the preciousness of time and try to live each day as if it were your last. You learn to appreciate and safeguard the simple gifts with which G-d endowed you, gifts that you come to realize are not so simple after all: marriage and children.

Marriage can be the greatest joy and source of fulfillment in your life, but it can also be the greatest source of anguish and pain. Torah wisdom can protect you from failure in marriage. It can inspire you to relate with *chesed*, compassion and sensitivity, to your mate. And most significant, Torah study teaches you how your marriage can become the most awesome experience through which you can realize your potential as a man or woman and impart a legacy to future generations.

It is my hope and prayer that through this book you, too, will embark upon this path of growth and come to view your marriage not so much as happy or unhappy, but rather as an opportunity for growth in kindness, wisdom, and love. If you do that, your marriage will provide you with the illusive happiness for which you yearn.

I leave you with the blessing of *Sholom bayis.* May G-d grant you peace and harmony in your home.

*Esther Jungreis*